PRESENTED TO _Joy - to show our appreciation for your special gift_

BY _Janice and Kurt Schmadeke_

DATE _October 21, 1977_

a field of diamonds

COMPILED BY
JOSEPH S. JOHNSON

DRAWINGS BY
PHYLLIS JOLLY

BROADMAN PRESS
Nashville, Tennessee

This book is dedicated to

THE LORD JESUS CHRIST,

without whom these thoughts
could never have come into being.

© Copyright 1974 ● Broadman Press
All rights reserved

4251-33

ISBN: 0-8054-5133-1
Dewey Decimal Classification: 808.8
Library of Congress catalog card number: 73-870-67
Printed in the United States of America

preface

A Field of Diamonds is a first for Broadman—the first anthology of prose and poetry in its publishing history. Here is a compilation of devotional gems encompassing all of Christian history from New Testament times to the present.

Included are giants of the faith like Augustine, Martin Luther, Fanny J. Crosby, Roger Williams, Charles Haddon Spurgeon, John Wesley, and George W. Truett—along with contemporary writers. Numerous selections appear in print for the first time within these pages.

Every effort has been made to give proper credit to every selection. Where an author is unknown there is no citation like "author unknown," "anonymous," or "selected." If by chance we have overlooked an author, this oversight will be corrected in subsequent printings, provided we receive notification.

Further, this anthology makes no attempt at uniform styling, since these materials are gleaned from hundreds of different sources and are published as close to the original styling and wording as possible.

The book is arranged in thirty-eight headings beginning with "Adoration" and going through "Youth." The compiler realizes that possible categories are virtually infinite and that no book can be exhaustive.

A Field of Diamonds is sent forth with a prayer that the inspiration and wisdom contained within will encourage and illumine its readers.

A Field of Diamonds owes its existence to countless writers of inspiration, those who have "followed the gleam" and those who have "sat in heavenly places with Christ Jesus."

Every impulse and idea in this book rest on the foundational truths of Almighty God as revealed in Jesus Christ. The gospel of Jesus Christ has directly or indirectly influenced every good motive and thought in the world. *A Field of Diamonds* reflects this affirmation.

Take. Read. Apply. Let these selections escort you through a field of diamonds provided by the Spirit. Read with a responsive heart and you cannot remain the same. Stand now "on heaven's tableland."

THE COMPILER

contents

ADORATION

A Field of Diamonds

CROWN HIM WITH MANY CROWNS
Crown Him with many crowns,
The Lamb upon the throne;
Hark, how the heavenly anthem drowns
All music but His own:
Awake, my soul, and sing
Of Him who died for thee,
And hail Him as the matchless King
Through all eternity.

Sir George J. Elvey

My God, my all! Who art Thou, my sweetest
Lord and God? And who am I? . . . Most holy
Lord, I would love Thee! Sweetest Lord, I
greatly desire to love Thee! Lord God, I have
given Thee all my heart and my body; and I
ardently long to do yet more for love of Thee, if
I but knew how! Amen.

Francis of Assisi

DOXOLOGY
Praise God, from whom all blessings flow;
Praise Him all creatures here below;
Praise Him above, ye heavenly host;
Praise Father, Son, and Holy Ghost.

Thomas Ken

And we poor whispering wayfarers heard,
   round about and o'er us,
The throbbing, thundering triumphs of the
   Hallelujah Chorus!

Fay Inchfawn

WORSHIP ONLY THEE
The dearest idol I have known,
   Whate'er that idol be,
Help me to tear it from Thy throne,
   And worship only Thee.

William Cowper

Praise Him! Jesus, our blessed Redeemer!

Fanny J. Crosby

HOLY, HOLY, HOLY
Holy, Holy, Holy, Lord God Almighty!
Early in the morning our song shall rise to Thee;
Holy, Holy, Holy, Merciful and Mighty!
God in Three Persons, blessed Trinity!

Reginald Heber

ALL PEOPLE THAT ON EARTH DO DWELL
All people that on earth do dwell,
   Sing to the Lord with cheerful voice;
Him serve with fear, His praise forth tell;
   Come before Him and rejoice.

William Kethe

MAJESTIC SWEETNESS
Majestic sweetness sits enthroned
   Upon the Saviour's brow;
His head with radiant glories crowned,
   His lips with grace o'erflow.

Thomas Hastings

ALL NATURE REFLECTS GOD'S GLORY
Every mountain tells of his majesty and every
crystal stream reminds us of the Water of life.
Each flower that opens pays homage to the Rose
of Sharon and Lily of the valley. His name is
written in the splendor all about us and his voice
is heard in the song of the robin or redbird as
each new spring arrives. His glory is told in the
fragrance of the jasmine and jonquil. The eagle
on wing is a reminder of the heights to which we
are invited. The music of the tossing waves and
their pause at twilight are a part of his orchestra.

Rosalee Mills Appleby

LOOK, YE SAINTS
Look, ye saints, the sight is glorious;
See the Man of sorrows now;
From the fight returned victorious,
Every knee to Him shall bow:
Crown Him, crown Him, crown Him, crown Him!
Crowns become the Victor's brow.

Thomas Kelly

O for a thousand tongues to sing,
My great Redeemer's praise,
The glories of my God and King,
The triumphs of His grace.

Charles Wesley

Art Thou not mighty, God Almighty, so as to
heal all the diseases of my soul! . . . I am still
imperfect; hoping that Thou will perfect Thy
mercies in me, even to perfect peace . . .

Augustine

BLESSED ART THOU
Blessed art thou, O Lord our God, King of the
universe, who openest the eyes of the blind.
Blessed are thou, O Lord our god, King of the
universe, who clothest the naked. Blessed art
thou, O Lord our God, King of the universe,
who loosest them that are bound. Blessed art
thou, O Lord our God, King of the universe,
who raisest up them that are bowed down.
Blessed art thou, O Lord our God, King of the
universe, who givest strength to the weary.

Hebrew Prayer

DO NOT SPARE THE IDOLS
Let us not spare our idols. It is to our interest to
demolish them. If we shatter them, there will
rain about our hearts the very treasures of
heaven, the gifts and graces of the Holy Spirit;
but if we spare our idols, we miss the riches un-
searchable. If you do not crown Him Lord of all,
you do not crown Him Lord at all.

John MacNeil

Each day I am filled with awe at the magnificent
beauty of God. A sunrise, a sunset, a season's
change, a breeze, a stream--and yet of what
worth am I that I should be given these gifts
from him?

Hubert Shipman

MY SONG IS LOVE UNKNOWN
My song is love unknown,
    My Saviour's love to me,
Love to the loveless shown,
    That they might lovely be.
        O who am I,
            That for my sake
            My Lord should take
        Frail flesh and die?

Here might I stay and sing,
    No story so divine;
Never was love, dear King,
    Never was grief like thine!
        This is my friend,
            In whose sweet praise
            I all my days
        Could gladly spend.

Samuel Crossman

KEEP SILENCE
Let all mortal flesh keep silence,
    And with fear and trembling stand;
Ponder nothing earthly-minded,
    For with blessing in his hand
Christ our God to earth descendeth,
    Our full homage to demand.

Ancient Liturgy

LO, GOD IS HERE!
Lo, God is here! let us adore,
    And own how dreadful is this place:
Let all within us feel his power,
    And silent bow before his face:
Who know his power, his grace who prove,
Serve him with awe, with reverence love.

Gerhard Tersteegen

THE HEART'S ADORATION
Vainly we offer each ample oblation,
    Vainly with gifts would his favour secure;
Richer by far is the heart's adoration,
    Dearer to God are the prayers of the poor.

Reginald Heber

A Field of Diamonds

LIKE OCEAN FLOOD-TIDES
Come, O Lord, like ocean flood-tides
Flowing inland from the sea;
As the waters fill the shallows,
May our souls be filled with Thee!

IN BREATHLESS ADORATION
Alone with Thee, amid the mystic shadows,
 The solemn hush of nature newly born;
Alone with Thee in breathless adoration,
 In the calm dew and freshness of the morn.

NO LUSTER OF OUR OWN
Lord of all life, below, above
Whose light is truth, Whose warmth is love,
Before Thy ever-blazing throne
We ask no luster of our own.

Wherever God's grace is discerned, and His love
is welcomed, there praise breaks forth, as surely
as streams pour from the cave of the glacier
when the sun of summer melts it, or earth
answers the touch of spring with flowers.
Alexander Maclaren

No earthly father loves like Thee,
 No mother e'er so mild,
Bears and forbears as Thou hast done
 With me, Thy sinful child.

LORD OF ALL BEING
Lord of all being; throned afar,
Thy glory flames from sun and star;
Centre and soul of every sphere,
Yet to each loving heart how near!

Sun of our life, Thy quickening ray
Sheds on our path the glow of day;
Star of our hope, Thy softened light
Cheers the long watches of the night.
Oliver Wendell Holmes

THE WORLD WILL EXTOL THEE
For thousands of years the world will extol thee.
Banner of our contradictions, thou wilt be the
sign around which will be fought the fiercest
battles. A thousand times more living, a thousand times more loved since thy death than
during the days of thy pilgrimage here below,
thou wilt become to such a degree the cornerstone of humanity, that to tear thy name from
this world would be to shake it to its foundations.
Ernest Renan

GLORY, GLORY, GLORY!
In one case I have in mind there was great pain,
as one lay upon his back with a broken leg in a
cast, but there was joy, such over-flowing joy
that the sufferer lay there with dancing eyes and
radiant face and throbbing heart shouting:
"Glory, glory, glory!"
R. A. Torrey

HOW INSIGNIFICANT WE FEEL
How insignificant we feel trying to sing a worthy
song to our King. How poor is the human language to express even a part of what the heart
feels! His marvels of grace, his matchless love,
his infinite power! What more can these lips add
to the universal chorus that praises him continu-
ously?
 The heavens declare his glory. In the dawn of
each new day the sun in all its splendor speaks of
the Light of the world. Night after night the
stars speak of the bright and morning Star.
Rosalee Mills Appleby

PLENTEOUS GRACE
Plenteous grace with Thee is found,
 Grace to cover all my sin;
Let the healing streams abound;
 Make me, keep me pure within.
Thou of life the fountain art,
 Freely let me take of Thee;
Spring Thou up within my heart,
 Rise to all eternity.

WORTHY OF WORSHIP

God rightly is called the Supreme Being. He is so much greater than any man that the differences between men fade into insignificance before him. He alone is worthy of worship. He alone is due the kind of serious respect that the Bible calls "the fear of the Lord." God is God. His own revelation of his gracious character never mitigates the unique quality of his Person. Seeing him calls us to reverent repentance and worship.

Joseph F. Green

Science and industry are not God's competitors. They must never be elevated to where they become our graven images. They cannot take God's place. But properly conceived and used, they are expressions of his goodness. They are part of the way he today prepares a table before us and anoints our head with oil. Therefore, he is as interested in what we do at our workbench as in what we do in church. As Brother Lawrence contended, to pick up a straw from a littered floor can be a service in his glory.

Clarence W. Cranford

STUPENDOUS FAITH

It is impossible for us to conceive of a Consciousness so all-inclusive that every person and all of that person is the immediate center of attention and care. Yet that is exactly what the Christian means by God. "Not a sparrow falls to the ground without your Heavenly Father." It is a dizzy conception, but it is a necessary one, if God is to be what revelation and the most comprehensive thinking of the Christian centuries declares Him to be—Creator, Sustainer, Redeemer, the Everlasting Father. It is a stupendous faith but it is the Christian faith as declared by our Lord Jesus Christ.

A. E. Day

O most Holy Trinity . . . it is my earnest intention . . . to praise, adore, and revere thee.

Gertrude the Great

MY LIFE FOR THEE

My feet to walk,
My eyes to see,
My ears to hear,
My life for Thee;
My heart to beat,
My hands to work,
My voice to teach
Of Heaven and eternity;
My mouth to eat,
My nose to smell,
My mind to think
And know of Thee;
My sense to use
In good judgment
In preparing for
A life with Thee.

Hubert Shipman

WORSHIP IS . . .

To worship is to quicken the conscience by the holiness of God, to feed the mind with the truth of God, to purge the imagination by the beauty of God, to open the heart to the love of God, to devote the will to the purpose of God.

William Temple

What God does with poor weak creatures like us, when He lifts up our weaknesses, and replenishes our weariness; pouring oil and wine into our wounds and a cordial into our lips, and sending us, with the joy of pardon, upon our road again; that is a greater thing than when He rolls Neptune in its mighty orbit round the central sun, or upholds with unwearied arms, from cycle to cycle, the circle of the earth.

Alexander Maclaren

Joyful, joyful, we adore Thee . . .

Henry van Dyke

Emotion, such as generated in a moving hour of worship, provides the mind with a kaleidoscope.

A Field of Diamonds

God does not sound the trumpets before Him.
He comes quietly, unobtrusively, in a casually
begun acquaintance, in the communication of a
seminal idea, in a book one happens upon, in a
word dropped by a friend, in a gleam that flickers
for a moment in the darkness and then vanishes,
leaving behind a new hope that there is light and
a sure path, opening not far ahead.

A. E. Day

For the evil pride we nourish,
    Making self the god we love,
We confess this sin most humbly,
    Seeking pardon from above.
To the waters Christ invites us,
    For the world a symbol clear
Of the healing, cleansing wonder,
    Given by the Saviour dear.

John Warren Steen

HIS PRESENCE
One day I came to myself and talked to the Lord
like this: "I did not come to China of my own
accord. In your Word you say that when we go
to tell people about you, you go with us, even
unto the end of the age. Now the end of the age
has not come, so this promise includes today,
right now!" And when I began to praise him for
his presence, he was there.

Bertha Smith

NIGHT HAS COME
Night has come once again
And I find once again it is time
To place my soul completely in God's hands.

Hubert Shipman

By faith I think of God as my Creator, I adore
Him as my Redeemer, I look for Him as my
Saviour.

Bernard of Clairvaux

BLESS THE NAME OF GOD
It is a profound thought that I can bless the Name
of God in prayer. The fact that we can bless God
with our mouths is confirmed in James 3:9,
"Therewith bless we God, even the father." The
Psalmist supports this when he says in 103:1-2,
"Bless the Lord, O my soul; and all that is within
me, bless his holy name. Bless the Lord, O my
soul, and forget not all his benefits." And again
he says, "Bless the Lord, O my soul, O Lord my
God, thou art very great: thou art clothed with
honour and majesty" (Psalm 104:1).

Jack R. Taylor

GOD'S MERCY LEADS TO . . .
Man who rejects God's goodness must experience
God's mercy. Only then can his heart be melted
and become as a cup running over with awe,
adoration, and joy at the goodness and mercy of
God that follow him all the days of his life and
promise to continue even into eternity itself.

Clarence W. Cranford

GLORIFICATION
But what is glorification to the Christian? Let me
repeat it again: that God having foreknown me,
did predestinate me, to be conformed to the
image of his Son, and nothing, but nothing shall
separate me from the final accomplishment of
that great fact. Let me say it like this. Glorification is ultimately to be like Jesus. "Oh," says the
song writer, "to be like him. More like Jesus
every day."

John R. Bisagno

MY GOD, HOW WONDERFUL THOU ART!
My God, how wonderful Thou art,
    Thy majesty how bright!
How beautiful Thy Mercy-seat
    In depths of burning light!

O worship the King, all glorious above . . .

Robert Grant

14

AGE

. . . Your old men shall dream dreams . . .

Joel 2:28

Now also when I am old and greyheaded, O God, forsake me not;
until I have shewed thy strength unto this generation, and thy
power to every one that is to come.

Psalm 71:18

Grow up as soon as you can. It pays. The only time you really live is from thirty to sixty.

Hervey Allen

GROW OLD TOGETHER

   Grow old along with me!
   The best is yet to be,
The last of life for which the first was made;
   Our times are in His hand
   Who saith: "A whole I planned—
Youth shows but half; trust God, see all nor be
   afraid."

Robert Browning

NEAR HOME

The soul's dark cottage, battered and decayed,
Let in new light through chinks that time has
   made.
Stronger by weakness, wise men become,
As they draw near to their eternal home.

Waller

HYMN OF MARRIAGE

John Anderson, my jo, John,
   When we were first acquent,
Your locks were like the raven,
   Your bonnie brow was brent;
But now your brow is bald, John,
   Your locks are like the snow;
But blessings on your frosty pow,
   John Anderson, my jo.
Now we maun totter down, John,
   And hand in hand we'll go,
And sleep thegither at the foot,
   John Anderson, my jo.

Robert Burns

A SERIOUS QUESTION

What's an old woman's reward for a life
Given to others as Mother and Wife,
Leaving her faltering, furrowed and scored—
What's an old woman's reward?

AGED FACE

As a white candle in a holy place,
So is the beauty of an aged face.

Joseph Campbell

MY TIMES IN THY HAND

So, take and use thy work:
Amend what flaws may lurk,
What strain o' the stuff, what warpings past the
   aim!
My times be in thy hand!
Perfect the cup as planned!
Let age approve of youth, and death complete
   the same!

Robert Browning

The fear of life is the favorite disease of the twentieth century. Too many people are afraid of Tomorrow—their happiness is poisoned by a phantom. Many are afraid of old age, forgetting that even if they should lose their bodily vigor, weakness itself may minister to them.

NEW WOOD

When Henry Wadsworth Longfellow was past seventy he was asked by an inquiring reporter for the secret of his continued youthful spirit and vigor. Pointing to an old apple tree near-by, which was a mass of blossoms, he said: "I try to be like that tree, I grow a little new wood every year." While it is true our human bodies must cease growing at a certain stage of life, it is also true that our minds and spirits may continue to improve even down to old age. "The path of the just is as the shining light, that shineth more and more unto the perfect day."

COUNTING YEARS

We do not count a man's years, until he has nothing else to count.

Ralph Waldo Emerson

FROM WESLEY'S DIARY

I am now an old man, decayed from head to foot. My eyes are dim; my right hand shakes much; my mouth is hot and dry every morning; I have a lingering fever almost every day; my motion is weak and slow. However, blessed be God, I do not slack my labour: I can preach and write still.—*Jan. 1, 1790*

LIVING PROOF

The question is asked, "Is there anything more beautiful in life than a boy and girl clasping clean hands and pure hearts in the path of marriage?" And the answer is given, "Yes—there is a more beautiful thing; it is the spectacle of an old man and an old woman finishing their journey together on that path. Their hands are gnarled but still clasped; their faces are seamed but still radiant; their hearts are tired and bowed down but still strong. They have proved the happiness of marriage and have vindicated it from the jeers of cynics."

LIFE BEGINS AT EIGHTY

Moses was eighty years of age when God called him to the leadership of Israel. Cato, at eighty, began the study of Greek; Tennyson, at eighty, wrote "Crossing the Bar;" George Bernard Shaw has written some of his most famous plays while in his eighties; Scott, the commentator, began the study of Hebrew at eighty-seven; Verdi wrote "Ave Maria" at eighty-five; many judges of the Supreme Court have been nearer eighty than seventy; Goethe wrote *Faust* when past eighty; Simonides won a prize for poetry when past eighty; Dr. Howard A. Kelly continued to be a world-famous cancer specialist when past eighty.

TAKE DOWN THIS BOOK

When you are old and gray and full of sleep,
And nodding by the fire, take down this book.
William Butler Yeats

O Lord, support us all the day long of this troublous life until the shadows lengthen and the evening comes, and the busy world is hushed, and the fever of life is over, and our work is done. Then in Thy mercy grant us a safe lodging and a holy rest, and peace at last. Amen.
Book of Common Prayer

CARRY-OVER INTO OLD AGE

It is possible for a man to carry the freshness, the buoyancy, the elastic cheerfulness, the joyful hope of his earliest days, right on through the monotony of middle-aged maturity, and even into old age, shadowed by the lovely reflection of the tones which the setting sun casts over the path.
Alexander Maclaren

FROM WESLEY'S DIARY

This day I enter on my eighty-sixth year. I now find I grow old. . . . What I should be afraid of, is, if I took thought for the morrow, that my body should weigh down my mind; and create either stubbornness, by the decrease of my understanding; or peevishness, by the increase of bodily infirmities: but Thou shalt answer for me, O Lord my God.—*June 28, 1789*

I think that old age is the best part of life, because you see things more truly and impersonally and less under the influence of party or interest or the world (having nothing to fear and nothing to hope for except rest with God) than you did in the days of youth. Also you have the opportunity of doing more good to others and to yourself, because you have more experience and knowledge. Nor is death a terror, but the prospect of it a pleasure and repose, when bodily troubles are beginning to weight you down.
Benjamin Jowett

Eternity sees all of our years at a glance.

A Field of Diamonds

GOD'S SOCIAL SECURITY
Too many people who continue to be active in their daily lives and work after retirement age think if they are getting a little tired, it is time to retire from God's service. So they just sort of get on God's Social Security. They figure after all those years of faithfulness they have in a sufficient number of quarters for God to continue to bless them with health, happiness and worldly goods—and they expect God to be right there with His Social Security check, and perhaps a little something extra, should any difficulties arise.

Iris O'Neal Bowen

The neglect of older people is becoming an increasing sin in America.

Billy Graham

RATHER LATE?
There is another kind of doubter. He is at the other end of the line. His favorite plaint is:

"Ah, but I am fifty. Rather late."

For what? For using a background of fifty years of experience for truer judgment? For erecting the house of which he has been laying the foundations? Have the great men of all times said that at seventy-five, eighty, or even ninety? At fifty a man's real life begins. He has acquired upon which to achieve; received from which to give; learned from which to teach; cleared upon which to build. "Rather late"? Rather early to cry "Wolf." Exactly the time to "cash in" upon the capacity that God has bestowed.

Edward W. Bok

BEAUTIFUL AT SIXTY
When at sixteen I was vain because someone praised me, my father said: 'They are only praising your *youth*. You can take no credit for beauty at sixteen. But if you are beautiful at sixty, it will be your own soul's doing. Then you may be proud of it and be loved for it.'

Marie Stopes

A SIXTY-NINE-YEAR-OLD DRIVER'S MIRACLE
Last evening as I was driving east,
    A beautiful sunset I did see.
And on and on to the east I drove,
    That sunset was in front of me.
Now I did not lose sense of direction,
    And from being confused I was far,
The sunset I saw while driving east
    Was in the mirror of my car.

Nell Roeder Lipham

But I am now in my seventieth year; what can be done ought not to be delayed.

Samuel Johnson

A DILAPIDATED HOUSE
When John Quincy Adams was eighty years old, a friend inquired, "How is John Quincy Adams today?" "Quite well, I thank you," replied Adams, "but the house in which he lives is becoming dilapidated, in fact, almost uninhabitable. I think John Quincy Adams will have to move out before long. But he himself is well, quite well."

Ere I had reached the age of sixty.
I spun, I wove, I kept the house, I nursed the sick,
I made the garden, and for holiday
Rambled over the fields where sang the larks,
And by Spoon River gathering many a shell,
And many a flower and medicinal weed—
Shouting to the wooded hills, singing to the
    green valleys.
At ninety-six I had lived enough, that is all,
And passed to a sweet repose.
What is this I hear of sorrow and weariness,
Anger, discontent, and drooping hopes?
Degenerate sons and daughters,
Life is too strong for you—
It takes life to love life.

Edgar Lee Masters

18

ASSURANCE

And we desire that every one of you do shew the same diligence to the full assurance of hope unto the end.

Hebrews 6:11

As I was with Moses, so I will be with thee: I will not fail thee, nor forsake thee.

Joshua 1:5

A FIRM LOVE
Not with doubting, but with assured consciousness, do I love Thee, Lord.

Augustine

BROKEN CHAINS OF DOUBT
I have lost that weary bondage of doubt, and almost despair, which chained me for so many years. I have the same sins and temptations as before, and I do not strive against them more than before, and it is often just as hard work. But whereas I could not before see why I should be saved, I cannot now see why I should not be saved if Christ died for sinners. On that word I take my stand, and rest there.

Frances Ridley Havergal

DRAFTS ON GOD'S BANK
The Bible is full of pictures of saints and beautiful poetry, but it has much more. To the believing child of God these are drafts on God's bank to be honored in the time of need. Every promise is a "Pay bearer on demand" of real practical value if we have faith to present it at God's bank.

ASSURANCE OF ETERNAL LIFE
The Word of God has power to give assurance of eternal life. In 1 John 5: 13, R. V., we read: "These things have I written unto you, that ye may know that ye have eternal life, even unto you that believe on the name of the Son of God." That is, the assurance of eternal life comes through what is "written." Suppose one has not assurance of salvation, what shall we do? Tell him to pray until he gets it? Not at all. Take him to some such passage as John 3:36, "He that believeth on the Son hath everlasting life . . ."

R. A. Torrey

Assurance begins with *as sure* . . .

CONFIDENCE IN THE PILOT
Were you ever at sea in a storm, when the ship reeled to and fro like a drunken man, and struggling, as for life in the arms of death, now rose to the top of the billow, and now plunged into the trough of the sea? Partially infected with others' terror, did you ever leave shrieking women and pale men below, to seek the deck and look your danger bravely in the face? In such circumstances I know nothing so reassuring as . . . the calm confidence that sits on the brow of that weather-beaten man who with iron strength leans upon the wheel and steers our ship through the roaring billows. Such, only much higher, is the confidence we draw from the confidence of God, as expressed in the words, "I have spoken, and I will do it."

Guthrie

WILL YOU TAKE CARE OF ME?
I remember, many years ago, a little boy on a trundle bed, having just retired for the night. Before going to sleep, he turned in the direction of the large bed on which his father lay, and said, "Father, are you there?" and the answer came back, "Yes, my son." I remember that that boy turned over and went to sleep without a thought of harm. Tonight that little boy is an old man of seventy, and every night before going to sleep he looks up into the face of his Heavenly Father, and says, "Father, are you there?" and the answer comes back, "Yes, my son." And then he asks in childish faith, "Will you take care of me tonight?" and the answer comes back, clear and strong, "Yes, my son." Whom need we fear, if God our Father be with us?

Henry Clay Trumbull

Blessed assurance, Jesus is mine!
Oh, what a foretaste of glory divine!
Heir of salvation, purchase of God,
Born of His Spirit, washed in His blood.

Fanny J. Crosby

HE IS WITH US

We can be sure of this, that God will be with us in all the days that lie before us. What may be round the next headland we know not; but this we know, that the same sunshine will make a broadening path across the waters right to where we rock on the unknown sea, and the same unmoving nightly star will burn for our guidance. So we may let the waves and currents roll as they list; or rather, as He lists, and be little concerned about the incidents or the companions of our voyage, since He is with us.

Alexander Maclaren

CHRIST WILL FIND THE WAY

Dr. H. Clay Trumbull used to tell with keen pleasure of the glimpse he once had of the secret of Napoleon's power over his soldiers. Happening to meet a French veteran who had served under the great commander, Dr. Trumbull asked him: "Did Napoleon's soldiers like him?" "Like him!" exclaimed the old French man, straightening up, his eyes snapping excitedly. "Like him! We believed in him. Napoleon say: 'Go to the Moon.' Every soldier start. Napoleon find the way." And we have a commander who is greater than Napoleon. Start out in the Christian life, friends, and Christ will find the way.

AN ASSURING THOUGHT

No one is so accursed by fate,
No one so utterly desolate,
    But some heart, though unknown,
    Responds unto his own.

Henry Wadsworth Longfellow

It isn't that I cling to Him
    Or struggle to be blest;
He simply takes my hand in His
    And there I let it rest.

Except for pressure a diamond would still be a piece of common coal.

THE GOD OF CONSOLATION

In a wonderful manner, difficult to explain, all that which had been taken from me was not only restored but restored with increase and with new advantages. In thee, my God, I found it all, and more than all! The peace which I now possess is all holy, heavenly, inexpressible. What I had possessed some years before, in the period of my spiritual enjoyment, was consolation and peace—the gift rather than the Giver. I might now be said to possess not merely consolation, but the God of consolation; not merely peace, but the God of peace.

Madame Guyon

PERSPECTIVE ON PESSIMISM AND THE FUTURE

The pessimist who hung his harp on the willow tree didn't have any perspective. He didn't see that although the exiles lost the Temple, they gained the synagogue. They lost worshipping multitudes but gained small study groups. They lost the ritual, but they gained an emphasis on torah (teaching or the law). They lost some dispensible elements but not their faith.
If religious customs change in the future, you may lose some of the old forms; but you can never lose your God. Jesus has promised that you will be secure in his hands. You can say, "I don't know what the future holds, but I know Who holds the future."

John Warren Steen

HIS SWEET CONSOLATION

For the kingdom of God is peace and joy in the Holy Ghost, and it is not given to the wicked. Christ will come to thee, and show thee His consolation, if thou prepare a worthy mansion for Him within thee. All His glory and beauty is from within, and there it pleaseth Him to dwell. He often visiteth the inward man and holdeth with him sweet discourse, giving him soothing consolation, much peace, friendship exceeding wonderful.

Thomas a Kempis

FAITH BRINGS ASSURANCE

Many people completely lack assurance because they have failed to understand a very necessary truth of the Christian experience: Faith brings assurance!

Billy Graham

RELIGION OF FOUR LETTERS

A friend of mine once said to another who was seeking peace by doing: "You have a religion of two letters. My religion is a religion of four letters." "How is that?" asked the other. "Your religion is do. My religion is done. You are trying to rest in what you do. I am resting in what Christ has done." There are many Christians today who have not permitted the blood of Christ to cleanse their consciences from dead works. They are constantly feeling they must do something to atone for sin. Oh, my brother, my sister, look at what God looks at, the blood, and see that it is all done, already done!

R. A. Torrey

NEVER LOST A MAN

A traveler, following his guide amid the Alpine heights, reached a place where the path was narrowed by a jutting rock on one side and a deep precipice on the other. The guide passed around, and then holding on to the rock with one hand, extended the other out over the precipice for the traveler to step upon, and so pass around the jutting rock. He hesitated, but the guide called back saying, "That hand has never lost a man." The traveler stepped onto the hand and was soon safely past the danger.

Mrs. Charles E. Cowman

A MIGHTY FORTRESS

A mighty fortress is our God,
  A bulwark never failing.
(Ein feste Burg ist unser Gott
  Ein gute Wehr und Waffen.)

Martin Luther

GOD KEEPS WATCH

Though the cause of evil prosper,
  Yet 'tis truth alone is strong;
Though her portion be the scaffold,
  And upon the throne be wrong—
Yet that scaffold sways the future,
  And behind the dim unknown
Standeth God within the shadow,
  Keeping watch above His own.

James Russell Lowell

LORDS OVER THE STARS

Luther and Melancthon once wanted to cross the Elbe at Torgau during a terrific storm. Timid Melancthon tried to dissuade Luther from making the dangerous crossing and said: "Martin, do not cross over, the stars are against us!" Luther answered: "We are the Lord's, consequently we are lords over the stars." What a rich fullness of comfort and trust lie in the words: "We belong to the Lord." There is no danger greater than he, no sin, not even death is greater. And what a call to us to be faithful, wakeful of our duty in these same words! They ennoble us and enrich our life. And that is the goal of salvation—to be his and to serve him.

A PERSONAL ASSURANCE

When Dr. James W. Alexander was dying, his wife sought to comfort him with precious words, as she quoted them to him: "I know in whom I have believed." Dr. Alexander at once corrected her by saying, "Not in whom I have believed; but 'I know whom I have believed.'" He would not even suffer a little preposition to be between his soul and his Saviour.

Charles Haddon Spurgeon

And God fulfils himself in many ways,
Lest one good custom should corrupt the world.
Comfort thyself: what comfort is in me?
I have lived my life, and that which I have done
May He within himself make pure!

Alfred Lord Tennyson

BIBLE

For the prophecy came not in old time by the will of man: but Holy men of God spake as they were moved by the Holy Ghost.

2 Peter 1:21

All scripture is given by inspiration of God, and is profitable for doctrine, for reproof, for correction, for instruction in righteousness.

2 Timothy 3:16

THE WORD OF GOD

The Bible says of itself that it is to be taught; appealed to; read; received; published; sought; searched; loved; longed for; and rejoiced in. It says that the Scriptures are inspired of God; approved of Christ; breathed by the Holy Spirit. That they are the Word of God; the book of law; the Holy Book; powerful; pure; perfect; true; timely; instructive; and comforting. I believe it is reasonable to begin by presuming the Bible to be the Word of God.

John R. Bisagno

When Sir Walter Scott lay dying, he cried, "Bring me the Book." His nephew said, "Which book, sir?" And Scott replied, "Young man, there is but one book, the Bible."

SHE KNEW THE AUTHOR

The finest reply ever given to a man yet who tried to throw doubt on the Bible was heard at a large dinner given in New York by a wealthy lady who sat beside a professor of science. In the course of conversation she said, quite naturally, "The Bible says so-and-so."

"The Bible!" remarked the professor. "You don't believe the Bible?"

"Yes, indeed, I believe it," replied his hostess.

"Why, I didn't suppose that any intelligent person today believed the Bible."

"Oh, yes," she said, "I believe it all. I know the Author."

The scientist was silenced. He had not a word to say.

The studious persual of the sacred volume will make us better citizens, better fathers, and better husbands.

Thomas Jefferson

The Bible is God's love letter to mankind.

THE BIBLE'S POWER

No greater moral change ever passed over a nation than passed over England during the years which parted the middle of the reign of Elizabeth from the meeting of the Long Parliament. England became the people of a book, and that book was the Bible. Its literary effects were great, "but far greater was the effect of the Bible on the character of the people at large." "One dominant influence told on human action." "The whole temper of the nation felt the change." "A new conception of life, a new moral and religious pulse spread through every class."

J. R. Green

Strange it is that so many prefer other books than the Bible; passing strange that some prefer books with the taint of the gutter in them; strange, very strange, that many are swimming through sewerage to get one drop of truth when the Bible, God's book, my mother's book, book that is still and will ever be the monarch among the trees, is near at hand. How tragic and sad that some should feed on carrion, or starve, when it is true, as many say, "O Lord, how sweet are Thy words unto my taste! yea, sweeter than honey to my mouth! More to be desired are they than gold, yea, than much fine gold, sweeter than honey and the droppings of the honeycomb!" (Ps. 19:10).

R. G. Lee

A TELESCOPE

The Bible is like a telescope. If a man looks *through* his telescope, then he sees worlds beyond; but if he looks *at* his telescope, then he does not see anything but that. The Bible is a thing to be looked through, to see that which is beyond; but most people only look at it; and so they see only the dead letter.

Phillips Brooks

For my part, I glory in the Bible.

Haile Selassie

THE QUEST

We search the world for truth, we cull
The good, the pure, the beautiful
From graven stone and written scroll,
From all old flower fields of the soul;

And, weary seekers of the best,
We come back laden from our quest
To find that all the sages said
Is in the Book our mothers read.

John G. Whittier

One of the saddest conditions of a human creature is to read God's Word with a veil upon the heart, to pass blindfolded through all the wondrous testimonies of redeeming love and grace which the Scriptures contain. And it is sad, also, if not actually censurable, to pass blindfolded through the works of God, to live in a world of flowers, and stars and sunsets, and a thousand glorious objects of nature, and never to have a passing interest awakened by any of them.

Dean Goulbourn

TEXTS OF GREAT MEN

The text from which John Bunyan preached to the multitudes—John 6:37

The text that saved William Cowper from suicide—Romans 3:24-25

The text that made Martin Luther the hero of the Reformation—Romans 1:17

The text that comforted the troubled soul of John Wesley—Mark 12:34

The text that made David Livingstone a missionary—Matthew 28:19-20

In the diamond-fields of South Africa a diamond was found; placed under a magnifying glass, you see enclosed in all its brilliancy a little fly, with body, wings, and eyes, in the most perfect state of preservation. How it came there no one knows, but no human skill can take it out. So in Holy Scripture the Spirit of God is found in a place from which no power of man can remove it.

BIBLICAL AUTHORITY

The Holy Scripture is the only outward standing rule and record . . . by which God witnesseth himself and his truth in the world; [the only] authority and sole external direction how to judge of all pretending Christs, prophets, doctrines, churches and spirits.

Roger Williams

USE—NOT ABUSE

A church member remarked to a minister that the Bible on the table was about worn out. It did indeed appear so, but a closer examination revealed that it was only worn on the outside; the inside was intact. The Bible had been *abused* rather than *used*. "What is in the Bible?" asked a kindergarten teacher of a little girl. She replied, "A lot of birthdays and dates of weddings and deaths, a lock of hair, some clippings from old newspapers, some snapshots, and two valentines." An unopened jar of food may be real food, but it will never satisfy.

CAST UPON THE WATERS

In 1855 a Japanese officer named Murata was hired for one purpose—to keep Japanese students, hungry for knowledge of the West, from leaving the country.

Murata, while on an inspection tour, found a little book floating on the water. In type, binding, and language, it was different from anything he had seen.

After many inquiries Murata learned that the little book told about the Creator of the universe, Jesus, who taught his mind and truth. Murata became a student of the little book's message.

Twelve years later, Murata and two others were baptized at Nagasaki by Verbeck—the first fruits of the gospel cast upon the water—literally—and used by the providence of God.

I believe the Bible because it finds me.

Samuel Taylor Coleridge

Those who feast upon the spiritual food God has provided in His Book will find strength to accomplish the tasks He assigns.

BIBLICAL PRESCRIPTION
If you have the "blues" read the 27th Psalm.
If your pocketbook is empty, read the 7th Psalm.
If people seem unkind, read the 15th chapter of Hebrews.
If you are discouraged about your work, read the 126th Psalm.
If you are all out of sorts, read the 12th chapter of Hebrews.

A LESSON FOR CHRISTIANS
The Mohammedans' sacred book is known as the Koran, a book smaller than our New Testament. It is written in Arabic, which is considered a sacred language. The Mohammedans never touch the book with unwashed hands, never carry it below the waistline, and never place it upon the floor—although it is customary to place everything else upon the floor in Mohammedan lands. Some Christians are not as reverent in their handling of the Bible as they might be.

WARNING
To lift the latch, to force the way;
But better had they ne'er been born,
Who read to doubt, or read to scorn.

I believe in Divine Creation; the Divinity of Jesus Christ and the Word of God.
Wernher von Braun

The man who studies the Bible and neglects all other books, will be wiser than the man who studies all other books and neglects the Bible. The man who studies the Bible will have more to say that is worth saying, and that wise people wish to hear . . .
R. A. Torrey

TRIBUTE TO THE BIBLE
It was the Bible that gave fire and nobleness to England's language; it was the Bible that turned a dead oppression into a living church; it was the Bible that put to flight the nightmare of ignorance before the rosy dawn of progress. . . . You might as well quench the sun, and suppose that the world can get along without light, as to think that men or that nations can do without God. . . . The world has no other Trumpet of Peace save Holy Scripture for souls at war; no other weapon to slay terrible passions; no other teachings to quench the heart's raging fires. This book alone makes mortals immortal, makes immortals gods.
Frederic W. Farrar

Knowing Jesus Christ, the Living Word, is the key that unlocks the Written Word, the Bible!

BIBLE READING
A great many have a superstitious feeling about reading the Bible. Men carry texts as Indians carry amulets, with the superstitious idea that God will bless them to their good. The mere reading of the Bible, or carrying of texts, will not do you any good. A man may own a farm, and yet go to the poorhouse. His land must be cultivated, or it will do him no good.
Henry Ward Beecher

The Bible, by many books, by many multitudes of books, has been outnumbered, but it has not been and cannot be outweighed. It is above and beyond all books as the river is beyond the rill in reach, as the sun is beyond and above the tallow dip in brightness, as the steel girder is above and beyond the wisp of straw in strength, as the ocean is beyond the mill pond in treasure and grandeur, as the grapevine is beyond the bramble in fruitbearing.
R. G. Lee

The Bible is a chart, not a charm.

THE BREAD OF LIFE
"Break Thou the bread of life, Dear Lord, to me,
As Thou didst break the loaves Beside the sea;
Beyond the sacred page I seek Thee, Lord;
My Spirit pants for Thee, O living Word.
Bless Thou the Truth dear Lord, To me—to me—
As Thou didst bless the bread By Galilee;
Then shall all bondage cease, All fetters fall;
And I shall find my peace, My All in all."

Mary Ann Lathbury

A college professor said to a young man on graduation day, "Now, my boy, understand that you are going to launch your craft on a dangerous ocean." "Yes, I know it," said the boy, and taking a Bible out of his pocket and holding it up he added, "but you see, I have a safe compass to steer by."

THE BOOK
The books men write are but a fragrance blown
    From transient blossoms crushed by human
        hands;
But, high above them all, splendid and alone,
    Staunch as a tree, there is a Book that stands.

WHAT A BOOK!
What a Book! Vast and wide as the world, rooted in the abysses of creation, and towering up behind the blue secrets of Heaven. Sunrise and sunset, promise and fulfillment, birth and death, the whole drama of humanity all in this Book!

Heinrich Heine

The Bible, unopened, will never feed a soul.

A Hindu woman said to a missionary, "Surely your Bible was written by a woman." "Why?" "Because it says so many kind things for women. Our pundits never refer to us but in reproach."

Bishop Hall

THE BIBLE IS IMPARTIAL
The agnostic, Robert G. Ingersoll, had a lecture on the subject, "The Mistakes of Moses." Commenting on this, a great educator once said: "I wouldn't give a nickel to hear Ingersoll on 'The Mistakes of Moses,' but I surely would give a lot to hear Moses on 'The Mistakes of Ingersoll.'" Of course Moses made mistakes, and no one, much less the Bible, has ever claimed otherwise. When Oliver Cromwell was having his portrait painted, he noticed that the artist had left off a big wart he had on his face. "Paint me as I am," said Cromwell, "wart and all." Thus does the Bible paint impartially.

"PLAYING AT BIBLE"
You who like to play at Bible,
    Dip and dabble here and there,
Just before you kneel, aweary,
    And yawn through a hurried prayer,
You who treat the crown of writings
    As you treat no other book—
Just a paragraph disjointed,
    Just a crude, impatient look—
Try a worthier procedure,
    Try a broad and steady view;
You will kneel in very rapture,
    When you read the Bible through!

Mark your Bible. It will emblazon glorious truths. Well-springs of inspiration will stand out like electric signs in the night.

Mrs. Charles E. Cowman

Within this awful volume lies
The mystery of mysteries:
Happiest they of human race,
To whom their God has given grace
To read, to fear, to hope, to pray.

Walter Scott

Sin will keep you from the Book, and the Book will keep you from sin.

GOD–BREATHED

The Bible is composed of sixty-six books, attributed to more than forty writers who lived over a period of about fifteen hundred years. They were men of varied interests, education, training, lands. . . . Yet when these men write they all speak of one theme, of one Person, *and none of their statements are contradictory.* There may be apparent contradictions, but they are only apparent. Further study always reveals them as perfectly harmonious.

Could you get forty physicians covering a period of fifteen hundred years to write on any medical topic and find leather strong enough to bind the book? Or forty lawyers? Or forty engineers? Or forty geologists? Or forty chemists? Or forty farmers? Then what is the explanation here? God! God, the Holy Spirit, breathed through Moses and Joshua and Samuel and David and John and Paul.

Marion McHull

MORNING CALL

Some minutes in the morning
    Take your Bible in your hand,
And catch a glimpse of glory
    From the peaceful promised land.
It will linger still before you
    When you seek the busy mart,
And like flowers of hope will blossom
    Into beauty in your heart.
The precious words like jewels
    Will glisten all the day
With a rare refulgent glory
    That will brighten all the way!

Jesus Christ is the heart of the Bible even in its earliest books. He is the *Shiloh* in Genesis; the *I AM* in Exodus; the *Star and Sceptre* in Numbers; the *Rock* in Deuteronomy; the *Captain of the Lord's Host* in Joshua; and the *Redeemer* in Job. He is David's *Lord and Shepherd* in the Psalms; in the Song of Songs He is the *Beloved.*

RESERVOIR OF POWER

The great reservoir of the power that belongeth unto God is His own Word—the Bible. If we wish to make it ours, we must go to that book. Yet people abound in the church who are praying for power and neglecting the Bible. *Men are longing to have power for fruit-bearing in their own lives and yet forget that Jesus has said: "The seed is the Word of God."*

R. A. Torrey

MY GUIDING FRIEND

The path is clearly marked from Youth to Age.
One need not lose the way. A hand leads on
From rosy morning's earliest breaking dawn
Till evening, and He promises a light
For that dim hour between the day and night.
He says, "I will be with you to the end."
I read His Word, I trust my guiding Friend.

The Bible, with its noble and simple language, I continued to read with a higher and truer understanding than I had ever before conceived. Its powerful verses had a different meaning, a more penetrative influence, in the silence of the wilds. I came to feel a strange glow while absorbed in its pages, and a charm peculiarly appropriate to the deep melancholy of African scenery.

H. M. Stanley

A popular and successful young minister in America became entangled in the meshes of infidelity, left the pulpit, joined an infidel club, and derided the name he had preached to others as the Savior of the world. But he sickened, and came to his death-bed. His friends gathered round him, and tried to comfort him with their cold and icy theories, but in vain. The old thought came back to him—the old experience came before him. He said, "Wife, bring me my Greek Testament."

Charles Haddon Spurgeon

CHARACTER

. . . be thou an example of the believers, in word, in conversation, in charity, in spirit, in faith, in purity.

1 Timothy 4:12

For even hereunto were ye called: because Christ also suffered for us, leaving us an example, that ye should follow his steps.

1 Peter 2:21

A Field of Diamonds

So let our lips and lives express
The holy Gospel we profess;
So let our works and virtues shine,
To prove the doctrine all divine.

Isaac Watts

THE GOSPEL ACCORDING TO YOU

There's a sweet old story translated for man
    But writ in the long, long ago—
The Gospel, according to Mark, Luke and John—
    Of Christ and his mission below.

Men read and admire the Gospel of Christ,
    With its love so unfailing and true;
But what do they say, and what do they think;
    Of the Gospel "according to you"?

'Tis a wonderful story, that Gospel of love,
    As it shines in the Christ life divine,
And, O, that its truth might be told again
    In the story of your life and mine.

Unselfishness mirrors in every scene,
    Love blossoms on every sod,
And back from its vision the heart comes to tell
    The wonderful goodness of God.

You are writing each day a letter to men,
    Take care that the writing is true,
'Tis the only Gospel that some men will read—
    That "Gospel according to you."

An honest man's the noblest work of God.

Robert Burns

The beautiful word, placed in the depths of mind, beautifies the language of life. Kind words, firm words, tender words, righteous words, loving words, draw on these elements of God, bringing them to bloom in human life, as the wick draws the oil and produces light.

"Work out" the Gospel that God has "worked in."

30

There lived once a young girl whose perfect grace of character was the wonder of those who knew her. She wore on her neck a gold locket which no one was ever allowed to open. One day, in a moment of unusual confidence, one of her companions was allowed to touch its spring and learn its secret. She saw written these words—*"Whom having not seen, I love."* That was the secret of her beautiful life. She had been changed into the same image.

Henry Drummond

And is our best too much? dear friends, we should
        remember
    How much our Lord poured out His soul for us,
And in the prime of His mysterious manhood
    Gave up His precious life upon the cross.
The Lord of lords by whom the worlds were
        made,
    Through bitter grief and tears, gave us the best
        He had.

CHRIST LIKENESS

The caterpillar of a moth, we are told, becomes like the color of the leaf upon which it feeds. Its color in this way indicates the character of the food it eats. If we would be like Christ we must feed on Him. Our moral character will always manifest the color of our mental food. Christ lived upon the Word of God His Father, and so maintained a life that was like God. If we would be His disciples we must come after Him in this matter.

James Smith

A. D. Brown, once the world's largest shoe manufacturer, was a devoted Christian. He had a framed motto in his office which read: "God first, family second, shoes third." He had another motto—"The greatest need in life is someone to make us do our best."

Christian character will shine for eternity.

SEVEN HINTS
Do nothing you would not like God to see.—1 Cor. 10:31.

Say nothing you would not like God to hear.—Ps. 141:3.

Sing nothing that will not be melodious in God's ear.—Eph. 5:19.

Write nothing you would not like God to read.—Ps. 139:2.

Go to no place where you would not like God to find you.—Ps. 139:3.

Read no book of which you would not like God to say, "Shew it Me."—Ps. 119:37.

A. T. Pierson

Kind words can never die;
  Cherished and blest,
God knows how deep they lie
  Stored in the breast,
Like childhood's simple rhymes,
Said o'er a thousand times,
Aye, in all lands and climes
  Distant and near.
Sweet thoughts can never die,
  Though, like the flowers,
Their brightest hues may fly
  In wintry hours;
But when the gentle dew
Gives them their charm anew,
With many an added hue
  They bloom again.

HIGH RESOLVE
I'll hold my candle high, and then
Perhaps I'll see the hearts of men
Above the sordidness of life,
Beyond misunderstandings, strife.
Though many deeds that others do
Seem foolish, rash and sinful too,
Just who am I to criticize
What I perceive with my dull eyes?
I'll hold my candle high, and then,
Perhaps I'll see the hearts of men.

MIRRORS OF CHRIST
With this explanation read over the sentence once more in paraphrase: We all reflecting as a mirror the character of Christ are transformed into the same Image from character to character—from a poor character to a better one, from a better one to one a little better still, from that to one still more complete, until by slow degrees the Perfect Image is attained. Here the solution of the problem of sanctification is compressed into a sentence: Reflect the character of Christ and you will become like Christ.

Henry Drummond

BEAUTY OF CHARACTER
A good many years ago there was born in Russia a boy who thought himself so ugly that he felt there was no happiness for such as he. He had a wide nose, thick lips, small grey eyes, and big hands and feet. When he grew to be a man he became a famous writer. In one of his books he tells that he was so anxious about this ugliness that he besought God to work a miracle, to turn him into a beauty. If God would do this the boy promised that he would give God all he then possessed, or would possess in the future.

That Russian boy was the great Count Tolstoi. Happily as he grew older he discovered that the beauty for which he sighed was not the only beauty, nor the best beauty. He learned to value more the beauty of a character strong and great and good in God's sight.

James Hastings

We turn our sad, reluctant gaze
  Upon the path of duty;
Its barren, uninviting ways
  Are void of bloom and beauty.
Though often dreary, dark, and cold
  It seems as we begin it,
As we press on, lo, we behold
  There's heaven in it.

Ella Wheeler Wilcox

The man who has not anything to boast of but
his illustrious ancestors is like a potato—
the only good belonging to him is underground.
                                    Sir Thomas Overbury

WHAT YOU GIVE
Fame is what you have taken,
   Character's what you give;
When to this truth you waken,
   Then you begin to live.

                                    Bayard Taylor

God will not look you over for medals, degrees
or diplomas, but for scars.
                                    Elbert Hubbard

VIRTUE
When we are planning for posterity, we ought to
remember that virtue is not hereditary.
                                    Thomas Paine

WHAT YOU ARE
Don't *say* things. What you *are* stands over you
the while, and thunders so that I cannot hear
what you say to the contrary.
                                    Ralph Waldo Emerson

A COMPLETE LOSS
When wealth is lost, nothing is lost;
when health is lost, something is lost;
when *character* is lost, *all* is lost!

CANDOR ABOUT CHARACTER
Charles Kingsley, British preacher and novelist,
was asked what kind of character he disliked the
most. He replied, "My own."

Be too large for worry, too noble for anger, too
strong for fear, and too happy to permit the
presence of trouble.

Fronting my task, these things I ask:
To be true, this whole day through;
To be content with honest work,
Fearing only lest I shirk;
To see and know, and do what's right;
To come, unsullied, home at night.

THE MAKING OF CHARACTER
My business is not to remake myself,
But make the absolute best of what God made.
                                    Robert Browning

If there is righteousness in the heart, there is
beauty in the character. If there is beauty in the
character, there will be harmony in the home. If
there is harmony in the home, there will be order
in the nation. When there is order in the nation,
there will be peace in the world.
                                    Chinese Proverb

CHRISTIAN CHARACTER
Under the right conditions it is as natural for character to become beautiful as for a flower; and if
on God's earth there is not some machinery for
effecting it, the supreme gift to the world has
been forgotten . . . Or in the deeper words of
an older Book: "Whom He did foreknow, He
also did predestinate . . . to be conformed to
the Image of His Son."
                                    Henry Drummond

LIKE THEE, DIVINE
"Lord, we are able," Our spirits are Thine
Remold them, make us like Thee, divine:
Thy guiding radiance above us shall be
A beacon to God, To love and loyalty.
                                    Earl Marlatt

The servant of God should so burn and shine
forth by life and holiness in himself, that . . .
he should reprove all the impious.
                                    Francis of Assisi

OUR NAMES

"Not as Cain," wrote James, and by so doing reminded us that names can be honored or debased, made popular or deprived of merit. Our names are solemn trusts, and even if we cannot give them luster we should keep them clean.

Donald F. Ackland

TRUE JUDGE OF CHARACTER

Jesus Christ saw in men what they could become. He looked beyond their frailties, shortcomings, hypocrisies, dishonesties, immoralities and saw what divine grace could do for them.

Leslie B. Flynn

CHARACTER IN THE CAR

One of the great needs of our time is to have Christians who are Christlike when they are behind the wheel of an automobile. We can use our automobiles to glorify God or we can let the devil use them as an instrument of destruction.

Willard Dawson

By our loyalty and meekness,
By our courage day by day,
By our kind consideration,
By forgiveness full and free,
By our just appreciation,
Lord, may we interpret Thee.

By our strength in overcoming,
By refusing selfish gain,
By response to those who struggle,
By relieving woe and pain,
Just by daily, helpful service
May we true disciples be,
Showing forth the love of Jesus,
Lord, and thus interpret Thee.

A man has to live with himself—see therefore that you are always in good company.

UPRIGHT CONVERSATION

Jesus admonished us to keep our conversation simple: a 'yes' or 'no' without expletives. On one occasion he prayed, "I thank you, Father, that you have hidden these things from the wise and prudent and revealed them unto babes."

Paul repeatedly spoke about the importance of Christian conversation. To the Ephesians he declared, "Let no corrupt communication proceed out of your mouth." He warned the Philippians: "Do all things without grumbling or disputing." To the Colossians he wrote, "Let the word of Christ richly dwell within you, with all wisdom, teaching and admonishing one another with psalms and hymns and spiritual songs, singing with thankfulness in your hearts to God."

"A word fitly spoken is like apples of gold in pitchers of silver."

Pawnee Martin

THOUGHTFULNESS

The roses on the desk were a lovely surprise; their blush of pink splashed color against the usually drab walls. Someone had thought to place them there, and that thoughtfulness was as nice as the flowers.

Thoughtfulness is a lovely virtue. Those who cultivate it add a great deal to the world—but not without a blessing in return. The word of appreciation—the smile of content . . . these things money cannot buy.

Man is thoughtful and benevolent only because he is made in the image of God. We think of others because we have first been the objects of God's thoughtfulness. The entrance of Jesus into the world, his death and resurrection, and his living presence, are like the blush of beautiful roses and the caress of helping hands. He came because God thought of us in our time of need.

John Jeffers

PRISON
Those prisons
   we make for ourselves are worst of all.
Though no bars or bunks or shelves or concrete
     walls
Enclose our physical beings,
Yet, our minds and souls
   are caged by pride and lies, or covetous
     greed, or hate bent on revenge.

Truth is the only key
   that unlocks the door of such a jail.
Love alone breaks the walls,
While kindness bends the bars to make us free.
And being free,
   We should never condemn
     Another to such a cell.
Jimmy Martin

THE VALUE OF PATIENCE
I compare patience to the most precious thing
that the earth produces—a jewel. Pressed by
sand and rocks, it reposes in the dark lap of the
earth. Though no ray of light comes near it, it
is radiant with imperishable beauty. Its
brightness remains even in the deep night; but,
when liberated from the dark prison, it forms,
united to gold, the distinguishing mark and
ornament of glory, the ring, the scepter, and
the crown.

Hillel

Beware of too sublime a sense
Of your own worth and consequence.
The man who deems himself so great,
And his importance of such weight,
That all around in all that's done
Must move and act for him alone,
Will learn, in school of tribulation,
The folly of his expectation.
William Cowper

Beautiful nature is the robe of God, woven on
the loom of His everlasting word.

PARADOXES OF LIFE
First, the way up is down. "He that humbleth
himself shall be exalted." Second, the way to
get rich is to become poor. "Blessed are the
poor in spirit: for theirs is the kingdom of
heaven." Third, the way to gain life is to lose
it. "He that loseth his life for my sake shall
find it."

You need not break the glasses of a telescope,
or coat them over with paint, in order to prevent
you from seeing through them. Just breathe
upon them, and the dew of your breath will shut
out all the stars. So it does not require great
crimes to hide the light of God's countenance.
Little faults can do it just as well.
Henry Ward Beecher

CHARACTER IN A NAME
And when God told His people His *name* He
simply gave them His character, His character
which was Himself: "And the Lord proclaimed
the Name of the Lord . . . the Lord, the Lord
God, merciful and gracious, long-suffering and
abundant in goodness and truth."
Henry Drummond

HOW OTHERS KNOW WE ARE CHRISTIANS
By our kindness and compassion,
By our help to those in need,
By our sympathetic patience,
By our willingness to heed,
By our happiness and gladness,
By unfailing charity.
By our tender ministrations,
Lord, may we interpret Thee.

When G. Campbell Morgan visited the home of
his then recently-married son, he remarked,
"Why, son, one could not tell from the pictures
on the walls whether you are Christians or not."
   Christians should pay attention to the details
of their lives.

CHILDHOOD

. . . Suffer the little children to come unto me, and forbid them not: for of such is the kingdom of God.

Mark 10:14

Train up a child in the way he should go: and when he is old, he will not depart from it.

Proverbs 22:6

Gentle Jesus, meek and mild,
Look upon a little child,
Pity my simplicity,
Suffer me to come to Thee.

Charles Wesley

But it was said, in words of gold
No time or sorrow ever shall dim,
That little children might be bold
In perfect trust to come to Him.

Child, you are like a flower,
    So sweet and pure and fair;
I look at you and sadness
    Comes on me, like a prayer.

I must lay my hands on your forehead
    And pray God to be sure
To keep you forever and always
    So sweet and fair—and pure.

Heinrich Heine

How dear to this heart are the scenes of my
        childhood,
    When fond recollection recalls them to view;
The orchard, the meadow, the deep-tangled
        wildwood
    And every loved spot which my infancy knew.

Samuel Woodworth

Each child must choose; may his heart yield
    To follow Christ in answer clear;
We bring him to thy temple, Lord,
    Then let him say, "Speak, Lord, I hear."

Marjorie Lou Stump

Shall I make my child go to Sunday School and
church? Yes! How do you answer Junior when
he comes to breakfast on Monday morning and
announces to you that he is not going to school
anymore? You know! Junior goes.

J. Edgar Hoover

The child is father of the man.

William Wordsworth

CHILD RECEIVING COMMUNION
Strange how his little freckled face
Is lighted up. He takes his place,
Half stumbling over others' feet.
Within his eyes are dreams so sweet
We scarce dare breathe to break the spell.
He is not here; we know it well.
For this brief space, withdrawn, apart,
He rests against our Savior's heart.

Geraldine Ross

THE INCOHERENT
He seated himself and explained:

"The children are not uttering strange words.
They are saying that which they feel nearest their
hearts.

There was once a time when you understood, but
that was long ago—before you lost yourselves so
completely,
    inventing horrible means of destruction;
    creating racial hatred;
    condoning international suspicion and conflict;
    fostering deceit;
    serving mammon;
    breaking marriages and marriage vows;
    trying to outdo one another in materialistic
        things;
    lusting after the flesh;
    nourishing selfishness.

These things have blinded you to the simplest and
most sincere of all statements.

It is you, not they, who are incoherent. They
want only to say, 'We love you.' "

A. B. Cothron

Parents do wrong by failing to exercise wise and
loving authority over their children.

Billy Graham

SOMETHING HEAVENLY

Jesus was indignant when the disciples thought children were not of sufficient importance to occupy his attention. Compared with the selfish ambition of grown-ups he felt something heavenly in children, a breath of the Kingdom of God. . . . To inflict any spiritual injury on one of these little ones seemed to him an inexpressible guilt.

Walter Rauschenbusch

HIS MERRY-GO-ROUND

Time used to be his merry-go-round
And ponies pranced when he closed his eyes;
Life was done in technicolor
And sparkled with gay surprise!
His thoughts so often scampered
Like lambs in the month of May
And on clouds of glorious fancy
He would exultantly drift away.

But now that winter has come,
From those billowy clouds he dismounts.
His lambs have turned to sheep—
And he methodically counts.
The merry-go-round has stilled somehow
And I quietly say my prayers . . .
Lest those dancing, prancing ponies
Suddenly turn to "mares."

Katherine Mills Johnson

FOR A SMALL BOY ANYWHERE, PLAYING WITH BLOCKS

Tossed aside, the tiny gun,
Wars forgotten, lost or won.
Ah, a house, a church; well done!
Learn to build, my little son.

Geraldine Ross

The beauty of democracy is that you never can tell when a youngster is born what he is going to do with you, no matter how humbly he is born . . .

Woodrow Wilson

CHILDREN AND EMOTIONAL UPHEAVALS

Children are not so much upset by physical insecurity as they are by emotional upheavals, or the lack of love. During World War II, when Britain was being bombed nightly, many British parents sent their children to the country where they could be safe from the bombings. But social studies made after the war showed that the children who stayed in London with their parents, where, despite the bombings, they could have the security of love and understanding, were less disturbed than those who were isolated from home in areas of comparative safety.

Billy Graham

TOO STUPID TO LEARN?

Was the mother "exceptional" whose six-year-old boy came home from school one day with a note from his teacher suggesting that he be taken from school as he was "too stupid to learn"?
"My boy is not stupid," said the mother to herself. "I will teach him myself."
She did and Thomas A. Edison was the result. "Exceptional"? In faith, yes!

Edward Bok

UNGRATEFUL CHILD

How sharper than a serpent's tooth it is
To have a thankless child!

William Shakespeare

REACH THEM AS CHILDREN

Recently in an audience of 4500 people I found that at least 400 of the audience came to Christ under 10 years of age; between 10 and 12, 600; between 12 and 14, 600; between 14 and 16, about 1000; between 16 and 20, fully one half, and in the entire audience not more than 25 people came to Christ after they were 30 years of age.

J. Wilbur Chapman

The laughter of a child is heavenly language.

A Field of Diamonds

WE THANK YOU FOR CHILDREN
Our Father,

We thank you for children.

We thank you for younger children,
   with their startling frankness,
   with their quick and solemn loyalties,
   with their unquestioning belief.

We thank you for older children,
   with their changing bodies,
   with their daring curiosity,
   with their anguished uncertainty.

We thank you for adolescents,
   with their crisp idealism,
   with their need for affirmation,
   with their emerging womanhood
   and manhood.

We thank you for children
and their spirit of renewal
which they give to the rest of us.

Thank you. Amen.

Francis Martin

A PRAYER FOR CHILDREN'S TEACHERS
We implore thy blessing, O God, on all men and women who teach the children and youth of the world. Into their hands are committed the true treasures of the nations. As they teach the children so shall the future of the nations be.

Walter Rauschenbusch

JESUS LOVES THEM
Jesus loves the little children,
All the children of the world;
Red and yellow, black and white,
They are precious in His sight;
Jesus loves the little children of the world.

C. G. Woolston

PARENTAL CRUELTY
The parent who does not teach his child to obey is being cruel to him.

Billy Graham

"Why do you pay attention to that newsboy?" President Garfield was asked by an associate. "Because," the President answered, "no one knows what is buttoned up in that boy's jacket."

BEATITUDES FOR TEACHERS OF CHILDREN
Blessed are you when your church says, "Teach our children," for then you are numbered among these who follow the great command, "Go, teach."
Blessed are you when children think of you as a trusted friend, for in establishing this relationship with the children you have attained one qualification of a good teacher.
Blessed are you when with the children you see beauty, love, truth, and live in righteousness, for as you teach, you will also learn and grow.

HOW TO CURB DELINQUENCY
Six suggestions on how to curb juvenile delinquency: 1–Take time with your children; 2–Set your children a good example; 3–Give your children ideals for living; 4–Have a lot of activities planned for your children; 5–Discipline your children; 6–Teach them about God.

Billy Graham

THE LAD I USED TO BE
Across the fields of yesterday
   He sometimes comes to me,
A little lad just back from play—
   The lad I used to be.

T. S. Jones, Jr.

YOU NEVER KNOW
A doctor did not want to make a call on a particularly bad night, but he went through a pouring rain to the home of a poor laborer. His services saved the life of a small child. Years later the doctor said: "I never dreamed that in saving the life of that child on the farm hearth I was saving the life of the leader of England, Prime Minister David Lloyd–George!"

38

CHRISTMAS

Joy to the world, the Lord is come:
Let earth receive her King;
Let every heart prepare him room,
And heaven and nature sing.

Isaac Watts

Almost 2,000 years ago there was a Man born
contrary to the laws of life. This man lived
in poverty and was reared in obscurity. He did
not travel extensively.

He possessed neither wealth nor influence.
His relatives were inconspicuous, and had neither
training nor formal education.

In infancy He startled a king; in childhood He
amazed the doctors!

The names of the past proud statesmen, scientists, philosophers, and theologians have come
and gone; but the name of this Man abounds
more and more. Though 1900 years have passed
since His crucifixion, yet He still lives. Herod
could not destroy Him, and the grave could not
hold Him.

He stands forth upon the highest pinnacle of
heavenly glory, proclaimed of God, acknowledged
by angels, adored by saints, feared by devils, as
the living, personal Christ, our Lord and Saviour.

HOW FAR TO BETHLEHEM?

And so we find the Shepherd's field
And plain that gave rich Boaz yield,
And look where Herod's villa stood.
We thrill that earthly parenthood
Could foster Christ who was all-good;
And thrill that Bethlehem Town to-day
Looks down on Christmas homes that pray.

It isn't far to Bethlehem Town!
It's anywhere that Christ comes down
And finds in people's friendly face
A welcome and abiding place.
The road to Bethlehem runs right through
The homes of folks like me and you.

THAT NIGHT

That night when in the Judean skies
The mystic star dispensed its light,
A blind man moved in his sleep—
And dreamed that he had sight!
That night when shepherds heard the song
Of hosts angelic choiring near,
A deaf man stirred in slumber's spell—
And dreamed that he could hear!
That night when in the cattle stall
Slept child and mother cheek by jowl,
A cripple turned his twisted limbs—
And dreamed that he was whole!
That night when o'er the newborn babe
The tender Mary rose to lean,
A loathsome leper smiled in sleep—
And dreamed that he was clean!

I know not how that Bethlehem's Babe
Could in the God-head be;
I only know the Manger Child
Has brought God's life to me.

H. W. Farrington

O holy Child of Bethlehem,
Descend on us, we pray;
Cast out our sin, and enter in,—
Be born in us today.
We hear the Christmas angels
The great, glad tidings tell;
O come to us, abide with us
Our Lord Emmanuel!

Phillips Brooks

CHRISTMAS BALLAD

As Joseph was a-wurkin',
Thus did the angel sing,
And Mary's Son at midnight
Was born to be our King.
Then be you glad, good people,
At this time of the year;
And light you up your candles,
For His star it shineth clear.

God rest you merry, gentlemen,
Let nothing you dismay,
For Jesus Christ, our Saviour,
Was born upon this day.

I heard the bells on Christmas Day
Their old familiar carols play,
And wild and sweet
The words repeat
Of peace on earth, good will to men.
Henry Wadsworth Longfellow

Have you any old grudge you would like to pay,
Any wrong laid up from a bygone day?
Gather them all now, and lay them away
When Christmas comes.
Hard thoughts are heavy to carry, my friend,
And life is short from beginning to end;
Be kind to yourself, leave nothing to mend
When Christmas comes.
William Lytle

THE CHRISTMAS SYMBOL
Only a manger, cold and bare,
Only a maiden mild,
Only some shepherds kneeling there,
Watching a little Child;
And yet that maiden's arms enfold
The King of Heaven above;
And in the Christ Child we behold
The Lord of Life and Love.

Silent night, holy night,
All is calm, all is bright,
Round yon Virgin Mother and Child,
Holy Infant so tender and mild,
Sleep in heavenly peace,
Sleep in heavenly peace.
Franz Gruber

You can have that "Christmas feeling" all year if
Christ is in your heart.

But with the woes of sin and strife
The world hath suffered long;
Beneath the angel-strain have rolled
Two thousand years of wrong;
And man, at war with man, hears not
The love-song which they bring;
O hush the noise, ye men of strife,
And hear the Angels sing!
Edmund H. Sears

The whole world that knows about Christ's
coming dates its whole life from it. Such is the
splendor and importance of the advent of Jesus
Christ.
Phillips Brooks

THE CHRISTMAS GIVER
Christ is the Christmas giver. Many of the richest
and sweetest joys human hearts can experience
were born into the world when Christ was born.
Let us name a few from among the many. One is
the joy of knowing the nature of God. Christ is
Immanuel, God with us; so near that we could
see and understand and know him. Before the
coming of Christ men's ideas of God were hazy
and indistinct, sometimes even crude.

It is Christmas on the highway,
In the thronging, busy mart;
But the dearest, truest Christmas
Is the Christmas in the heart.

Hark the herald angels sing;
Glory to the new-born King;
Peace on earth, and mercy mild,
God and sinners reconciled.
Charles Wesley

That night when in the manger lay
The Sanctified who came to save,
A man moved in the sleep of death—
And dreamed there was no grave!

NO ROOM

Candy canes of red and white;
Holly wreath upon the door;
Relatives for overnight;
Inns are filled as before.
Sleds for children coasting;
Taffy for their candy–pull;
Making dinner . . . hurrying,
Asking what have we forgot?
Still, the Inns are full!

Helen Felts Brown

CHRISTMAS PRESENCE

Only an altar high and fair,
    Only a white-robed priest,
Only Christ's children kneeling there
    Keeping the Christmas feast;
And yet beneath the outward sign
    The inward Grace is given—
His Presence, who is Lord Divine
    And King of earth and heaven.

GRANDMA'S CHRISTMAS

Whenever Christmas comes . . . Christmas Day
at Grandma's . . . All the kith and kin . . .
From here and there and everywhere . . . Came
a-trippin' in . . . Through lanes and drifts they
brought their gifts . . . And smiles and words
of cheer . . . From out the storm a welcome
warm . . . To gladden all the year . . .
Christmas Day at Grandma's seems so long
ago . . . But it's here and just as dear as that we
we used to know . . . For I'm a grandpa now
you see . . . And Grandma's house is mine . . .
And girls and boys still bring Christmas joys . . .
And words of love divine.

In a thousand ways I cause the weary world to
look up into the face of God, and for a little
moment forget the things that are small and
wretched.
    I am the Christmas spirit!

E. C. Baird

Everywhere, everywhere, Christmas tonight!
For the Christ-child who comes is the Master of
    all;
No palace too great, no cottage too small.

Phillips Brooks

All round about our feet shall shine
A light like that the wise men saw,
If we our loving wills incline
To that sweet Life which is the law.
So shall we learn to understand
The simple faith of shepherds then,
And clasping kindly hand in hand
Sing, "Peace on earth, good will to men!"
And they who do their souls no wrong,
But keep at eve the faith of morn,
Shall daily hear the angel song,
"Today the Prince of Peace is born!"

James Russell Lowell

'Most all the time, the whole year round, there
    ain't no flies on me,
But jest 'fore Christmas I'm as good as I kin be!

Eugene Field

APPALACHIAN CAROL 2

How quiet falls December's snow
upon the brown-leaf earth;
it lays a blanket woven new
for little Jesus' birth.
The radiance of the star defines
the pine-topped mountain's height
and paints a peaceful stillness on
the valleys with its light.
The goldfinch on a holly bough,
the spotted yearling deer--
no smallest creatures move to break
the spell of waiting here.
And if our hearts are waiting still
to catch the distant strain,
the mountains will resound with joy
of angel songs again.

Bettie M. Sellers

CHURCH

This is a great mystery: but I speak concerning Christ and the church.

Ephesians 5:32

And he is the head of the body, the church: who is the beginning, the firstborn from the dead; that in all things he might have the preeminence.

Colossians 1:18

I am decked with loving tears, crowned by loving hands and hearts.

In the minds of the greatest men on earth I find a constant dwelling place.

I live in the lives of the young and in the dreams of the old.

I safeguard man, with a friendly hand for the man in fine linen and the man in homespun.

I am the essence of good fellowship, friendliness, and love.

I have gifts that gold cannot buy. They are given freely to all who ask.

I bring back the freshness of life, the eagerness, the spirit of youth, which feels that it has something to live for ahead.

I meet you with outstretched arms and with songs of gladness.

I am your comforter and best friend.

I am calling you!

I am the church.

A UNIQUE INSTITUTION

The church was founded by Christ to promote his kingdom of righteousness, peace, and joy in the world. It is the only institution that takes Jesus Christ seriously, teaches his Word, observes his ordinances, promotes his program, and seeks to exemplify his spirit. The church is the one institution that seeks the allegiance of men for their own sakes and gives its primary concern to the souls of men, seeking to prepare them for the best in time and eternity.

EXCUSES FOR A CLOSED MIND

"It's against church policy" . . . "That's not our problem" . . . "Runs up the overhead" . . . Let's give it more thought" . . . "We've always done it this way" . . . "It can't be done" . . . "It won't work in our church" . . . "It's never been tried before" . . . "We're not ready for that" . . . "It's impossible" . . . It's too much trouble to change."

I BELIEVE IN THE CHURCH

I believe more profoundly in the church every hour that I live. A man can make his testimony go further through the church than through any independent movements. He can make his money go further, his testimony, all his work go further. He can do more constructive work, than any other way in the world.

George W. Truett

GROWTH

Located in a university science building are some little cell-like cubicles called growth chambers. By using electric power most any combination of climatic and atmospheric conditions can be simulated in these chambers making it possible to determine how plants may fare under certain conditions.

Artificial, you may say? Follow the touch of human hand that sets the thermostat and flips the switch, through the wires of the building back to the transformer, to the powerline, to the generator, to the turbine, to the river, the rains, the clouds, and you stand ultimately in the presence of God. He is still the power that germinates and nurtures in growth.

The church is the Christian's growth chamber, but conditions can't be made exactly right here by the flip of a switch—too many personalities involved. Its members must provide the right conditions—reverence, good teaching, effective prayer, service, meaningful worship, and vital fellowship. These like heat, light and moisture are not of our own making; they reside in God, the source of all life, both physical and spiritual.

John Jeffers

A GIFT

My church represents Christ's best gift to me. I have united with it in solemn covenant that it shall have my best in attendance, prayer, service, sacrifice, zeal, giving, patience, and love. To be loyal to Christ I must be loyal to His Church.

QUALITY
Whitefield often affirmed that he would rather have a church with ten men in it right with God, than one with five hundred at whom the world would laugh up its sleeve.

Joseph Cook

COME AND GO
At a Salvation Army congress in London, General Booth told of a sympathetic clergyman who said to a young woman, a captain in the general's forces, that he admired their work, but disliked their drum. "Sir," said she in reply, "I don't like your bell." "What!" said he, "not the bell that says 'come to the house of God'?" "The bell may say 'Come!'" said she, "but the drum says 'Go and fetch them!'" The program of the church calls for Christians both to come and go. We are to come to the church where our souls are strengthened, then go in strength to the place of service.

SEVEN PROBLEMS OF THE CHURCH
1. The Unbended Knee
2. The Unread Book
3. The Unattended Service
4. The Unpaid Tithe
5. The Unrealized Cross of Christ
6. The Uncompassionate Heart
7. The Unconcern for Lost Souls

SOME BIRD!
When some churches want a new minister they want one with
> the strength of an eagle,
> the gentleness of a dove,
> the grace of a swan,
> the eye of a hawk,
> the friendliness of a sparrow,
> the night hours of an owl,
> the industry of a woodpecker,
> the attractiveness of a peacock,
> the tough skin of a gander,

and when they get the bird they want him to live on the food of a canary!

GOD'S GRIEF
The unused ability of the church is the exultation of hell, the surprise of heaven, the loss of man, and the grief of God.

W. B. Hinson

THE MAJOR TASK
Dr. L. R. Scarborough once suggested that the churches must not only recognize evangelism as their major task, but must organize and consecrate their manpower to that end: "Our supreme challenge is massing, mobilizing, and utilizing our millions of men and money, millions of missionary-minded women and youth under the direction of the Holy Spirit for the winning of the lost."

BUILDING THE CHURCH
When a contractor wants an old building demolished to make way for improvements he puts a gang of unskilled laborers at the task. Men do not need to be skilled in order to tear things to pieces. But when the site is cleared and the construction of the new building is begun, skilled mechanics are put to work. This illustrates a fact in church work. To tear things to pieces one doesn't have to know much, nor does he have to have religion, principle, or character. Those who build the church of Jesus Christ must study to show themselves approved unto God, workmen that need not be ashamed. They must acquire skill; mere goodness is not enough. They must know what they want to build and ways and means to build it.

Dr Len G. Broughton tells of a church which reported as follows: "Members received, none. Dismissed, none. Died, none. Married, none. Given to missions during the year, nothing. Brethren, pray for us that during the next year we may hold our own."

The Church rallies round the Cross.
Bishop Matthew Simpson

The church needs a fresh sense of its eternal destiny. While faith may seem to be losing ground today, God will ultimately triumph. He does not have to win every battle. Eternity is on his side.

Joseph F. Green

PLANNING GOD OUT

Our Father,
We plan our church life
so completely that
we wonder if our plans
put an end to you.

    Do we organize you
    into a neat package
    so that
    you are not at home with us?

    Father,
    sometimes, we feel that
    our organizing
    to communicate your love
    is a lot like
    the adolescent who
    mimeographed his love letters
    to his girl friends.

Forgive us when
our plans put an end to you.

Lead us to plan and to organize
to meet the real needs
or real persons,
even as you met
the real needs
of real persons
through the life and ministry
of our Lord, Jesus Christ.
Amen.

Francis Martin

The revival we long for must begin in our churches.

Billy Graham

GOD'S OWN JERUSALEM

O Thou not made with hands,
    Not throned above the skies,
Nor walled with shining walls,
    Nor framed with stones of price,
More bright than gold or gem,
God's own Jerusalem!

Not throned above the skies,
    Nor golden-walled afar,
But where Christ's two or three
    In his name gathered are,
Lo, in the midst of them,
God's own Jerusalem!

Francis Turner Palgrave

You take the church out of America, and see what kind of hell you'd have here overnight.

Billy Graham

THE CHURCH CONQUERING

What can be said of the church? It is the only institution fashioned and founded by our divine Saviour and Lord. He said, "The gates of hell shall not prevail against it," and they have not through the long centuries. Though sorely persecuted, the church has endured through fire and sword, and has risen up from the debris and has gone on conquering and to conquer.

George W. Truett

NOT JESUS' INSTITUTION

The national church . . . a state church, whether explicit as in Old England, or implicit as in New, is not the Institution of the Lord Jesus Christ.

Roger Williams

If one expects to answer "when the roll is called up yonder," he should be present when the roll is called down here.

The devil is perfectly willing that the Church should multiply its organizations and its deftly contrived machinery for the conquest of the world for Christ, if it will only give up praying.

R. A. Torrey

STEPS TO A FRIENDLIER CHURCH

Here are five simple steps to a friendlier church: (1) Speak to the other person first. Don't wait for someone else to take the initiative. (2) If you don't know him, introduce yourself. (3) Wear a pleasant expression. If you have to be grumpy and sour, do it somewhere besides at church. A great church was never built on frowns. (4) Take Will Rogers' testimony as your motto, "I never met a man I didn't like." (5) Memorize and practice Proverbs 18:24, "A man that hath friends must show himself friendly."

THINK IT OVER

1. How many times a month would there be no services at the church if everyone attended as you attend?
2. How much power would there be in the church work if everyone prayed as you pray?
3. Would the church ever be able to meet its obligations if no one ever gave any more than you do?
4. What opinion would people have of your church if no one praised it any more than you do?
5. How far would the church get with its teachings and training if no one gave any more time to it than you do?

By-and-by, as the young church became strong, it began to make its existence and its presence felt in the world. and then it stood in its genuine character and distinctive spirit, face to face with Rome. Once met, they instinctively recognized each other as its natural and irreconcilable enemy.

Islay Burns

MY CHURCH

My church is the agency of God's salvation for mankind. It is the expression of the love of God as it is revealed in Jesus Christ our Lord.

My church seeks to build the Kingdom of God, beginning here and now, and continuing forever. It seeks to do God's will "on earth as it is in heaven."

My church is composed of human beings, sinners saved by grace. It has no perfect people, but it seeks to make all men better. It offers no promise of easy living. Rather, it challenges persons to venture forth to live for God in the spirit of Christ.

My church needs me and I need my church. For this is the means God uses to carry forward his redemptive work—through human beings, who are His own creation.

My church needs my prayers, and I need its support in all experiences of life.

MORBUS SABBATICUS

Morbus sabbaticus is a disease peculiar to church membership. (1) The symptoms vary, but it never interferes with the appetite. (2) It never lasts more than twenty-four hours at a time. (3) No physician is ever called. (4) It always proves fatal in the end—to the soul. (5) It is very contagious. The attack comes on suddenly every Sunday; no symptoms are felt on Saturday night, and the patient awakes as usual, feeling fine, and eats a hearty breakfast. About nine o'clock the attack comes on and lasts until around noon. In the afternoon the patient is much improved and is able to take a ride, and read the Sunday papers. The patient eats a hearty supper, but the attack soon comes on again and lasts through the evening. The patient is able to go to work Monday as usual.

The church is not a dormitory for sleepers, it is an institution for workers; it is not a rest camp, it is a front line trench.

Billy Sunday

THE ROLE OF CHURCHES

The eleventh and twelfth centuries were in many ways great centuries in the history of Christendom. It was a period when the massive Gothic cathedrals flourished, the Abbey was built in London, and Chartres had just been completed. The monasteries were growing larger, accumulating more property, and generating more wealth. Outwardly the established church appeared to be at the peak of her power. But inwardly it was a different story. The hierarchy too often was obsessed with power and position. The people were often neglected.

At that time a little man called Francis, born in Assisi, said to the church, "First cleanse the inside of the cup." When proof of piety requires bricks piled high, the piety itself is suspect. Churches are not buildings; they only meet in them. Churches are fellowships people create from their common love for the Lord. The New Testament says that churches are Christ's body in the world.

If they are his body, then it follows they will be doing his bidding. I cannot recall reading in the New Testament where Jesus erected a building, but I do recall the word that he went about doing good (Acts 10:38).

Ralph L. Murray

Henry Sloane Coffin has declared that the church must be (1) a fellowship of free persons under the law of Christ, (2) a redemptive fellowship, (3) a supra-national fellowship, (4) a supra-class fellowship, (5) a supra-racial fellowship, and (6) an eternal fellowship.

THE CHURCH IS GOD'S

We render to Caesar the things that are Caesar's, and to God the things that are God's. To Caesar tribute is due, we deny it not; the Church is God's, and must not be given up to Caesar, because the Temple of God cannot by right be Caesar's.

Ambrose

After the riot, a fire in the ghetto of Washington, D. C.; but Alan didn't understand what God was trying to tell him: and after the fire God spoke gently to Alan.

When the Lord spoke, Alan pulled his sweater over his head and hid once again in his room. And the Lord said, "Alan, what are you doing here?"

And he answered, "Lord, I've always tried to do what you wanted me to, but the church refuses to minister to all people; it continues to build bigger buildings and neglect persons; it dismisses its clergy if they attempt to speak prophetically. Lord, they refuse to follow you, and now they won't listen to my suggestions."

And the Lord said, "Alan, you have no business hiding here. You have work to do. You're not alone, nor have I forsaken the church. Go back into the world."

Ed Seabough

A distraught student wrote to Dr. William L. Self of Atlanta: "Lately, God and the church have played a very small part in my life. Through my despair, though, I can see no other way. God's love must be the answer. But will God's church, as the supposed embodiment of committed believers in that love, provide a way? Will this wretched world be shown salvation? Will we express love, through sacrifice, sweat, tears,—and sometimes blood? I fear for myself, for my generation, for my nation, for my world."

My church stands as a beacon on the shoals of time. It is the lighthouse pointing to eternal life.

COMFORT

Comfort ye, comfort ye my people, saith your God.

Isaiah 40:1

I will not leave you comfortless: I will come to you.

John 14:18

A Field of Diamonds

SINGING AMONG DEAD TREES
I heard a bird at bread of day
    Sing from the autumn trees
A song so musical and calm,
    So full of certainties,
No man, I think, could listen long
    Except upon his knees.
Yet this was but a simple bird
    Alone among dead trees.

HOLD MY HAND
It isn't that I cling to Him
    Or struggle to be blest;
He simply takes my hand in His
    And there I let it rest.
So I dread not any pathway,
    Dare to sail on any sea,
Since the handclasp of Another
    Makes the journey safe for me.
Hold Thou my hand, dear Lord,
    Hold Thou my hand!

Be still, sad heart! and cease repining;
Behind the clouds is the sun still shining.
                Henry Wadsworth Longfellow

Abide with me: fast falls the even-tide;
The darkness deepens: Lord with me abide:
When other helpers fail, and comforts flee,
Help of the helpless, O abide with me!
                Henry F. Lyte

Ask the Saviour to help you,
    Comfort, strengthen, and keep you;
He is willing to aid you,
    He will carry you through.
                H. R. Palmer

God is before me, he will be my guide,
God is behind me, no ill can betide;
God is beside me, to comfort and cheer,
God is around me, so why should I fear?

When I laid down the Book, my mind commenced to feed upon what memory suggested. Then rose the ghosts of bygone yearnings, haunting every cranny of the brain with numbers of baffled hopes and unfulfilled aspirations. Here was I, only a poor journalist, with no friends, and yet possessed by a feeling of power to achieve! How could it ever be! Then verses of Scripture rang iteratively through my mind as applicable to my own being, sometimes full of glowing promise, often of solemn warning.
                H. M. Stanley

OUR LORD HAS BEEN THERE
Dr. S. D. Gordon once wrote: "Our Lord has been everywhere that we are called to go. His feet have trodden down smooth a path through every experience that comes to us. He knows each road, and knows it well—the steep path of temptation down through the rocky ravines and slippery gullies, the dizzy road along the heights of victory, the old beaten road of commomplace daily routine."

PROMISES
On every package sent out by a certain printer in a large city is an impressive trade-mark. It is simply a circle within which is his name and the words, "I never disappoint." Every promise of the Lord ever made to his people might have borne that legend.

If we could see beyond today
    As God can see;
If all the clouds should roll away,
    The shadows flee,
O'er present griefs we would not fret,
Each sorrow we would soon forget,
For many joys are waiting yet
    For you and me.

You cannot have roses without thorns.

50

OUR GOOD
All that He blesses is our good
  An unblessed good is ill;
And all is right that seems most wrong
  If it be His sweet will.

CLOUDS
Once there lived an old woman who was always so cheerful that everyone wondered at her. "But you must have some clouds in your life," said a visitor.

"Clouds?" she replied. "Why of course; if there were no clouds, where would the blessed showers come from?"

Though the Christian may sometimes have a "rough passage," he is assured a safe landing; for the promise is immutable: "It shall be well with them that fear God!"

PILOT AND CAPTAIN
Wild blasts upon my vessel sweep,
  From my weak grasp the wheel would tear,
I feel beside my hands His hands,
  Master of sky and sea and air.
I cannot plot my onward way;
  He holds all things in His control,
Jesus, the Master of my fate,
  Pilot and Captain of my soul.

THE ONE REALITY
Show me Thy face—my faith and love
  Shall henceforth fixed be,
And nothing here have power to move
  My soul's serenity.
My life shall seem a trance, a dream,
  And all I feel and see
Illusive, visionary—Thou
  The one reality!

The mountain that cannot be climbed may be tunneled.

AN OVERCOMER
When your good is evil spoken of, when your wishes are crossed, your taste offended, your advice disregarded, your opinion ridiculed, and you take it all in patience and loving silence, YOU ARE AN OVERCOMER.

When you never care to refer to yourself in conversation or to record your own good works, or itch after commendation; when you can truly "love to be unknown," YOU ARE AN OVER-COMER.

Mrs. Charles E. Cowman

HE KEEPS THE KEY
Is there some earnest prayer unanswered yet,
Or answered not as you had wished 'twould be?
God will make clear his purpose by-and-by,
  He keeps the key.
Unfailing comfort sweet and blessed rest,
To know—to every door He keeps the key;
And that at last, just when he thinks is best,
  He'll Give It Thee.

SORROWS
Our sorrows, like the passing keel of vessels upon the sea, leave a silver line of holy light behind them, afterward.

Charles Haddon Spurgeon

HIS CHILD AND HE
"Coward and wayward and weak,
  I change with the changing sky;
Today, so eager and brave,
  Tomorrow, not caring to try:
But He never gives in; so We Two shall win!
    —Jesus and I.
"Strong and tender and true,
  Crucified once for me;
Ne'er will He change, I know,
  Whatever I may be.
But all He says I must do—
  Ever from sin to keep free;
We shall finish our course, and reach Home at last!
    —His child and He."

This is my hope and my only comfort, to fly unto Thee in all tribulation, to hope in Thee, to call upon Thee from my heart and patiently wait for Thy loving kindness.

Thomas a Kempis

It has been well said that no man ever sank under the burden of the day. It is when tomorrow's burden is added to the burden of today that the weight is more than a man can bear. Never load yourselves so, my friends. If you find yourselves so loaded, at least remember this: it is your own doing, not God's. He begs you to leave the future to Him, and mind the present.

George MacDonald

NEVER BROKEN-HEARTED

They weep, you weep—it must be so;
  Winds sigh as you are sighing,
And Winter sheds its grief in snow
  Where Autumn's leaves are lying:
Yet, these revive, and from their fate
  Your fate cannot be parted:
Then, journey on, if not elate,
  Still *never* broken-hearted!

Emily Bronte

GOD'S WAY

It is not God's way that great blessings should descend without the sacrifice first of great sufferings. If the truth is to be spread to any wide extent among the people, how can we dream, how can we hope, that trial and trouble shall not accompany its going forth?

John Henry Newman

I wish you could convince yourself that God is often (in some sense) nearer to us, and more effectually present with us, in sickness than in health. Whatever remedies you make use of, they will succeed only so far as He permits.

Brother Lawrence

If it were not for hope the heart would break.

CASTING CARE UPON THEE

See, Lord, I cast my care upon Thee, that I may live, and consider wondrous things out of Thy law. Thou knowest my unskilfulness, and my infirmities; teach me, and heal me.

Augustine

An old man's prayer: "O Lord, help me to remember that nothin' is goin' to happen to me today that You and me together can't handle."

GOOD MEN WEEP EASILY

"Good men weep easily," says the Greek poet; and the better any are, the more inclined to weeping, specially under affliction. As you may see in David, whose tears, instead of gems, were the ornaments of his bed; in Jonathan, Job, Ezra, Daniel, etc. "How," says one, "shall God wipe away my tears in heaven if I shed none on earth? And how shall I reap in joy if I sow not in tears? I was born with tears, and I shall die with tears; and why then should I live without them in this valley of tears?"

Thomas Brooks

Cleave thou to Jesus in life and death, and commit thyself unto His faithfulness, who, when all men fail thee, is alone able to help thee.

Thomas a Kempis

May He support us all the day long, till the shades lengthen, and the evening comes, and the busy world is hushed, and the fever of life is over, and our work is done! Then in His mercy may He give us a safe lodging, and a holy rest, and peace at the last!

Ralph Waldo Emerson

COURAGE

. . . Be strong and of a good courage; be not afraid, neither be thou dismayed: for the Lord thy God is with thee whithersoever thou goest.

Joshua 1:9

Finally, my brethren, be strong in the Lord, and in the power of his might.

Ephesians 6:10

Courage consists not in blindly overlooking danger, but in seeing it and conquering it.

Jean Paul Richter

Yes, as my swift days near their goal,
  'Tis all that I implore:
In life and death a chainless soul,
  With courage to endure.

Emily Bronte

Oh! great is the hero who wins a name,
But greater many and many a time
Some pale-faced fellow who dies in shame
And lets God publish the thought sublime,
And great is the man with the sword undrawn,
And good is the man who refrains from wine,
But the man who fails and yet still fights on,
Lo, he is a twin brother of mine.

Joaquin Miller

Build to-day, then, strong and sure,
  With a firm and ample base,
And ascending and secure
  Shall to-morrow find its place.
Thus alone can we attain
  To those turrets, where the eye
Sees the world as one vast plain,
  And one boundless reach of sky.

Henry Wadsworth Longfellow

With every rising of the sun,
Think of your life as just begun,
The past has cancelled and buried deep
All yesterdays: there let them sleep.
Concern yourself with but today;
Grasp it and teach it to obey
Your will and plan.
Since time began, today has been
The friend of man.
You and today: a soul sublime
And the great heritage of time.
With God himself to bid the twain,
"Go forth, brave heart; attain! Attain!"

CHRISTIAN COURAGE

But Christianity has done more; it has marked the limits of it in the awful graves of the suicide and the hero, showing the distance between him who dies for the sake of living and him who dies for the sake of dying. And it has held up ever since above the European lances the banner of the mystery of chivalry: the Christian courage, which is a disdain of death; not the Chinese courage, which is a disdain of life.

G. K. Chesterton

MARCHING ORDERS

Go forth, then, ye ransomed ones, and remember that you bear through the world the image and superscription of Jesus Christ; in whatever company of men ye stand, forget not that His signature is upon you.

NOT BY COWARDS

Let us insist on having our say. We but half express ourselves, but ever draw diagonals between our own thought and the supposed thought of our companion, and so fail to satisfy either. Now God made the model and meant we should live out our ideal. It may be safely trusted as proportionate and of good issues, so that it be faithfully expressed, but God will not have his work made manifest by cowards. And so it takes a divine man to exhibit anything divine.

Ralph Waldo Emerson

Dare to be different! Dare to stand alone. Dare to stand up for your convictions even though the crowd may move as one body the other way.

It is only through labor and painful effort, by grim energy and resolute courage, that we move on to better things.

Theodore Roosevelt

Courage is the power of being mastered by and possessed with an idea.

Phillips Brooks

BE A HERO
In the world's broad field of battle,
    In the bivouac of Life,
Be not like dumb, driven cattle!
    Be a hero in the strife!

Henry Wadsworth Longfellow

BELIEVE IN THE HEROIC
"Ah!" said Coningsby, "I should like to be a great man!"
    The stranger threw at him a scrutinizing glance. His countenance was serious. He said in a voice of almost solemn melody:—
    "Nurture your mind with great thoughts. To believe in the heroic makes heroes."

Benjamin Disraeli

COURAGE!
Courage! What if the snows are deep,
And what if the hills are long and steep,
And the days are short, and the nights are long,
And the good are weak, and the bad are strong!
Courage! The snow is a field of play,
And the longest hill has a well-worn way,
There are songs that shorten the longest night,
There's a Day when wrong shall be ruled by right,
So courage! Courage! 'Tis never so far
From a plodded path to a shining star.

FOUNDED BY THE BOLD
This country was founded by the bold and cannot be maintained by the timid.

Theodore Roosevelt

Cowards die many times before their deaths;
The valiant never taste of death but once.

William Shakespeare

There's a call for men who are brave and true—
On! on with the song!

Quit you like men, be strong;
    There's a year of grace,
    There's a God to face,
There's another heat in the great world race—
Speed, speed with a song!

William Herbert Hudnut

When we live for the eyes of God, we do not fear the lips of men!

COURAGE TO FIGHT THE WOLF
No man can accomplish that which benefits the ages and not suffer. Discoverers do not reap the fruit of what they discover. Reformers are pelted and beaten. Men who think in advance of their time are persecuted. They who lead the flock must fight the wolf.

Henry Ward Beecher

Two things stand like stone—
Kindness in another's trouble,
    Courage in our own.

Adam Lindsay Gordon

SNOWFLAKES
If Snowflakes have the courage to leave Heaven's warm bed of comfort and travel an uncharted course to their final destination, couldn't you and I to be a little braver?

Ruth McPherson Kilby

I do not ask to walk smooth paths
Nor bear an easy load.
I pray for strength and fortitude
To climb the rock strewn road.
Give me such courage I can scale
The hardest peaks alone
And transform every stumbling block
Into a stepping stone.

Gail Brook Burket

A Field of Diamonds

BRAVE LUTHER
What! shall one monk, scarcely known beyond
his cell,
Front Rome's far-reaching bolts, and scorn her
frown?
Brave Luther answered, "Yes." That thunder's
swell
Rocked Europe, and discharmed the triple crown.
James Russell Lowell

REGIMEN OF A HERO
The hero is not fed on sweets,
Daily his own heart he eats;
Chambers of the great are jails,
And headwinds right for royal sails.
Ralph Waldo Emerson

But there is something deeper than that. "Depend upon it," said old Carlyle, "the brave man has somehow or other to give his life away."
. . . What we may pray for and desire is courage, to live eagerly in joy and not less eagerly in sorrow; to be temperate in happiness and courageous in trouble.
Arthur Christopher Benson

AN INDEPENDENT SPARK
Courage—an independent spark from heaven's
bright throne,
By which the soul stands raised, triumphant,
high, alone.
George Farquhar

LIFE, JOY, EMPIRE, VICTORY
To suffer woes which hope thinks infinite;
To forgive wrongs darker than death or night;
To defy power which seems omnipotent;
To love and bear; to hope till hope creates
From its own wreck the thing it contemplates;
. . . is to be
Good, great and joyous, beautiful and free;
This is alone life, joy, empire, and victory.
Percy Bysshe Shelley

The Courage we desire and prize is not the Courage to die decently, but to live manfully.
Thomas Carlyle

Be strong!
Say not the days are evil—who's to blame?
And fold the hands and acquiesce—O shame!
Stand up, speak out, and bravely,
In God's name.

Be strong!
It matters not how deep entrenched the wrong,
How hard the battle goes, the day how long,
Faint not, fight on!
Tomorrow comes the song.
Maltbie D. Babcock

Courage is resistance to fear, mastery of fear—not absence of fear.
Mark Twain

PACESETTERS
When you are called to get into the game, get into it good and strong. There's no fun in going through life spoon-fed; in finding the soft-seat. That makes a man soft, and a soft man is an abomination before God and men. Find your place and hold it: find your work and do it. And put everything you've got into it. Take hold and carry the biggest load your shoulders can carry, and then carry it right. Set the pace for others; don't let them set it for you.
Edward W. Bok

THE REWARD
Garibaldi, the great Italian reformer, urged thousands of Italy's young men to fight for the freedom of their homeland. One timid fellow approached him, asking, "If I fight, sir, what will be my reward?" Came the uncompromising answer: "Wounds, scars, bruises, and perhaps death. But remember that through your bruises Italy will be free."
Mrs. Charles E. Cowman

56

CREATION

Poems are made by fools like me,
But only God can make a tree.
Joyce Kilmer

To see a world in a grain of sand,
   And a heaven in a wild flower,
To hold infinity in the palm of your hand,
   And eternity in an hour.
William Blake

The poetry of earth is never dead; . . .
The poetry of earth is ceasing never.
John Keats

To me the meanest flower that blows can give
Thoughts that do often lie too deep for tears.
William Wordsworth

The account of the Creation indicates an orderly, systematic procedure in the development of the universe. And this is an object lesson in the divine character of order. Pope asserts that "order is heaven's first law," and the more we study God's universe, the better we see the beauty of this law. Whittier speaks of "the calm beauty of an ordered life."

At last with evening as I turned
Homeward and thought what I had learned
And all that there was still to probe—
I caught the glory of His robe
Where the last fires of sunset burned.

AWESOME WONDERS
In the beauty of a moment,
Is found time.
In the majesty of the horizon,
Is found the future.
In the simpleness of a flower,
Is found peace.
In the boldness of the dawn,
Is found hope.
Pam Herrell

A GNAT'S EYE
The circle that is in a gnat's eye is as true a circle as the one that holds within its sweep all the stars; and the sphere that a dew-drop makes is as perfect a sphere as that of the world.
Alexander Maclaren

ETERNAL SPRING
Soft fluffs of foam
drift dreamily with wandering winds
beneath a sky-blue dome.
Jonquil breath is faint upon the air.
On yonder branch an infant bud expands.
Below red robin tilts his sleuthing ear
and hears within the thawing ground
a welcome sound.
On sheltered bank bright crocus arms
stretch sunward.
Earth's sap is rising fast . . .
Winter is no more,
for spring is gently rapping
at resurrection's door.
Louise Barker Barnhill

TO A SKYLARK
Hail to thee, blithe Spirit!
   Bird thou never wert,
That from Heaven, or near it,
   Pourest thy full heart
In profuse strains of unpremeditated art.
Percy Bysshe Shelley

One impulse from a vernal wood
May teach you more of man,
Of moral evil and of good,
Than all the sages can.
William Wordsworth

The pots are mine,
   The flowers are God's.
      The enjoyment is yours.
John Warren Steen

There is beauty in the sunlight
  And the soft blue beams above.
Oh, the world is full of beauty
  When the heart is full of love.

The silent skies are full of speech
  For who hath ears to hear;
The winds are whispering each to each,
The moon is calling to the beach,
And stars their sacred wisdom teach
  Of Faith, and Love, and Fear.
                    Bernard of Clairvaux

I wandered lonely as a cloud
That floats on high o'er vales and hills,
When all at once I saw a crowd,
A host, of golden daffodils;
Beside the lake, beneath the trees,
Fluttering and dancing in the breeze.
                    William Wordsworth

NIGHT SOUNDS
Midnight on my mountain
and night sounds quiet the hurt and heat of day.
Below, by the tumbling creek,
frog songs faintly throb with calming pulse,
and cicadas of late summer lightly stir
in tall grasses moistening with dew.
The night plane droning west across the Milky
    Way
and the truck climbing the low grade to a distant
    gap
offer no intrusion,
only faraway accompaniment to the drowsy bird
muttering in the nearby pine thicket.
My house sleeps,
asking nothing more of me for this day now past.
The last lights go out in the valley below.
Soon I shall sleep,
but for a moment more I sit hushed
in the healing dark.
                    Bettie M. Sellers

WITHIN THESE WALLS

Within these walls the lush of pasture green
Lies like a wide-spread carpet in between
Two aged peaks. A shepherd tends his sheep.
Softly one walks beside the keeper's feet.

Within these walls are waters deep and still
Whose edge is fringed with silent trees that spill
Patterned shadows when bending low to drink.
By quiet pools the soul abides to think.

Within these walls there is a forest hall
Where tread of step is mute and woodthrush call
Softens the edge of night with plaintive trill.
In woodland depth the soul finds peace, is still.

Within these walls a tall cathedral spire
Points silently to heaven's blue attire.
Beneath its weathered dome, at altar shrine,
One kneels to pray, to touch a hem divine.

Within these walls there is the strength of calm
Where thought probes deep, and anchored faith
    the balm
For deadly fear. These walls that merge with sod
Shelter the still small voice of Almighty God!
                    Louise Barker Barnhill

HARVEST
When the breath of God breaks the seam of the
    pod,
You will hear the call of the quail
And the loud "Caw! Caw!" of the ebony daw,
As they feed on new seed by the trail.
                    Mrs. Anna Walker Robinson

One touch of nature makes the whole world kin.
                    William Shakespeare

WORKING WITH CREATION
I bring fresh showers for the thirsting flowers,
  From the seas and the streams;
I bear light shade for the leaves when laid
  In their noonday dreams.
                    Percy Bysshe Shelley

THE WORK OF GOD

The grass springs up; the bud opens; the leaf extends; the flowers breathe forth their fragrance as if they were under the most careful cultivation. All this must be the work of God, since it cannot even be pretended that man is there to produce these effects. Perhaps one would be more deeply impressed with a sense of the presence of God in the pathless desert or on the boundless prairie, where no man is, than in the most splendid park or the most tastefully cultivated garden which man could make. In the one case, the hand of God alone is seen; in the other, we are constantly admiring the skill of man.

Quoted by Charles Haddon Spurgeon

DAWN . . .

Dawn slips a pale shawl about the room.
A mockingbird announces daybreak.
I realize I have been awake a while,
Yet the family and house are quiet.
Now is the time for prayer . . .

Iris O'Neal Bowen

THOUGHTS FROM A DREAMER

Snowflakes tumbled from Heaven's sleepy bed and frolicked earthward covering the land with crystal-white happiness. The hour was marked by that invisible moment when night and dawn struggle for ultimate supremacy.

Unlike the patter of raindrops announcing their arrival, snowflakes tiptoe to one's doorstep and await in quiet splendor for that magic instant of discovery!

Well nigh into the day, snowflakes drifted earthbound and the glory of one's vision could be measured only by the miracle of nature's wonderment of enchantment.

Each day Nature promises a new setting, a bounty of colors and a rustle of winds to remind her inhabitants that constant change is just as inevitable as the breath of life itself.

Ruth McPherson Kilby

When lilacs last in the dooryard bloom'd,
And the great star early droop'd in the western
    sky in the night,
I mourn'd, and yet shall mourn with ever-
    returning spring.

Walt Whitman

MY AWAKENING

This morning just at seven
I awoke with all good will:
There was a chirp, a twitter,
And then a clear sweet trill!
A new kind of alarm, I mused—
A peaceful sort of thrill.

It was like a lovely symphony
Played in perfect rhythmic rime;
The notes were so well blended
The effect was more sublime
Than anything I'd heard all winter—
Or, it seemed, at any time.

Surely I must have been dreaming
Of some fairyland afar
Where no shrill sounds or scheming
Would all my senses jar!
"Where the best laid plans of mice or men"
Would only seem bizarre.

I needed no alarm this morning—
I awakened just before its ring,
Such a sweet melodious sound
I think it must be Spring!

Katherine Mills Johnson

COOPERATE WITH THE CREATOR

Come away from the
   competitions of the world,
    the ambiguities of life,
     and the fickleness of people—
Work in a garden of flowers or vegetables;
Cooperate with the Creator.
Watch out for unannounced miracles.

John Warren Steen

SUNDOWN

Now fades the glimmering landscape on the sight,
And all the air a solemn stillness holds.

Thomas Gray

DAWN . . .

Night's candles are burnt out, and jocund day
Stands tip-toe on the misty mountain-tops.

William Shakespeare

And down the long and silent street,
The dawn, with silver-sandalled feet,
Crept like a frightened girl.

Oscar Wilde

ILLUSTRATIONS FROM NATURE

Jesus saw spiritual truth in all of Creation. To
him the lily spoke of his Father's care, the leaven
that he saw in his mother's house spoke to him
of the way in which the Kingdom of God grew in
this world. The mustard seed was an illustration
of the growth of truth. Many of his most simple
and precious teachings were drawn thus from
nature. Sparrows, seed and tares, fig-tree, salt,
and many other objects of nature told him of
things unseen.

There is beauty in the forest
    When the trees are green and fair,
There is beauty in the meadow
    When wild flowers scent the air.

To hear the lark begin his flight,
And singing startle the dull night,
From his watch-tower in the skies,
Till the dappled Dawn doth rise;
Then to come, in spite of sorrow,
And at my window bid good-morrow,
Through the sweet-briar or the vine,
Or the twisted eglantine . . .

John Milton

BEAUTIFUL MUD!

A minister and his young friend were out for a
hike. Pausing to rest at a woodland stream, the
minister plunged his arm into the water and
brought up a handful of black mud. He looked
at it, then said to his companion, "Beautiful
mud." But the younger man did not agree.
"Mud isn't beautiful," he said. "None of us
really like it. I don't believe in kidding myself.
We wash mud out of our clothes because it's
dirty. We clean it out of our rugs."

The minister smiled. "Many millenniums
ago," he said, "God created the earth. The wind
blew over it and ground its rock into dust. God
dropped seed into it. Green shoots climbed to
the sun. In the autumn, a field of wheat waved in
the wind, and the hungry had bread to eat. After
all, as you'll find out, the meaning and beauty of
anything are determined by what it produces.
Beautiful mud!"

His young friend saw the point. "I guess
you're right," he agreed. "I never looked at it
that way, but I suppose a thing is evil when it is
used to create what is evil, and good when it is
used to produce what is good."

A FRIEND TO NATURE

Where rose the mountains, there to him were
    friends;
Where rolled the ocean, thereon was his home;
Where a blue sky, and glowing clime, extends,
He had the passion and the power to roam;
The desert, forest, cavern, breaker's foam,
Were unto him companionship . . .

Lord Byron

The year's at the spring
And day's at the morn;
Morning's at seven;
The hill-side's dew-pearled;
The lark's on the wing;
The snail's on the thorn;
God's in his heaven—
All's right with the world!

Robert Browning

The mountains are God's thoughts piled up. The ocean is God's thoughts spread out. The flowers are God's thoughts in bloom. The dew drops are God's thoughts in pearls.

Sam Jones

Study nature as the countenance of God.

Charles Kingsley

This earth on which we live is big or little, according to perspective. Compared with what we can see of the landscape and horizon, it is huge and we marvel at its immensity. But compared with the universe it is only a tiny speck. The earth as compared with the sun is like a one-inch ball compared with a globe nine feet in diameter. The sun is 866,000 miles in diameter and 93,000,000 miles from the earth. The sun is a star, but shines so brightly because it is relatively close to the earth. There are multiple other stars, many of them hundreds of times bigger than the sun, but they shine dimly because they are much farther away. David, the stargazer, cried, "When I consider thy heavens, the work of thy fingers, the moon and the stars, which thou hast ordained; what is man, that thou art mindful of him?"

When we worship God and live by His spiritual values, the knowledge and infinite complexity of science are channeled by a wisdom beyond human capability. Then, instead of making us the slaves of its industries, science sharpens the higher senses by removing the drudgery from life. Then, instead of smothering religion with its masses of data and logic, it intensifies religious truth by cleansing it of ignorance and superstition. Then science gives us the material strength to protect our spiritual values, and its machines, instead of turning cities into mounds of blood and rubble, become vehicles which carry man beyond the horizons he has known.

Charles A. Lindbergh

GOD MADE IT ALL!
However, you're a man, you've seen the world—
The beauty and the wonder and the power,
The shape of things, their colours, lights and
    shades,
Changes, surprises—and God made it all!

Robert Browning

Nature is the glass reflecting God, as by the sea reflected is the sun, too glorious to be gazed on in his sphere.

John Young

CAUSING ADMIRATION AND AWE
Two things fill me with constantly increasing admiration and awe, the longer and more earnestly I reflect on them: the starry heavens without and the moral law within.

Immanuel Kant

All things bright and beautiful,
    All creatures great and small,
All things wise and wonderful,
    The Lord God made them all.

Cecil F. Alexander

NOTES IN THE GREAT CONCERT
To exist is to bless; life is happiness. In this sublime pause of things all dissonances have disappeared. It is as though creation were but one vast symphony, glorifying the God of goodness with an inexhaustible wealth of praise and harmony. We question no longer whether it is so or not. We have ourselves become notes in the great concert; and the soul breaks the silence of ecstasy only to vibrate in unison with the eternal joy . . .

Henri Frederic Amiel

God Almighty first planted a garden. And, indeed, it is the purest of human pleasures.

Francis Bacon

CROSS

But God forbid that I should glory, save in the cross of our Lord Jesus Christ, by whom the world is crucified unto me, and I unto the world.

Galatians 6:14

And, having made peace through the blood of his cross, by him to reconcile all things unto himself; by him, I say, whether they be things in earth, or things in heaven.

Colossians 1:20

A Field of Diamonds

IN THE CROSS OF CHRIST I GLORY
In the cross of Christ I glory,
Tow'ring o'er the wrecks of time,
All the light of sacred story
Gathers round its head sublime.

John Bowring

THE OLD RUGGED CROSS
On a hill far away stood an old rugged cross,
The emblem of suffering and shame;
And I love that old cross where the dearest and
    best,
For a world of lost sinners was slain.

George Bernard

THERE IS A FOUNTAIN
There is a fountain filled with blood
    Drawn from Emmanuel's veins,
And sinners plunged beneath that flood
    Lose all their guilty stains.

William Cowper

Can there no help be had?
Lord, Thou art holy, Thou art pure:
    Mine heart is not so bad,
So foul, but Thou canst cleanse it sure.
Speak blessed Lord, wilt Thou afford
    Me means to make it clean?
I know Thou wilt: Thy blood was spilt.
    Should it run still in vain?

Christopher Harvey

The world has many symbols, but none is so
precious as the cross. It stands for God's love,
shown us in His Son. It stands for the love of
Jesus Christ, shown us in His death for us on
Calvary. It stands for our salvation from sin and
for the gift of eternal life. It stands for the
blessings of heaven. Whenever we see the cross,
our hearts leap with thanksgiving.

Amos R. Wells

WHEN I SURVEY THE WONDROUS CROSS
When I survey the wondrous cross,
On which the Prince of glory died,
My richest gain I count but loss,
And pour contempt on all my pride.

Isaac Watts

There is a green hill far away,
    Without a city wall,
Where the dear Lord was crucified,
    Who died to save us all.

Cecil F. Alexander

He died for me, he tasted death,
    Its woe and all its hell;
How much he suffered when he died
    No human voice can tell.
He died for me, for me he died,
    Oh, let me say it more;
For me he died, he died for me,
    My soul doth him adore.

Thus we see that the Cross was substitutionary.
On the Cross, where the history of human guilt
culminates, he was wounded for our transgressions. On the Cross, where purposes of divine
love are made intelligible, he was bruised for our
iniquities. As our substitute on the Cross, where
the majesty of the law is vindicated, he bore the
penalty of our transgressions and iniquities.
"Who his own self bare our sins in his own body
on the tree" (1 Peter 2:24). Only as a substitute
could he have borne them. As Abraham offered
the ram instead of Isaac his son, so Christ was
offered once to bear the sins of man (Heb. 7:27).

R. G. Lee

Grace is flowing from Calvary,
    Grace as fathomless as the sea,
Grace for time and eternity,
    Grace enough for me!

E. O. Excell

64

THE SINLESS SUFFERER

But His bearing is no easy tolerance of the intolerable. His love for us is hot with wrath for them. In that unwrathful recoil of love is our hope that He will not cease until all that is ungodlike in our own and the world's life is abolished. The sinless Sufferer on the cross, in His oneness with His brethren, felt their wrong doing His own, confessed in His forsakenness that God would have nothing to do with it save destroy it, felt that it separated between men and God, and that He was so at one with us that He was actually away from God. "That was hell," said a Scotch theologian.

Henry Sloane Coffin

THE HIGHEST AND LOWEST

The New Testament, generally, represents the cross as the very lowest point of Christ's degradation; John's Gospel always represents it as the very highest point of His glory. And the two things are both true; just as the zenith of our sky is the nadir of the sky for those on the other side of the world.

Alexander Maclaren

Christ is the basis upon which God can deal in mercy with the whole world. All of God's dealings in mercy with man are on the ground of the shed blood of Christ!

Amid all his defenses of Divine Sovereignty, Calvin never ignored or belittled the Atonement.

Cowper sang of it among the water lilies of the Ouse.

Spurgeon thundered this glorious doctrine of Christ crucified into the ears of peer and peasant with a voice like the sound of many waters.

NO DATE

Calvary has no date. "The Lamb slain from the foundation of the world."

"CHRISTIANITY" WITHOUT BLOOD

Christianity without atoning blood, is a Christianity without mercy for the sinner, without settled peace for the conscience, without genuine forgiveness, without justification, without cleansing, without boldness in approaching God, without power. It is not Christianity but the devil's own counterfeit. If we would know fulness of power in Christian life and service, we must first of all know the power of the blood of Christ, for it is that which brings us pardon, justification, and boldness in our approach to God.

R. A. Torrey

DOUBLE-DYED

Certain scarlet cloth is first dyed in the grain, and then dyed in the piece; it is thus double-dyed. And so we are with regard to the guilt of sin; we are double-dyed for we are all sinners by birth, and sinners by practice. Our sins are like scarlet, yet by faith in Christ they shall be as white as snow: by an interest in Christ's atonement, though our offences be red like crimson, they shall be as wool; that is, they shall be as white as the undyed wool.

Friendly Greetings

THE PRICE IS SET

There are some who would have Christ cheap. They would have Him without His cross. But the price will not come down!

Samuel Rutherford

God loves you. You're rebellious, you cheat, you commit immorality, you're selfish, you sin, but God loves you with an intensity beyond anything that I could describe to you. He loves you, and He loves you so much that He gave His only son Jesus Christ to die on that cross and the thing that kept Christ on that cross was love, not the nail.

Billy Graham

WHATEVER THE STREET—CALVARY

Here windows flaunt their colored wares,
A hundred lights blaze forth at once,
To win the coins of millionaires,
To pick the pockets of the dunce.
Here, greedy hands grasp with delight,
The rich man's gold, the poor man's mite.

Here where the offerings are flung
Before the gods of gain, I see
A small, a faded picture hung,
The Christ in dark Gethsemane.
Alone, ignored by avid eyes,
His gaze is fixed on endless skies.

A Magdalene who swaggers by,
A priest who pauses for a breath,
A drudge who passes with a sigh,
A furtive thug who deals in death,
They all must pass and go their ways
While Christ hangs there and prays—and prays.

Geraldine Ross

THE BLOOD FOR ALL

The blood of Christ in a certain measure avails
for all, for unbelievers, for the vilest sinner and
the most stubborn unbeliever and blasphemer.
In 1 John 2: 2, R. V., we read: "And He is the
propitiation for our sins, and not for ours only,
but also for the whole world."

R. A. Torrey

FOR GOD, the Lord of earth and heaven
SO LOVED, and longed to see forgiven,
THE WORLD, in sin and pleasure mad
THAT HE GAVE the greatest gift he had:
HIS ONLY BEGOTTEN SON to take our place
THAT WHOSOEVER - oh, what grace!
BELIEVETH, placing simple trust
IN HIM, the Righteous and the Just,
SHOULD NOT PERISH - lost in sin
BUT HAVE EVERLASTING LIFE in Him.

Simply to Thy cross I cling.

Augustus M. Toplady

THE CROSS

During World War II, it was announced that a
certain city would undergo a practice blackout
on a given night. It fell my lot to be returning
home from work on a city bus when the signal
for the blackout sounded. The driver pulled to
the curb and we watched the lights of the city go
out; first, the neons, then the street lamps, finally
the traffic signals. For a moment everything was
dark and strangely silent.

Then I noticed a reflection, in the store window to my right, which startled me at first because it was the reflection of a lighted cross,
towering in the sky. I looked up Sixth Avenue
and there it was, shining brilliantly atop the
Church of the Advent. Someone had overlooked
one switch and a city that would otherwise have
been in total darkness looked up to a cross in the
sky.

Even so must a world in darkness look to the
cross for its salvation---so must individuals, in-
cluding you and me, look to the cross of Jesus
for life abundant and eternal.

John Jeffers

THE TWO CROSSES

I saw a cross upon a hill,
    A cross made from a tree;
Upon it hung the Son of God,
    His blood poured out for me.

I turned and saw another cross,
    Not fashioned from a tree;
And felt it lean upon my back,
    For it was meant for me.

R. Paul Caudill

"I paint," cried Raphael.
"I build," was the boast of Michelangelo
"I rule," cried Caesar.
"I sing," cried Homer.
"I conquer," cried Alexander.
"I *seek and save*," cried Jesus Christ.

GOD'S GREATEST
God [the greatest lover] so loved [the greatest degree] the world [the greatest number] that he gave [the greatest act] his only begotten Son [the greatest gift] that whosoever [the greatest invitation] believeth [the greatest simplicity] in him [the greatest person] should not perish [the greatest deliverance], but [the greatest difference] have [the greatest certainty] everlasting life [the greatest possession].

THE PARADOX OF THE CROSS
In the cross of Christ we glory, because we regard it as a matchless exhibition of the attributes of God. We see there the love of God, desiring a way by which He might save mankind, aided by His wisdom, so that a plan is perfected by which the deed can be done without violation of truth and justice. In the cross we see a strange conjunction of what once appeared to be two opposite qualities—justice and mercy. We see how God is supremely just; as just as if He had no mercy, and yet infinitely merciful in the gift of His Son.
Charles Haddon Spurgeon

AWED AT CALVARY
When we look at Jesus of Nazareth hanging on the cross, our hearts go out to Him and cling to Him and give Him their all in adoring devotion. He is the divinest we know or can conceive of. His conscience and His love bow us before Him. We cannot think of Calvary without becoming awed.
Henry Sloane Coffin

God loved the world of sinners lost
  And ruined by the fall;
Salvation, full, at highest cost,
  He offers free to all!
Mrs. M. Stockton

The cross means death or life, according to your perspective.

WHAT SEEST THOU?
What seest thou, oh sinful man,
  Thine eyes upon yon cross?
"I can but see a dying man,
  His cause now stayed and lost."

What seest thou, oh dreamer,
  Thine eyes fixed on the tomb?
"I can but see the moulding clay
  And the midnight of its doom."

And what seest thou, oh Christ-like man,
  Thine eyes raised to the sky?
"I can but see a risen Lord
  Too powerful to die."

"A Christ Who rolled the rock away
  That blind men might see;
A Christ Who locked death in the grave
  And gave to me the key."
M. F. Graham

THE MISSION OF JESUS
Jesus will take care of you. He is a friend who will stick closer than any brother. Even if your own parents have discarded you, He will take you up out of the deepest gutter of sin. He is the one who will get you into right relations with God. It was out of infinite love that the Father sent the Son on this great mission, and out of infinite love the Son came on such mission. Oh, what a gospel we Christians have! What a gospel!
George W. Truett

Under this standard shalt thou conquer.
(In hoc signo vinces.)
Emperor Constantine, Motto assumed by him, A.D. 312

Crosses point to the heavens.
Crosses dangle from necks.
Crosses in icing are put on buns.
We are far removed from the Via Dolorosa—
But even farther away from the agony of Calvary.

THE DRAMA OF REDEMPTION

At a place called "Golgotha" (the place of a skull) they nailed him to a cross and raised him up between two thieves. All heaven and earth converge upon that central cross. The drama of redemption reached its amazing climax when human sin rose up and divine love reached down to that cross on Calvary!

Wayne Ward

THE MEANING OF CALVARY

What does Calvary mean to you?

The Jewish chief priests and scribes would have an answer. They would say it meant riddance of an imposter who threatened to stir up the people against them.

The Roman soldiers who nailed him to the cross would say the cross was an instrument of punishment.

The Christian would point to Calvary as the place where Jesus became our substitute and suffered the full penalty for our sins (2 Cor. 5:21).

Willard Dawson

THE NECESSITY FOR THE CROSS

The necessity for the cross, then, lies in the power of sin and God's desire to rescue man from it. God chose it because nothing less was adequate to break sin's hold on man. In verses such as this that interpret Christ's death, "blood" means that he died sacrificially. Giving his blood not only fit the Hebrew sacrificial pattern but expressed the completeness of his sacrifice. He went all the way for us, even to the point of giving his lifeblood.

Joseph F. Green

THE PASSION OF CHRIST

And so our redemption is that supreme love manifested in our case by the passion of Christ, which not only delivers us from the bondage of sin, but also acquires for us the liberty of the sons of God; so that we may fulfil all things from the love rather than from the fear of Him . . . .

Peter Abelard

The Cross of Christ reveals the love of God at its best, and the sin of man at its worst.

C. N. Bartlett

SIN CARPENTERED THE CROSS

Sin carpentered the Cross, and wove the thorns, and drove the nails—*our* sin! And a story too, in red—bright-flowing red—the story of love, his love that yielded to the Cross and nails and shame for us! And only the passion of His love burning within will make us hate sin, as only His blood can wash it out.

S. D. Gordon

THE RED CORD OF THE ATONEMENT

Napoleon, after conquering almost the whole of Europe, put his finger on the red spot on the map representing the British Isles, and said, "Were it not for that red spot, I'd conquer the world!" So says *Satan* about the place called Calvary, where Jesus Christ shed His Blood. Every true preacher of the Gospel strings all his pearls on the Red Cord of the Atonement.

T. L. Cuyler

AT CALVARY

Oh, the love that drew salvation's plan,
Oh, the grace that brought it down to man,
Oh, the mighty gulf that God did span
　　　At Calvary!

William R. Newell

AMAZING LOVE

And can it be that I should gain an interest in the
　　　Saviour's blood?
Died He for me, who caused His pain? For me,
　　　who Him to death pursued?
Amazing love! how can it be that Thou, my Lord,
　　　shoulds't die for me?

Charles Wesley

Does God love you?
　　　The cross answers.

DEDICATION

I beseech you therefore, brethren, by the mercies
of God that ye present your bodies a living sacrifice,
holy, acceptable unto God, which is your reasonable
service.

Romans 12:1

. . . the Holy Ghost said, Separate me Barnabas and
Saul for the work whereunto I have called them.

Acts 13:2

A Field of Diamonds

Here I give my all to Thee—
Friends and time and earthly store,
Soul and body Thine to be—
Wholly Thine for evermore.

W. H. McDonald

THE BEST WE HAVE
God wants our best. He in the far-off ages
    Once claimed the firstling of the flock, the
        finest of the wheat;
And still He asks His own, with gentlest pleading,
    To lay their highest hopes and brightest
        talents at His feet.
He'll not forget the feeblest service, humblest
    love;
    He only asks that of our store, we give the
        best we have.

WHAT YOU HAVE GIVEN AWAY
Count your wide conquests of sea and land,
    Heap up the gold and hoard as you may—
All you can hold in your cold, dead hand
    Is what you have given away.

E. M. Poteat, Jr.

ETERNITY IN A MINUTE
I have only just a minute,
Only sixty seconds in it,
Thrust upon me, can't refuse it,
Didn't seek it, didn't choose it,
But it's up to me to use it.
I must suffer if I lose it,
Give account if I abuse it.
Just a tiny little minute,
But Eternity is in it.

Let God have your life. He can do more with it
than you can.

D. L. Moody

FIND YOUR PURPOSE
Find your purpose and fling your life out into it;
and the loftier your purpose is, the more sure you
will be to make the world richer with every
enrichment of yourself.

Phillips Brooks

ATTEMPT AND EXPECT
No! rather, strengthen stakes and lengthen cords,
Enlarge thy plans and gifts, O thou elect,
And to thy kingdom come for such a time!
The earth with all its fullness is the Lord's.
Great things attempt for Him, great things expect,
Whose love imperial is, whose power sublime.

Charles Sumner Hoyt

A CROSS FOR ME
Must Jesus bear the cross alone,
And all the world go free?
No; there's a cross for every one,
And there's a cross for me.

Thomas Shepherd

One of the most beautiful Christians of the past
was Madame Guyon of France, a deeply consecrated woman who, in the corrupt times of
Louis XIV, was imprisoned because of her spiritual life and teachings. Even this did not daunt
her spirit, for while in prison she could write:
    A little bird I am,
    Shut from the fields of air;
    And in my cage I sit and sing
    To Him who placed me there;
    Well-pleased a prisoner to be,
    Because, my God, it pleases Thee.

Rosalee Mills Appleby

That is no true alms which the hand can hold;
He gives only the worthless gold
    Who gives from a sense of duty.

James Russell Lowell

THE NEAREST VESSEL

Nearness to God is essential if we are to be used of God. He chooses the vessel nearest His hand. This has always been true. The apostles, martyrs, missionaries, and saints who have finished their work and have gone on before, as well as those who live to-day, prove the statement that we must be in closest relationship with Christ if we are to be entrusted with the gift of power. It is when we are in the secret place of the Most High that we learn God's will concerning us.

J. Wilbur Chapman

HE WANTS ME, TOO!

Why should I give? What can God need from me?
When His are all the earth and sky and sea?
What worth to Him my little all would be!
    He wants me, too!

Why should I pray? My feeble voice Him move?
Bends He a listening ear to me in love?
Yet, when I cry He answers from above,
    He wants me, too!

Crown Him as your Captain
    In temptation's hour,
Let His will enfold you
    In its light and power.

CROWNED, NOT CRUCIFIED

I knelt in tears at the feet of Christ,
    In the hush of the twilight dim,
And all that I was, or hoped, or sought,
    Surrendered unto Him.
Crowned, not crucified; my heart shall know
    No king, but Christ who loveth me so.

J. Hussey

One sage has suggested that a Christian's prayer should be: "Lord, do not only count me—but count on me."

You may do miracles by persevering.

Robert Burns

O Lord, how I long to be centered in Thee, so completely centered in Thee that I do not realize it.

Oswald Chambers

IS OUR BEST TOO MUCH?

And is our best too much? dear friends, we
    should remember
How much our Lord poured out His soul for us,
And in the prime of His mysterious manhood
Gave up His precious life upon the cross.
The Lord of lords by whom the worlds were
    made,
Through bitter grief and tears, gave us the best
    He had.

DIVINE ENERGY

Give me the love that leads the way,
The faith that nothing can dismay,
The hope no disappointments tire,
The passion that will burn like fire.
Let me not sink to be a clod:
Make me Thy fuel, Flame of God.

THE ONLY WAY TO JOY

This is the only way to find fulness of joy,—complete, unconditional surrender to God. "Yield yourselves unto God." There is no very great measure of joy in a half-hearted Christian life. Many so-called Christians have just "enough religion to make them miserable." They can no longer enjoy the world and they have not entered into the "joy of the Lord."

R. A. Torrey

Not the sundown hours of my life, but all the hours of my life—God's!

You and today: a soul sublime
And the great heritage of time.
With God himself to bid the twain,
"Go forth, brave heart; attain! Attain!"

WHO IS WORSE?

One who does not believe in God, or
One who believes in Him, but does not serve Him?
One who does not believe the Bible, or
One who believes in the Bible but does not read it?
One who does not believe in prayer, or
One who believes in prayer but never prays?
One who does not believe in church, or
One who believes, but never attends, does not support it regularly, does not pray for it and very often criticizes it?

LABORERS TOGETHER

The chisel cannot carve a noble statue—it is only cold, dead steel. Yet neither can the artist carve the statue without the chisel. When, however, the two are brought together, when the chisel lays itself in the hands of the sculptor, ready to be used by him, the beautiful work begins. We cannot do Christ's work—our hands are too clumsy for anything so delicate, so sacred; but when we put ourselves into the hands of Christ, his wisdom, his skill, and his gentleness flow through us, and the work is done.

Phillips Brooks

Set apart for Jesus!
    Is not this enough
Though the desert prospect
    Opens wild and rough?
Set apart for His delight,
    Chosen for His holy pleasure,
    Sealed to be His special treasure:
Could we choose a nobler joy?
    And would we if we might?

The heights by great men reached and kept
Were not attained by sudden flight,
But they, while their companions slept
Were toiling upward in the night.

Henry Wadsworth Longfellow

GO ALL OUT

If you decide to live for Jesus Christ and go all out for Him, He'll be in your heart and He'll be there when every moral choice is made to help you over the humps and problems and difficulties and temptations. He'll give you a new power and new strength to resist temptation.

Billy Graham

CONSECRATION OF SELF

True conversion to God involves the consecration of ourselves and of all that we have to him, so far as we understand what is implied in this. But, at first, converts are by no means aware of all that is involved in the highest forms of consecration. To gain such knowledge is a work of time; and growth in the favor of God is conditioned on making a full surrender and consecration to God of everything we are, and have, and desire, and love, as fast as these objects are presented to thought.

Charles G. Finney

GOD'S DELIGHT

Purify the temple, and abandon your pleasures and careless ways, like the flower of a day, to the wind and fire; but labour in wisdom for the harvest of self-control, and present yourself as first-fruits to God, in order that you may be not only His work, but also His delight. Both things are necessary for the friend of Christ . . .

Clement of Alexandria

Day by day His tender mercy,
    Healing, helping, full and free,
Brought me lower, while I whispered,
    "Less of self, and more of Thee."
Higher than the highest heavens
    Deeper than the deepest sea,
"Lord, Thy love at last has conquered;
    None of self and all of thee!"

Theodore Monod

EASTER

And they shall scourge him, and put him to death: and the third day he shall rise again.

Luke 18:33

He is not here: for he is risen, as he said. Come, see the place where the Lord lay.

Matthew 28:6

HALLELUJAH!

"Christ the Lord is risen to-day,"
Sons of men and angels say:
Raise your joys and triumphs high;
Sing, ye heavens, and earth, reply.

Charles Wesley

In the bonds of Death He lay
    Who for our defence was slain;
But the Lord is risen to-day.
    Christ hath brought us life again,
Wherefore let us all rejoice,
Singing loud, with cheerful voice,
    Hallelujah!

Martin Luther

GO, TELL

Go quickly and witness for Jesus,
    Go, tell of his matchless love;
That for us He now makes intercession
    At the throne of the Father above.

"Come, see," and "go, tell," is the challenge
    Of Easter, to you and to me—
Come, see for yourself and be happy,
    Go, tell that salvation is free.

P. E. Holdcraft

HOPE LIGHTS THE DAWN

The sun hung at the rim of ending light
And moved dark shadows out across the earth . . .
Three rugged crosses faced approaching night
And shaded, with the sun, the lilies' birth.
Great sorrow-shadows fell across each heart
Of those who knelt beneath the stricken tree,
Obscuring faith that soon would be a start
Of hope that blossoms for eternity.
Then Christ was planted in a borrowed tomb
To wait new life on Resurrection Day,
And lilies that were resting burst in bloom
To brighten cross-made shadows where they lay.
Today, the shadow of the cross is gone,
And hope--as Easter lilies, lights the dawn.

Iris O'Neal Bowen

TO THE RISEN LORD

The three sad days have quickly sped;
He rises glorious from the dead;
All glory to our risen Head!
        'Alleluia!'
He brake the fast-bound chains of hell;
The bars from heaven's high portals fell;
Let hymns of praise His triumph tell.
        'Alleluia!'
Lord, by the stripes which wounded Thee,
From death's dread sting Thy servants free,
That we may live, and sing to Thee,
        'Alleluia!'

Translated from the Latin by F. Pott

POST-RESURRECTION WORDS

The first words that ever Christ spake after His resurrection to them He appeared to, were, "Woman, why weepest thou?" It is a good question after Christ's resurrection. What cause of weeping remains now that Christ is risen? Our sins are forgiven, because He, our Head and Surety, hath suffered death for us; and if Christ be risen again, why weep we? If we be broken-hearted, humbled sinners, that have interest in His death and resurrection, we have no cause to grieve.

Richard Sibbes

HOW TO SUCCEED IN RELIGION

There was a Frenchman by the name of Lepaux, who wanted to found a new religion. It was not long when he complained to the statesman Talleyrand of his ill-success. The statesman replied, "That you have difficulty in introducing your new religion does not surprise me. But I believe I can show you how to succeed." "I should be grateful for being shown," the new religionist said, rather curious and eager. This was the information he recieved: "The way to succeed in teaching religion is: Go and perform miracles; heal the sick of every variety; raise the dead; then be crucified and rise up again from the grave on the third day. When you shall have done all this, you may succeed."

THE EASTER LIGHT

Springtime, pulsating with vibrant new life, is
    reborn;
And all creation awaits the sunrise on Easter
    morn;
In the first rays of light,
The sweet lily glistens so pure and white;
The dew drops a tear of joy on the face of a rose;
And the sounds of spring are a symphony all
    nature knows;
As the spirit of new life surges through the earth,
    Winter's death is gone;
But there is an Easter light far greater then the
    golden rays of dawn;
It glowed two thousand years ago in a cold,
    dark tomb;
Where there was no sound . . . no sun . . . no
    sweet bloom;
Christ, the light of God in the world, conquered
    death and lived again;
And He is living now in the hearts of men:
The Christ-light's wondrous beams lift the spirit
    of man and revive his soul;
Then gently lead him to a higher goal;
No greater light shall ever be, no other can,
Than the Christ-light's wondrous beams in the
    heart of man.

Eva Adams

THE WONDER OF AN EMPTY TOMB

Suppose the tomb still held its prey
    as once it did that day
    far gone in time's escape –
Suppose the stone was yet in place
    and sorrow deepened for all who mourned
    their loss –
Suppose the angel's reassuring word had not
    been said when seeking ones bent low
    to peer within –
Suppose supernal joy had been denied these three
    whose hope was burning still.
Would we have known today of Bethlehem –
    his place of lowly birth?
    of love that masters self to shed
    its warmth on foe and friend the same?
Would we have heard the truth as was revealed
    by sea, on mountaintop, or plain?
Would we have known of Calvary –
    of how One bore the cross of suffering
    and shame to save mankind from wrong
    and soul condemnation?
An earthquake came that dawn.
An angel of the Lord then rolled the stone
    away,
    and they who came in search of Him
    were told that He was risen from the dead.
The wonder of an empty tomb remains.

Louise Barker Barnhill

BODILY RESURRECTION

The Bible teaches the bodily resurrection of
Christ. It is not simply a spiritual resuscitation,
as some would have us believe. His very body
was raised by God from the dead, and some day
we shall see the nailprints in His hands.

Billy Graham

I know that my Redeemer liveth,
And on the earth again shall stand;
I know eternal life He giveth,
That grace and power are in His hand.

Jessie Brown Pounds

RESURRECTION

Casting away the shroud, I come outside
Into the sunlight and the garden's cool
And call your name, desiring that you know
At last the time has come for which I cried
When in the darkness and the lonely rule
Of death. I thought there was no way to go
Beyond that prison and its final bier.
But then you brought Him there, the One, who
Cried out, "Come forth!" And here at last I stand,
Reeking of damp and darkness, yet I hear
His voice, "Come forth and find a life that's new."
There's love and grace and joy in his command.
I shall bow down this resurrection morn
In praise, for tombs, places to be reborn.

Ida Nelle Hollaway

ABSOLUTE PROOF

There are many historical facts in the world that were not attended by one-tenth as many witnesses as was the resurrection of Jesus Christ. Therefore I need not beg anybody's pardon for what I believe. I believe with all my heart that Jesus, the Christ, is risen indeed. I believe that He was seen after His resurrection, by 641 eye witnesses. During those forty days, Jesus appeared to different men under different circumstances at various places. He ate with them, walked with them, and talked with them. They positively could not have been deceived. Such deception would be without parallel in history and without an analogy in the annals of men. Christ's enemies became the charter members of His church, in Jerusalem on the day of Pentecost. Account for that fact if you deny the resurrection.

Scoville

Easter is the way across the dark river of death. Because Jesus lives we shall live also.

RESURRECTION EVIDENCE

There is more evidence that Jesus rose from the dead than there is that Julius Caesar ever lived or that Alexander the Great died at the age of thirty-three.

Billy Graham

A Mohammedan said, "You Christians do not even have a tomb to which you can point, where your Jesus lies buried. We have the tomb of Mohammed in Mecca." The Christian replied, "That is just the point; your prophet is dead and lies buried; our Christ is risen and is with us always."

Jesus' resurrection has provided for ours.

The greatest past tense in history is: "Come see the place where the Lord *lay*."

HOPE LIGHTS THE DAWN

The sun hung at the rim of ending light
And moved dark shadows out across the earth . . .
Three rugged crosses faced approaching night
And shaded, with the sun, the lilies' birth.
Great sorrow-shadows fell across each heart
Of those who knelt beneath the stricken tree,
Obscuring faith that soon would be a start
Of hope that blossoms for eternity.
Then Christ was planted in a borrowed tomb
To wait new life on Resurrection Day,
And lilies that were resting burst in bloom
To brighten cross-made shadows where they lay.
Today, the shadow of the cross is gone,
And hope, as Easter lilies, lights the dawn.

Iris O'Neal Bowen

Earth to earth, ashes to ashes, dust to dust, in sure and certain hope of the resurrection.

Book of Common Prayer

The Holy Scripture tells us that Jesus was seen five times on the resurrection day. He was seen of Mary; He was seen of the women: He was seen by two disciples on the road to Emmaus; He was seen by the apostles as they sat at meat. Later, He was seen by seven apostles by the sea, and by above five hundred at another time. He was seen by James, and last of all, He was seen by Paul, earth's chiefest apostle. The evidences external and internal that Christ rose from the grave are overwhelming. That is our hope in the face of broken humanity; that is our hope in the face of life; that is our hope in the face of death.

George W. Truett

Belief in the resurrection of Jesus is the motive power of all Christian mankind.

Dmitrii Merezhkovskii

The Easter message "de-stings" death.

FAITH

Now faith is the substance of things hoped for, the evidence of things not seen.

Hebrews 11:1

. . . and this is the victory that overcometh the world, even our faith.

1 John 5:4

A Field of Diamonds

REAL FAITH
Believing where we cannot prove.
Alfred Lord Tennyson

THE STEPS OF FAITH
Nothing before, nothing behind;
 The steps of faith
Fall on the seeming void, and find
 The rock beneath.
John Greenleaf Whittier

TRUE FAITH
True faith is simply taking God at His word and
personally and unreservedly casting one's self
into the open and waiting arms of Jesus!

IF WE COULD SEE
"If we could see, if we could know,"
 We often say,
But God in love a veil doth throw
 Across our way;
We cannot see what lies before
And so we cling to Him the more,
He leads us till this life is o'er;
 Trust and obey.

A MAN LIVES BY BELIEVING
A man lives by believing something; not by
debating and arguing about many things.
Thomas Carlyle

LINK WITH DIVINITY
Faith links me with Divinity. Faith clothes me
with the power of Jehovah. Faith insures every
attribute of God in my defense. It helps me to
defy the hosts of hell. It makes me march triumphant over the necks of my enemies. But without faith how can I receive anything from the
Lord?
"If thou canst believe, all things are possible to
him that believeth."
Charles Haddon Spurgeon

AVENUE TO SALVATION
Faith is the avenue to salvation. Not intellectual
understanding. Not money. Not your works.
Just simple faith. How much faith? The faith of
a mustard seed, so small you can hardly see it.
But if you will put that little faith in the person
of Jesus, your life will be changed. He will come
with supernatural power into your heart. It can
happen to you.
Billy Graham

FAITH TELLS US SO
If we could know beyond today
 As God doth know,
Why dearest treasures pass away
 And tears must flow;
And why the darkness leads to light,
Why dreary paths will soon grow bright;
Some day life's wrongs will be made right;
 Faith tells us so.

FAITH—GOD FELT BY THE HEART
It is the heart which experiences God, and not
the reason. This, then, is faith: God felt by the
heart, not by the reason.
Faith is a gift of God; do not believe that we said
it was a gift of reasoning. Other religions do not
say this of their faith. They only give reasoning
in order to arrive at it, and yet it does not bring
them to it.
Rene Pascal

All I have seen teaches me to trust the Creator
for all I have not seen.
Ralph Waldo Emerson

WE GO IN FAITH
We go in faith, our own great weakness feeling,
 And needing more each day Thy grace to
  know:
Yet from our hearts a song of triumph pealing;
 We rest on Thee, and in Thy name we go.

BELIEVING WHAT GOD SAYS
A little girl in Sunday school was asked, "What is faith?" and she said, "Believing what God says without asking any questions."

J. V. Updike

BELIEVE—LIVE
Inscribed upon the portal from afar
Conspicuous as the brightness of a star,
Legible only by the light they give
Stand the soul-quickening words
Believe and Live.

SAFE TO TRUST
My cherished plans and hopes may fail
   My idols turn to dust,
But this I know, my Father's love
   Is always safe to trust:
These things are dear to me, but still
   Above them all I love His will.

THE PROMISES . . .
Live upon them, not upon emotions. Remember feeling is not faith. Faith grasps and clings to the promises. Faith says, "I am certain, not because feeling testifies to it, but because God says it."

Mandeville

The Christian life is dependent upon faith. We stand on faith; we live by faith. Without faith, there is nothing.

Billy Graham

FAITH GIVES WINGS
The reason why birds can fly and we can't is simply that they have perfect faith, for to have faith is to have wings.

J. M. Barrie

Only those who see the invisible shall do exploits!

Faith is sufficient for itself, and in its own possession is rich enough.

Ambrose

I read the Word of God; it starts a flame
Within my heart; His Word that I can claim
Forever as my own, and always I
Find in its glow a fire to warm me by.
I find my strength and courage in His Word,
My hope is kindled and my heart is stirred
To stronger, growing faith.

FAITH IS THE KEY
Faith is the key to every door,
It opens hearts and fills them with love.
Faith is the hub of every wheel,
God makes it roll and men take the reigns.

Pam Herrell

I believe because it is impossible.
(Credo quia impossible.)

Tertullian

THE MASTER-KEY
Thanks be to Him that has loved us with an everlasting love, there is a way of escape for us all. The key is here, and it is not beyond our reach. Nay, into our hands he has thrust the master-key which will open every door the devil may shut against us. It is the key of faith in Jesus Christ.

E. L. Vincent

The only faith which makes a Christian is that which casts itself on God for life or death.

Martin Luther

Faith is an act and an affirmation of that act that bids eternal truth to be present fact.

Jack R. Taylor

OPTIMISTIC FAITH

I find daily life not always joyous, but always interesting. I have some sad days and nights, but none that are dull. As I advance deeper into the vale of years, I live with constantly increasing gusto and excitement. I am sure it all means something; in the last analysis, I am an optimist because I believe in God. Those who have no faith are quite naturally pessimists and I do not blame them.

William Lyon Phelps

A "RISKY" FAITH

God has guided the heroes and saints of all ages to do things which were ordinarily regarded by the community as ridiculous and mad. Have you ever taken any risks for Christ?

Charles E. Cowman

The price of the Scripture is our faith, for it is according to the intelligence and will of each that what we read therein is valued.

Ambrose

BELIEVE!

Believe! and the feeling may come or may go,
Believe in the Word, that was written to show
That all who believe their salvation may know;
Believe and keep right on believing.

A man at his wit's end is not at his faith's end.

Matthew Henry

All the scholastic scaffolding falls, as a ruined edifice, before one single word—faith!

Napoleon I

I have never been able to bring a man back to sanity and right thinking until I have brought him first to faith in God.

Dr. David Seabury

FAITH'S HABITAT

Shout on, proud men of State,
    I hear your haughty voices outside--
The ruthless, threatening, boisterous tones
    Of frenzied, war-mad earthly powers,
Who boast of gory carnage!

One thing alone sustains,
    Amidst the all-engulfing spate
Of treacherous, hate-born, sanguine fiats;
    I know I dwell within the walls
Of faith's glad habitation!

R. Paul Caudill

A WORD FOR FAITH

When John Paton, the pioneer missionary to the New Hebrides, was translating the Scriptures into the language of the people of the Southern seas, he had great difficulty in securing a word for faith; there seemed to be no equivalent in their language. He made it a special matter of prayer, and one day one of his workers came in from a hard day's work, and leaning back on a lounge chair, said, "Oh, I'm so tired, I feel I must lean my whole weight on this chair." "Praise God," said Paton, "I've got my word, 'God so loved the world that He gave His only begotten Son, that whosoever leaneth his whole weight on Him shall not perish, but have everlasting life.'"

Act on what faith you have. Don't worry about what you haven't.

LITTLE BUT TRUE

It is not the quantity of thy faith that shall save thee. A drop of water is as true water as the whole ocean. So a little faith is as true faith as the greatest. A child eight days old is as really a man as one of sixty years; a spark of fire is as true fire as a great flame . . .

Charles Haddon Spurgeon

Even "mustard seed" faith is colossal.

80

HOW TO GROW FAITH
If you want your faith to grow, there are four rules that you must adopt. First, be willing to have a great faith. Second, use the faith you have; the child with its slender arm muscles, will not be able to wield the sledgehammer unless he begins step by step to use them. Third, be sure to put God between yourself and circumstances. Everything depends on where you put God. Fourth, live a life of daily obedience to God's will. Observe these rules and your faith will grow.

F. B. Meyer

ROAD BETWEEN THE SOUL AND HEAVEN
Am I in trouble? I can obtain help for trouble by faith. Am I beaten about by the enemy? My soul on her dear Refuge leans by faith. But take faith away, then in vain I call to God. There is no other road betwixt my soul and Heaven. Blockade the road, and how can I communicate with the Great King?

Charles Haddon Spurgeon

Faith is the soul riding at anchor.

H. W. Shaw

FAITH OF THE MOUNTAINS
Teach me the faith of the mountains, serene and
    sublime,
The deep-rooted joy of just living one day at a
    time;
Leaving the petty possessions the valley-folk buy
For the glory of glad wind-swept spaces where
    earth meets the sky.
Teach me the faith of the mountains, their
    strength to endure,
The breadth and the depth of their vision, un-
    swerving and sure,
Counting the dawn and the starlight as parts of
    one whole
Wrought by the Spirit Eternal, within His control.

FAITH AND THE DIVINE ORDER
There is an order, a divine order, . . . true, whatever we may think or deny, find or miss. Faith does not create this order. It realizes it. It is the loyal and loving acceptance of it. What we think and do is only a tardy response to the thought of God, and to what He has been ever doing for us.

Robert E. Speer

FAITH BY THE WORD OF GOD
"I suppose that if all the times I have prayed for faith were put to together, it would amount to months. I used to say, "What we want is faith; if we only have faith we can turn Chicago upside down, or rather right side up. I thought that some day faith would come down and strike me like lightning. But faith did not seem to come. One day I read in the tenth chapter of Romans, "Faith cometh by hearing, and hearing by the Word of God." I had closed my Bible and prayed for faith. I now opened my Bible and began to study, and faith has been growing ever since."

D. L. Moody

WALK BY FAITH
And there are times and circumstances in the believer's life when, if he would keep himself from sinful doubts, if he would keep himself from falling into despair, he must, as it were, shut his eyes, lay the bridle on the neck of Providence, commit his way to God, and, however things may look, make this his comfort, "He will never leave me, nor forsake me." In such circumstances the only thing is to trust in God; "Walk by faith, not by sight."

Kenneth Sylvan Guthrie

One elderly Christian said, "I just fall flat on the exceeding great and precious promises, and I have all that is in them." So, "fall flat on the promises."

A Field of Diamonds

WHAT IS FAITH?

Faith is taking God at His word. It does not require a big army as in the case of Gideon, or the ability to see ahead as when Abraham went out into a new land, but it does require a change in direction as in Paul's life—also a clean life as in Joseph's life.

Faith involves belief but is more than belief. It is an unseen spiritual principle which enables us to cooperate with God so things can be accomplished that could not without Him. With God directing, great things can happen.

Those who have faith show evidence of it. Many spiritual giants have lived by faith. God acted through them to keep Christianity alive through persecution and the fall of many so called great nations. His Word will endure.

Sue Rogers Mitchell

FAITH IS RECEIVING AND BELIEVING

Faith is believing that God has done it and that we have it. Thus, the act of faith is receiving what we have. Faith enables the believing soul to treat the future as present, the invisible as visible. Abraham had faith, when, "having not seen, he believed." Mary accepted God's will with an affirmation of faith, "be it unto me according to thy word" (Luke 1:38). Jesus said, "Therefore I say unto you, What things soever ye desire, when ye pray, believe that ye receive them [literally, *are receiving*] and ye shall have them" (Mark 11:14).

Jack R. Taylor

Faith, mighty faith, the promise sees,
    And looks to that alone,
Laughs at impossibilities,
    And cries, 'It shall be done!'

True faith produces faithfulness. This principle is so certain that Christ will be able to judge our faith by the measure of faithfulness it has produced.

Joseph F. Green

FAITH IN THE FACE OF DEATH

A few years ago I had a friend, a devout Christian lawyer, whose doctor diagnosed his energy problem as the effect of leukemia at work in his body. Upon hearing of his illness, I wrote a letter expressing my concern and pledging my prayers.

In response there came back to me a letter full of high courage and strong faith. A paragraph of that letter not only reflects my friend's triumph over fear, but sets out for us the liberation Christian faith can give in any of life's boundary situations. He wrote:

"The other day a friend called by the office and asked me, 'Isn't there any cure for what you have?' I replied, 'Is there any cure for what you have?' He thought for a moment, and grinning said, 'I guess you're right.' Most of us have never honestly faced the fact of death, but the truth is that it is much more certain than living." Elsewhere in the same letter he wrote:

"I have had a full and complete life . . . Whatever the Lord wills about my continued life is perfectly satisfactory with me. Compared with eternity, I can see very little difference between 50 and 70." Only faith can help a person face the the fear of death like that. More particularly, only faith in the God who raised Jesus from the dead.

Ralph L. Murray

NOT ON FEELINGS

The fact of our salvation does not depend upon our own feelings. They are the least reliable of all things to rest upon; they are treacherous and not to be trusted. As surely as we rest upon these frauds—our feelings—the Lord will see fit to withdraw them, in order that we may learn to rest upon Him. Therefore stay your faith upon Christ Himself and His written promises. Whenever you are in doubt, perplexed, and unhappy, go at once to the Lord and His unfailing Word, and God's truth will disperse any mists of darkness which surround your soul.

Mrs. Charles E. Cowman

82

FELLOWSHIP

For your fellowship in the gospel from the first day until now . . .

Philippians 1:5

But if we walk in the light, as he is in the light, we have fellowship one with another, and the blood of Jesus Christ his Son cleanseth us from all sin.

1 John 1:7

LOVE HIM

Dost thou see a soul that has the image of God in him? Love him, love him; say, "This man and I must go to heaven together one day."

John Bunyan

You cannot despise a brother, without despising him that stands in a high relation to God, to His Son Jesus Christ, and to the Holy Trinity.

William Law

I SHALL NOT PASS THIS WAY AGAIN

Through this toilsome world, alas!
Once and only once I pass;
If a kindness I may show,
If a good deed I may do
To a suffering fellow man,
Let me do it while I can.
No delay, for it is plain
I shall not pass this way again.

No one is useless in this world who lightens the burden of it to anyone else.

Charles Dickens

COUNT THAT DAY LOST

If you sit down at set of sun
And count the acts that you have done,
  And, counting find
One self-denying deed, one word
That eased the heart of him who heard;
  One glance most kind,
That fell like sunshine where it went—
Then you may count that day well spent.
But if, through all the livelong day,
You've cheered no heart, by yea or nay—
  If, through it all
You've nothing done that you can trace
That brought the sunshine to one face—
  No act most small
That helped some soul and nothing cost—
Then count that day as worse than lost.

George Eliot

WORLD CITIZENS FOR CHRIST

And there is another great universal question which men are asking: "How shall a man relate himself to his fellowmen . . . ?" Then comes the Golden Rule: "Do unto others as ye would that they should do unto you." Christ gave us the parable of the Good Samaritan. Do you want to know who your neighbor is? Anybody who needs you is your neighbor. He may live next door to you, or across your state or your nation; he may live in the wilds of Africa, or in mystical India. He may never have heard of your country, nor of you. But wherever in the world he may be, if he really needs you, he is your neighbor. We are all to be world citizens. To follow Christ is to be a world citizen for Christ.

George W. Truett

God gave us five senses to appreciate his world
And a sixth sense to appreciate our friends.

John Warren Steen

If you really want to help your fellow-man, you must not merely have in you what would do them good if they should take it from you, but you must be such a man that they can take it from you. The snow must melt upon the mountain and come down in spring torrent, before its richness can make the valley rich.

Phillips Brooks

God, who hast given us the love of women and the friendship of men, keep alive in our hearts the sense of old fellowship and tenderness; make offences to be forgotten and services remembered; protect those whom we love in all things and follow them with kindnesses, so that they may lead simple and unsuffering lives, and in the end die easily with quiet minds.

Robert Louis Stevenson

Yes, you are your "brother's keeper," but more importantly you are your "brother's brother."

ONE COMMON LIFE
We are Christians, who not only profess to love one another, but are actually leading one common life; our pulses beat in harmony; we meet each other in love and sympathy, deriving support and counsel from our mutual intercourse. Were it not for this sympathy life would have no meaning.

Leo Tolstoy

ONE COMMON HEART
Man is dear to man: the poorest poor
Long for some moments in a weary life
When they can know and feel that they have been
Themselves the fathers and the givers-out
Of some small blessings; have been kind to such
As needed kindness, for the single cause
That we have all of us one common heart.

William Wordsworth

FRIENDSHIP
Friendship favors no condition,
    Scorns a narrow-minded creed,
Lovingly fulfills its mission,
    Be it word or be it deed.

Friendship cheers the faint and weary,
    Makes the timid spirit brave,
Warns the erring, lights the dreary,
    Smooths the passage to the grave.

Friendship—pure, unselfish friendship,
    All through life's allotted span,
Nurtures, strengthens, widens, lengthens,
    Man's relationship with man.

Let every man pray that he may in some true sense be a soldier of fortune, that he may have the good fortune to spend his energies and his life in the service of his fellow-men in order that he may die to be recorded upon the rolls of those who have not thought of themselves but have thought of those whom they served.

Woodrow Wilson

IN A WORLD OF STRIFE
In a world of strife and discord,
    Tempting us to hate mankind,
We look vainly for an answer,
    For the problems that we find.
Only in God's laws eternal
    Can we see how wars shall cease.
In a brotherhood of learning
    We shall serve the Prince of Peace.

John Warren Steen

BROTHERS' BROTHERS
We need to realize that we are not our brothers' keepers, but we are our brothers' brothers.

Boyd M. McKeown

LEVEL GROUND
When Chief Justice Charles Evans Hughes presented himself for membership in the Calvary Baptist Church of Washington, D. C., a Chinese laundryman came down another aisle to join at the same time. The pastor, so it is reported, said in receiving them, "The ground around the cross is wonderfully level." That is one place where all classes and nationalities meet on an equality.

AN INDICTMENT
A clergyman had preached about recognition of our friends in heaven. One of his hearers remarked: "I wish the pastor would soon preach on recognizing our friends on earth. I've attended this church six years, but do not recollect having been greeted outside of the church by any of its members."
Is it not true that there is far too little real fellowship in our churches? People sit in the same pew on Sundays, they commune at the Holy Table, they hope to spend eternity in Heaven, but in spite of these facts there seems to be a barrier between them here so that one is inclined to doubt whether their hope will be realized.

PREACHING NOT ENOUGH

Preaching is not enough, it is sometimes too general; the impressions of a song may soon be effaced, but the personal touch, the tear in the eye, the pathos in the voice, the concern which is manifested in the very expression of one's countenance; these are used with great effect, and thousands of people are to-day in the Kingdom of God, or in special service, because of such influences being brought to bear upon their lives.

J. Wilbur Chapman

GIFT WITHOUT GIVER—BARE

Not what we give, but what we share,
    For the gift without the giver is bare:
Who gives himself with his alms feeds three,
    Himself, his hungering neighbor, and Me.

James Russell Lowell

ROBBER AND MURDERER

He who withholds but a pennyworth of worldly goods from his neighbour, knowing him to be in need of it, is a robber in the sight of God. . . . Further I declare, who spares a penny for himself to put it by against a rainy day, thinking, I may need that for to-morrow, is a murderer before God.

Meister Eckhart

PRAYER FOR OTHERS

This will fill your heart with a generosity and tenderness, that will give you a better and sweeter behaviour than anything that is called fine breeding and good manners. By Considering yourself as an advocate with God for your neighbours and acquaintance, you would never find it hard to be at peace with them yourself. It would be easy for you to bear with and forgive those for whom you particularly implored the divine mercy and forgiveness.

William Law

HIS CHILD?

I find no concept quite so hard to grasp
And yet so full of comfort, joy, and love
As this—that the Eternal Lord, our God
Should welcome me before his throne above
And let me call him Father, as a child,
Beloved, forgiven, nurtured as his own,
Reminding me the blood his Son has shed
Has bought for me a place beside his throne.
But yet another truth stands parallel:
I have no right to call him Father, still,
Unless I can accept the simple fact
That every single creature in his will
Is his child, too---loved as any other,
Each one, my Father's child—each, my brother.

Ida Nelle Hollaway

I'm sick of hate and the waste it makes.
Let me be my brother's friend.

And throughout all Eternity
    I forgive you, you forgive me.

William Blake

FRIENDSHIP

Friendship, peculiar boon of Heav'n,
    The noble mind's delight and pride,
To men and angels only giv'n,
    To all the lower world denied.

Samuel Johnson

BUNDLE OF LIFE

We are bound together "in the bundle of life." No member of human society can dare say to another member of human society, nor can one race dare say to another race, nor can one country dare say to some other country: "I have no relation to you and I go on my way ignoring you." The Bible everywhere assumes the inescapable fact of human responsibility.

George W. Truett

GOD

In the beginning God created the heaven and the earth.

Genesis 1:1

And thou shalt love the Lord thy God with all thine heart, and
with all thy soul, and with all thy might.

Deuteronomy 6:5

GOD IS HIS OWN MOTIVE
God is His own motive, as His own end. As His Being, so His Love (which is His Being) is determined by nothing beyond Himself, but ever streams out by an energy from within, like the sunlight whose beams reach the limits of the system and travel on through dim, dark distances, not because they are drawn by the planet, but because they are urged from the central light.

Alexander Maclaren

GOD'S CHARACTERISTICS
The Bible tells us that God is Omnipotent. That means that He has all power. The Bible tells us that He is Omnipresent. That means that He is everywhere at the same time. The Bible tells us that He is Omniscient. That means that He has all knowledge. He knows everything that you do. "His eye is on the sparrow," and if God the Spirit is watching the sparrow, how much more He is watching you every moment.

Billy Graham

Happy is that soul with whom God findeth His resting-place, and in whom as in a tabernacle He is at rest.

Bernard of Clairvaux

GOD AND MAN'S FREE WILL
God, having placed good and evil in our power, has given us full freedom of choice; he does not keep back the unwilling, but embraces the willing.

John Chrysostom

JUSTIFY THE WAYS OF GOD
What is in me dark,
Illumine; what is low, raise and support;
That to the height of this great argument
I may assert Eternal Providence,
And justify the ways of God to men.

John Milton

THE GOODNESS OF GOD
O, the goodness of God! Who can so withstand this great love, that he does not love and praise Thee with all his powers? This work of our redemption makes Thee dear to us above all things. It is a work which has no like; humility unbounded, grace undeserved, a gift without return. This work claims our love, draws our wills gently, and unites our desires firmly and justly to Thee.

John Tauler

CAN YOU DOUBT?
Can you sit on top of a hill in spring,
And watch the birds sailing by on the wing,
And see the clouds drifting on in the sky,
And doubt there's a God who dwells on high?

GOD WORKS IN READY HEARTS
Although God is Almighty, He can only work in a heart when He finds readiness or makes it. He works differently in men than in stones. For this we may take the following illustration: if we bake in one oven three loaves of barley-bread, of rye-bread, and of wheat, we shall find the same heat of the oven affects them differently; when one is well-baked, another will be still raw, and another yet more raw. That is not due to the heat, but to the variety of the materials. Similarly God works in all hearts not alike but in proportion as He finds them prepared and susceptible.

Johannes Eckhart

. . . I was torn piecemeal, while turned from Thee, the One Good, I lost myself among a multiplicity of things. As among the powers in man's society, the greater authority is obeyed in preference to the lesser, so must God above all.

Augustine

A marvelous miracle—God is!

TO GLORIFY GOD
The older I grow, and now I stand upon the brink of eternity, the more comes back to me the sentence in the catechism which I learned when a child, and the fuller and deeper its meaning becomes: "What is the chief end of man? To glorify God and enjoy him forever."

Thomas Carlyle

OUR HIGHEST DESTINY
We and God must have business one with the other, and in opening our hearts to him our highest destiny is fulfilled.

William James

WHERE HIS LOVE CANNOT FALL
God's love can no more fall on rebellious hearts than the pure crystals of the snow can lie and sparkle on the hot, black cone of a volcano.

Alexander Maclaren

God is the denial of denials.

Meister Eckhart

God loves all existing things.

Thomas Aquinas

What can mud become when God takes it in hand? Well, what is mud? First of all, mud is clay and sand, and usually soot and a little water. When God takes it in hand He transforms the clay into a sapphire, for a sapphire is just that; and the sand into an opal, for that is the analysis of an opal; and the soot into a diamond, for a diamond is just carbon which has been transformed by God; and the soiled water into a bright snow crystal, for that is what the crystals are when God takes the water up into the heaven and sends it back again.

John Ruskin

THE BLIND "SEE"
If the blind put their hand in God's, they find their way more surely than those who see but have not faith or purpose.

Helen Keller

MUST HAVE A MAKER
Suppose I had found a watch upon the ground . . The mechanism being observed, . . . the watch must have a maker; . . .

William Paley

Thou Great First Cause, least understood,
　　Who all my sense confin'd
To know but this, that thou art good,
　　And that myself am blind.

Alexander Pope

Man proposes, but God disposes.
(Homo proponit, sed Deus disponit.)

Thomas a Kempis

GOD IS . . .
God is the supreme personal Spirit; perfect in all His attributes; who is the source, support, and end of the universe; who guides it according to the wise, righteous, and loving purpose revealed in Jesus Christ; who indwells in all things by His Holy Spirit, seeking ever to transform them according to His own will and bring them to the goal of His kingdom.

E. Y. Mullins

The Bible not only reveals God as Spirit, undiscerned by human hearts and untouched by human hands, but the Bible also reveals God as a Person. Everywhere in the Bible we read: "God loves"; "God says"; "God does." Everything that we attribute to a person is attributed to God.

Billy Graham

LOVE BEYOND UNDERSTANDING
For the love of God is broader
    Than the measure of man's mind;
And the heart of the Eternal
    Is most wonderfully kind.

Frederick W. Faber

SKY TOUCHERS

Grain elevators haughtily surveying
lesser beings
Self assuredly standing firm
Against the sky.

From our foreign perspective
they touch the sky
these sky touchers.

Yet
none touches so high
as the one not seen
Man's soul
touching sky with God.

Harvey Nowland

WITH ALL OUR HEARTS
Martin Luther, commenting on the First
Commandment, asks, "What means it to have a
God, or what is God?" and answers, "Whatever
thy heart clings to, and relies upon, that is properly thy God," and "to have a God is nothing
else than to trust and believe in Him with all our
hearts."

Henry Sloane Coffin

HE SHALL NOT BE MOVED
The seas shall arid be, the skies shall roll away;
Rocks shall turn to dust, mountains shall decay,
But His Word's fixed, His saving power remains,
For He shall not be moved; the Great Jehovah
reigns.

Anna Walker Robinson

"He lives within my heart" is the most telling
proof of God's existence.

COSMIC SLOT MACHINE

Our Father,

Some of us look for you
and see a cosmic slot machine
into which we drop a prayer
and take our chances.

Some of us look for you
and see a simple-minded social worker
who overlooks who we are and
provides us with unmerited handouts.

Some of us look for you
and see a cruel, super parent
who must punish and reward us
according to our behavior.

Some of us look for you
and don't see much, but
keep looking for you anyway,
hoping to see you as you are.

Some of us look for you
and see you: in ourselves,
in other persons, in your world,
and in the person of Jesus Christ.

Amen.

Francis Martin

A THOUSAND QUESTIONS
I had a thousand questions to ask God; but when
I met him, they all fled and didn't seem to
matter.

Christopher Morley

HIS FOOTPRINT
I took a day to search for God,
And found Him not. But as I trod
By rocky ledge through woods untamed,
Just where one scarlet lily flamed
I saw His footprint in the sod!

Quoted by R. G. Lee

Ours is a Jesus-like God. "God was in Christ,
reconciling the world unto Himself," and through
Jesus' reconciling love for us, we know God.

Henry Sloane Coffin

LET GOD REPAIR

Give to God all the pieces of your
    broken heart;
  Hold not one for grief or despair;
Take each and every precious part
  And send them up to God in prayer;
Have faith . . . surrender to His will;
  Do not bind your heart with sorrow;
Trust His mending and let your heart refill
  With hope and courage for tomorrow;
His love can heal each aching part;
But give to God all the pieces of your
    broken heart.

Eva Adams

GOD KNOWS

Is there some problem in your life to solve,
  Some passage seeming full of mystery?
God knows, Who brings the hidden things to
    light.
      He keeps the key.

Is there some door closed by the Father's hand
  Which widely opened you had hoped to see?
Trust God and wait—for when He shuts the door,
    He keeps the key.

THE TEMPLE OF GOD

Deal with thyself as with a temple of God, inasmuch as there is that within thee which is like unto God. The highest honour indeed that can be rendered to God is to venerate Him and to imitate Him.

Bernard of Clairvaux

HOW DO YOU KNOW?

"How do you know whether there be a God?" was once asked of a Bedouin; and he replied, "How do I know whether a camel or a man passed my tent last night? By their footprints in the sand." "The heavens declare the glory of God" (Ps. 19:1).

GOD IS LOVE

Where Love is, God is. He that dwelleth in Love dwelleth in God. God is Love. Therefore *love*. Without distinction, without calculation, without procrastination, love.

Henry Drummond

God made us to soar like eagles, but we are content to scratch like sparrows.

GOD INDEED

Know that the Lord is God indeed;
  Without our aid he did us make;
We are His flock, He doth us feed,
  And for His sheep he doth us take.

William Kethe

GOD'S EQUALITY

The roses bloom just as fair
  Beside the cottage door,
As they bloom by castle wall
  Far flung across the moor.

The robin lifts with vigor
  His precious melody
The same from stable door
  As from a mansion's magnolia tree.

The lilacs give their fragrance
  Just as freely to the air
From the cracked bowl of blue
  As from golden vase by curving stair.

The water that flows by Shantytown
  Leaps as gaily on its way,
As when it passes Londontown
  With rich ships in the bay.

The sunbeams and the moonbeams
  Shine alike on us all,
For God in his own goodness
  Considers none too small.

Helen Felts Brown

GOD

How often have I seen a little child throw its arms around its father's neck, and win, by kisses and importunities and tears, what had else been refused. Who has not yielded to importunity, even when a dumb animal looked up in our face with suppliant eyes for food? Is God less pitiful than we?

Kenneth Sylvan Guthrie

WHY DID GOD . . . ?

As we went around busily, the Chinese co-workers would ask, "Why did God, in whom we were trusting, permit those bombs to drop here on our mission grounds?"

I had known the Lord since before they were born and could answer, "We never ask 'Why' about anything that God permits. He knew that we were here and he knew that we were trusting him. We may not understand in this life, but this is not evil. The Lord permitted this for some purpose. He, the mighty God, does not have to explain himself to human beings—at least not now now."

Bertha Smith

I believe that man's concept of God began with our first parents, because we are told in the Bible that they were created by God.

Billy Graham

MAN—IN THE IMAGE OF GOD

Such divine, God-given glimpses into the future reveal to us more than all our thinking. What intense truth, what divine meaning there is in God's creative word: "Let us make man in our image, after our likeness!" To show forth the likeness of the Invisible, to be partaker of the divine nature, to share with God His rule of the universe, is man's destiny. His place is indeed one of unspeakable glory.

GOD IS LOVE

We've a message to give to the nations,
That the Lord who reigneth above,
Hath sent us His Son to save us,
And show us that God is love,
And show us that God is love.

Colin Sterne

All the gracious transactions between God and His people are through Christ. God loves us through Christ; He hears our prayers through Christ; He forgives us all our sins through Christ.

Ralph Robinson

GOD TAKES CARE OF HIS OWN

He compasses thee round and bears thee in His arms . . . He looks tenderly upon thy hands and thy feet; He hears thy voice, the beating of thy heart, and thy very breathing. Thou dost not love thyself better than He loves thee. Thou canst not shrink from pain more than He dislikes thy bearing it. Thou art chosen to be His, even above thy fellows who dwell in the East and South. What a thought is this—a thought almost too great for our faith!

John Henry Newman

GOD'S LIGHT

God is looking into His sanctuaries
Seeing many professing Him.
Then He looks into the world
Dusky and afar.
Lives that could possess Him
Stumble,
And fall,
With the world.
He reaches with His light
Few respond.
Darkness will prevail
Until many join hands
Reaching for the light,
God's light
To penetrate the darkness.

Sue Rogers Mitchell

GOSPEL

For I am not ashamed of the gospel of Christ: for it is the power of God unto salvation to every one that believeth . . .

Romans 1:16

But ye shall receive power, after that the Holy Ghost is come upon you: and ye shall be witnesses unto me . . .

Acts 1:8

WHAT THE GOSPEL OFFERS

The Gospel offers a man life. Never offer men a thimbleful of Gospel. Do not offer them merely joy, or merely peace, or merely rest, or merely safety; tell them how Christ came to give men a more abundant life than they have, a life abundant in love, and therefore abundant in salvation for themselves; and large in enterprise for the alleviation and redemption of the world. Then only can the Gospel take hold of the whole of a man, body, soul, and spirit, and give to each part of his nature its exercise and reward.

Henry Drummond

GOSPEL SWEETNESS

The milk and honey of the gospel affect the hearts of sinners more than the gall and wormwood of the law; Christ on Mount Zion brings more to repentance than Moses on Mount Sinai.

William Greenhill

THE MINISTRY OF RECONCILIATION

He came forth to reconcile the world unto God. In this task He was faithful unto death and wrought a great redemption. Now He has gone into the Heavens and committed unto us the ministry of reconciliation. He says, "Go ye into all the world and preach the gospel to every creature." Even now, two thousand years later, it appears as though the task has just begun!

F. W. Boreham

Jesus shall reign where'er the sun
Does his successive journeys run;
His kingdom spread from shore to shore,
Till moons shall wax and wane no more.

Isaac Watts

The Gospel works anywhere and everywhere. It has been declared on every continent of the earth, under every possible social and economic condition, and it always produces the same fruit.

Billy Graham

A STORY TO TELL

We've a story to tell to the nations,
That shall turn their hearts to the right;
A story of truth and sweetness,
A story of peace and light,
A story of peace and light.

For the darkness shall turn to dawning,
And the dawning to noon-day bright,
And Christ's great kingdom
Shall come on earth,
The kingdom of love and light.

Colin Sterne

Run, run, and work, the law commands,
But gives me neither feet nor hands;
But sweeter sounds the gospel brings,
It bids me fly, and gives me wings.

I HAVE TO GIVE

So long as there is heartache
Or suffering anywhere;
So long as men are homeless
With burdens I can share
        Where shadows live . . .
So long as life abundant
Is lived by Oh, so few;
So long as the Kingdom calls
Some things I have to do . . .
        I have to give!

SPEAK OUT

You call yourself a Christian
    And like the Gospel plan . . .
Then why not speak for Jesus,
    And speak out like a man?
Are you ashamed of Jesus
    And the story of the cross,
That you lower His pure banner
    And let it suffer loss?
Have you forgot His suffering?
    Did He die for you in vain?
If not, then live and speak for Jesus,
    And speak out like a man.

AROUND THE CORNER

Sophie Brugman, a German girl living in New York, wanted to be a foreign missionary and prayed for the way to open. One day a voice seemed to ask her, "Who lives on the floor above?" She answered, "A family of Swedes." "And who lives in the rear?" "Some Italians." "And who lives a block away?" "Chinese." Then she said to herself, "And I have never said a word to these people about the blessed Jesus. No wonder I am not sent to the heathen, thousands of miles away, when I do not care enough for those at home even to speak to them of Jesus." Some want to go around the world to China for Christ but they won't go around the corner to the Chinese laundryman for Christ.

WHY WIN SOULS?

One thus follows closely in the footsteps of our Saviour. He was the chiefest of winners.

It will bring the highest compensations for some of the hardships and losses of life.

It may mean not only the salvation of the soul but the salvation of life and the usefulness of an immortal being.

It will put the richest crown on the head of the Saviour and the chief soul-winner of God's universe.

L. R. Scarborough

I WILL STILL BE YOUR MISSIONARY

Who does not thrill to read the testimony of saintly James Chalmers, missionary to New Guinea, who proclaimed with triumph his unalterable choice: "Recall the twenty-one years, give me back all its experiences, give me its shipwrecks, give me its standings in the face of death, give me back my surroundment of savages with spears and clubs, give me back again the spears flying about me with the club knocking me to the ground—give it all back to me, and I will still be your missionary!"

HEAR THE MESSAGE

An expectant hush prevailed throughout the great sanctuary as the conductor stood to signal the choir to sing. Presently the harmony of half a hundred voices fell upon the ears of the congregation—but some ears didn't hear.

In a remote corner of the auditorium a woman stood between the choir and a small group of "listeners." She made movements with her hands and fingers conveying the message of the song. They were receiving the message without hearing the music. Music without sound! Amazing!

Jesus was concerned about people with healthy hears, but who still couldn't hear. Some, like the packed soil of the wayside, simply refused to hear until they couldn't. Some, like the shallow soil over a rock ledge, heard his words, but not his message. Some, like soil occupied by thorns, were too busy listening to trash to hear the word of life.

It is ironical that a deaf person can get the message of a song and never hear a note while others hear the music but never get the message. How fortunate is the person with good ears on either side of his head and also in his soul. He hears both the music and its message. "He that hath ears to hear, let him hear."

John Jeffers

WHAT IS EVANGELISM?

It is the sob of God.
It is the anguished cry of Jesus as He weeps over a doomed city.
It is the cry of Paul, "I could wish that myself were accursed from Christ for my brethren, my kinsmen according to the flesh."
It is the declaration of John Wesley, "The world is my parish."
It is the prayer of Billy Sunday, "Make me a giant for God."
It is the sob of parents in the night, weeping over a prodigal child.
It is the secret of a great church.
It is the secret of a great preacher and of a great Christian.

A Field of Diamonds

EVANGELISM

We must major on evangelism. That is the first note in the marching orders of our risen Saviour and Lord. Evangelism is the missionary spirit in action. It is the forerunner and builder of churches. It is essential to all Christian expansion and must give its benign influence to all sound teaching in the churches.

George W. Truett

BELIEVERS INACTIVE PERMIT

The bearer of this certificate is disqualified from the service of introducing others to Jesus Christ inasmuch as:

* He already has enough religious duties.
* He doesn't feel called as a soul-winner.
* He has fears which hinder such a work.
* He feels it really is the pastor's job.

CERTIFIED:

Satan

RESULTS BELONG TO GOD

Paul intimated that he and Apollos had their part to play in the work of the Kingdom of Christ, but they were not responsible for results. The increase was to come from God. Christians will not be held responsible if their efforts come to nought, but they are responsible for efforts. If we do our honest, earnest best to do God's will we may leave the rest with him. We are not charged with the responsibility of bringing the world to Christ, but we are commissioned to take Christ to the world. We are not ordered to bring men to the cross, but to lift Christ up and he will draw all men unto himself.

As a Christian, you are held responsible for those who have not accepted Him as their Saviour. Christ has no body on earth but yours, no hands but yours, no feet but yours. Yours are the eyes through which Christ's compassion must look out over the world. Yours are the feet with which He must go about doing good.

CHRISTLIKENESS

The wrapping around the new fishing lure said: "When this minnow is cast into the water and retrieved at the proper speed, it is guaranteed to look and behave exactly like a live minnow." The effectiveness of a fishing lure depends upon its ability to duplicate the real thing. When Jesus sent out his disciples he instructed them to go into the villages and cities and do exactly what they had seen him do---"preach, heal the sick, cleanse the lepers, raise the dead, cast out devils" (Matthew 10:7-8). After his death, the religious leaders of Jerusalem "marvelled" at the disciples and "took knowledge of them that they had been with Jesus" (Acts 4:13). Our effectiveness in fishing for men will depend in large measure on how accurately our daily lives reflect Jesus. The "lure" for "men fishing" is the Christ-like life. If we aren't getting results, we had better check on the behavior of the lure. It may be entangled with the tiny weeds of sin or tarnished with the rust of indifference. "Ye are my witnesses," said Jesus.

John Jeffers

WORLD AS A PARISH

I look upon all the world as my parish; thus far I mean, that, in whatever part of it I am, I judge it meet, right, and my bounden duty, to declare unto all that are willing to hear, the glad tidings of salvation.

John Wesley

IS IT ALL?

If I could see Jesus now face to face,
    Would I place in His hand this offering,
And say, "It is all that I have to bring
    To spread the blest work of redeeming grace"?

Brightly beams our Father's mercy,
From His lighthouse evermore
But to us He gives the keeping
Of the lights along the shore.

Philip P. Bliss

96

EXHIBITION OF THE GOSPEL'S POWER

Like the air which in the lungs needs to be broken up into small particles and diffused ere it parts with its vitalising principle to the blood; so the minute acts of obedience, and the exhibition of the power of the Gospel in the thousand trifles of Christian lives, permeating everywhere, will vitalise the world and will preach the gospel in such a fashion as never can be done by any single and occasional, though it may seem to be more lofty and more worthy, agency.

Alexander Maclaren

SO SEND I YOU

As my Father sent me to feed the hungry, to visit the fatherless, to minister with loving hands to the sick, even so send I you. As he sent me to heal the broken-hearted, to still the tempest, to bring peace and good will, even so send I you. As he sent me to sacrifice, to give without thought of return, to love without reward, so send I you. As he sent me to be a fisher of men, to multiply loaves for famished lives, to call sinners to repentance, even so send I you. As he sent me to spend nights in prayer, to agonize over a lost world, to suffer and know an aching heart, even so send I you. As he sent me to sanctify the home, to glorify womanhood and motherhood, to be a blessing to little children, to see life as a glorious opportunity, so send I you. As he sent me to lift up the fallen, to give hope to those who despair, to cast out evil, even so send I you.

Rosalee Mills Appleby

The thrust of the Gospel is Go.

The heralds of the cross continue to speak in "other tongues." In order to obey the Master's command to "Go, teach," his disciples have mastered almost every language spoken on the earth. The gospel has been translated in whole or in part into far more than a thousand languages and dialects.

THE GOSPEL THROUGH A TEACHER

I used to attend a Sunday School class, and one day, I recollect, my teacher came around behind the counter of the shop I was at work in, and put his hand upon my shoulder, and talked to me about Christ and my soul. I had not felt that I had a soul till then. I said to myself, "This is a very strange thing. Here is a man who never saw me till lately, and he is weeping over my sins, and I never shed a tear about them."

D. L. Moody

EMPHASIS ON THE WRONG WORLD

When David Livingstone's body was brought back to England, crowds thronged the streets to pay tribute to the noble missionary. An elderly man among them was heard to sob aloud, and the people wondered at his deep grief. It was revealed that he and Livingstone had been friends in their youth, and, as an ambitious young man, he had scorned Livingstone's choice to give his life for Christ in Africa. With a life of selfish interest behind him, the man saw with regret who had made the wiser choice, and he cried out, "I put the emphasis on the wrong world."

I reckon him a Christian indeed that is neither ashamed of the gospel nor a shame to it.

Matthew Henry

IF . . .

If all the sleeping folk—will wake up;
And all the lukewarm folk—will fire up;
And all the dishonest folk—will confess up;
And all the disgruntled folk—will sweeten up;
And all the discouraged folk—will cheer up;
And all the depressed folk—will look up;
And all the estranged folk—will make up;
And all the gossipers—will hush up;
And all the members—will pray up;
WE WILL HAVE A REVIVAL AND IT WILL
CONTINUE IN OUR CHURCH AND
COMMUNITY.

Christ, alone, can save the world;
But Christ cannot save the world alone.

WEARING AWAY THE SERPENT'S TEETH
Dr. John Hall, in one of his sermons, compared the attacks of infidelity upon Christianity to a serpent gnawing at a file. As he kept on gnawing, he was greatly encouraged by the sight of the growing pile of chips; till, feeling pain, and seeing blood, he found that he had been wearing his own teeth away against the file, but the file was unharmed.

Pollok

THE GOSPEL CHAIN
Years ago a missionary physician in one of China's hospitals cured a man of a cataract. A few weeks later forty-eight blind men, from one of China's interior provinces, each holding onto a rope held in the hand of the man who had been cured, came to the hospital. Thus in a chain they had walked 250 miles to the doctor, and nearly all were cured.

Does not this incident give a picture of our share in the missionary enterprise? The first blind man came to the physician, put his trust in him, received his sight and then went out to lead others to him.

A YOUTH MOVEMENT
The work of modern missions was begun by young people, and has been carried throughout the years by *youth*. You may live to see the literal fulfillment of Isaiah 58:12: "And they that shall be of thee shall build the old waste places: thou shalt raise up the foundations of many generations; and thou shalt be called, The repairer of the breach, The restorer of paths to dwell in."

Ye Christian heralds! Go, proclaim
Salvation thro' Immanuel's name . . .

Bourne H. Draper

MISSIONS AND STEWARDSHIP
Missions must wait upon stewardship. Mission zeal can never go beyond stewardship loyalty. Stewardship is the handmaiden of missions. Mission movements halt because they have not been supported by stewardship teaching and practice. Giving, persistent and perennial giving, must base itself upon stewardship. If the Christian world would produce a generation of givers, the Christian world must first produce a generation of stewards.

P. E. Burroughs

LESSONS FROM MISSIONARIES
The lessons I learn from the lives of missionaries are invaluable. J. Hudson Taylor teaches me the supremacy of childlike faith; Mackay, of Formosa, the transforming power of consecrated forces and the preaching of Jesus; Paton, of the New Hebrides, how holy a passion is love for souls; Andrew Murray and George Muller, that prayer availeth; Sheldon Jackson and Egerton Young that the frozen North cannot cool a flaming zeal for Christ. . . . These missionaries teach me that enduring hardship inspires love and quickens zeal. The cold of Greenland could not keep the Moravians away from their noble work there. The fever and heat did not daunt Livingstone. The dread of a living death among the lepers was not enough to hold Mary Reed in the homeland. Bill Wallace gave his life in a Communist jail . . .

SHINING SOUL–WINNERS
That those who have been faithful in soul-winning on earth will shine in the effulgence of God's glory forever in the world to come, we are assured in this passage: "And they that are wise shall shine as the brightness of the firmament; and they that turn many to righteousness as the stars for ever and ever" (Dan. 12:3).

If we would reach the lost, we must manifest this love for sinners regardless of the seriousness of their sins.

HEAVEN

. . . whosoever liveth and believeth in me shall never die. Believest thou this?

John 11:26

And I John saw the holy city, new Jerusalem, coming down from God out of heaven, prepared as a bride adorned for her husband.

Revelation 21:2

A Field of Diamonds

Some day you will read in the papers that D. L. Moody of East Northfield, is dead. Don't you believe a word of it! At that moment I shall be more alive than I am now; I shall have gone up higher—that is all—out of this old clay tenement into a house that is immortal, a body that death cannot touch, that sin cannot taint, a body fashioned like unto His glorious body.

D. L. Moody

EPITAPH
Bide not beside this rock to speak of Death—
    But rather sow within this mound some seed,
        some pod
That, bursting forth from out this prison clay,
    Lifts high its leafy head to God
        And says to all the world that likewise
    I, from out this shell, this planted seed,
Shall rise to dwell with Him in some more
        beauteous form,
    Unknown to mortal eye.

M. F. Graham

DEATH
They call me death,
For when I come, I bear away
Those whom they love,
As though they were my own.

But over those who know the Lord,
I have no power;
They are His own!

R. Paul Caudill

My heav'nly Home is bright and fair,
    Nor pain, nor death can enter There;
Its glitt'ring towers the sun outshine,
    That heav'nly mansion shall be mine!

William Hunter

Those bound for heaven will display a heavenly character here on earth.

LIFE IS EVER LORD OF DEATH
Alas for him who never sees
The stars shine through the cypress trees!
Who, hopeless, lays his dead away,
Nor looks to see the breaking day
Across the mournful marbles play!
Who hath not learned, in hours of faith,
    The truth to flesh and sense unknown,
That Life is ever Lord of Death,
    And Love can never lose its own!

James Russell Lowell

Soar we now where Christ has led,
    Following our exalted Head;
Made like Him, like Him we rise;
    Ours the Cross, the Grave, the Skies.

Charles Wesley

Home is everywhere to thee,
Who canst thine own dwelling be;
Yea, though ruthless Death assail thee,
Still thy lodging will not fail thee:
Still thy Soul's thine own; and she
To an House removed shall be;
An eternal House above,
Wall'd, and roof'd, and paved with Love.

Joseph Beaumont

I chatter, chatter as I flow
    To join the brimming river,
For men may come and men may go,
    But I go on for ever.

Alfred Lord Tennyson

Happy he whose inward ear
Angel comfortings can hear,
    O'er the rabble's laughter;
And while Hatred's fagots burn,
Glimpses through the smoke discern
    Of the good hereafter.

Walt Whitman

100

ARE YOU READY?

In these critical days, when world history well may be moving toward its climax, only those who know Jesus Christ as Lord and Savior, through an experience of personal salvation, are ready for whatever eventualities may come to men. Jesus said, "Therefore be ye also ready: for in such an hour as ye think not the Son of man cometh" (Matt. 24:44).

Joe T. Odle

NOT HOW THE WORLD WILL END

A generation ago, Orson Welles terrified a nation with a radio drama of an invasion from Mars. A college friend of mine was in his dormitory room on Sunday night when the broadcast was aired. He was petrified by the realistic accounts of waves of Martian giants "wading the Gulf of Mexico, devastating New York, sweeping across the land." He ran to the nearest church and stalked down the aisle interrupting the sermon and shouting, "The end of the world has come." As he gave the horrifying details of imminent destruction, the wise old pastor responded, "This may be true. But it is not the end of the world! *That* is not the way *God has said* this world will end! So, please sit down, young man. We have important work to do! Let me get on with the business of preaching the gospel."

Wayne Dehoney

HEAVEN — A PLACE

Heaven is a place (John 14:2), but the Bible does not locate it. However, it is where God and Christ are, and that will be heaven enough. It is a place of glory. Gold and precious stones (Rev. 21:18 ff.) suggest moral values; white robes (Rev. 6:11) imply purity; there will be leaves for healing (Rev. 22:2) and crowns for victory (Rev. 4:10). The "unclean" will not be there (Rev. 21:27).

Herschel Hobbs

Heaven projects itself into the life of the Christian now!

For the Christian, the grave is not the end; nor is death a calamity, for he has a glorious hope—the hope of Heaven.

Billy Graham

THE NATURE OF HEAVEN

In Revelation 21 John shares with us what God revealed to him about heaven.

He starts his disclosure by listing some things that will not be in heaven. These include tears, death, sorrow, and pain. Then he awes us with the glorious splendor of the majestic New Jerusalem.

Yet, these desired negatives and glorious surroundings would mean nothing without the personal presence of God and Jesus. Jesus went back to the Father to prepare a place for his own so they could be with him.

Willard Dawson

HEAVEN AND SALVATION

When Christmas Evans was about to die, several ministers were standing around his bed. He said to them: "Preach Christ to the people, brethren. Look at me; in myself I am nothing but ruin. But look at me in Christ; I am heaven and salvation."

Death hovers near as a dear one
Lies wide-eyed and suffering, unable to speak.
Her pain and our knowledge that she is going
Is nearly more than we can bear.
Now is the time for prayer . . .

Iris O'Neal Bowen

CLOSER TO HEAVEN

If a man would think of God as much as he thinks of himself, think what security and comfort he would find in day-to-day living. If a man would try to be a Christian as much as he tried to be someone else, how much closer to heaven he would be!

Hubert Shipman

A Field of Diamonds

AFRAID TO DIE?
Therefore, if one is afraid to die, one of three circumstances must be responsible for the fear: (1) he is *unsaved* and, therefore, not prepared to meet God; (2) he is *unconsecrated,* following Christ afar off in personal living and, therefore, ashamed to face God; (3) he is *uninformed* concerning the true nature of death for the Christian and, therefore, erroneously afraid of death.

Chester Swor

A MORNING IN THE SPRING
And then at last, if grace to us be given,
In that fair place of which the poets sing,
Oh heart of mine, God grant when we reach
   Heaven,
It will be on a morning in the Spring.

And there shall be a stretch of open country,
With meadows, where the thrush and robin sing,
And willows, like a green mist by the river,
Shall tell us it is morning in the Spring.

And you and I, just you and I together,
Shall wander down a road 'neath boughs that
   swing
Low, laden with a riot of pink blossoms,
And it shall be a morning in the Spring.

And you and I, just you and I together,
Shall find the joy we missed, and there shall
   spring
From out the Winter of long years of waiting
The rapture of a morning in the Spring.

So then at last, if grace to us be given,
To realize the dream to which we cling,
Oh heart of mine, God grant when we reach
   Heaven,
It will be on a morning in the Spring.

Maie Everett Wright

"I'm not homesick for heaven," one Christian remarked. Maybe he ought to examine his heart.

In heaven the *Son* will furnish the light.

WHEN THE LORD COMES
When the Lord comes, we and the sainted dead shall be changed in a moment, in the twinkling of an eye, at the last trump (1 Corinthians 15:52). When all of us are taken to be with the Lord, then we shall go with our Savior into glory and there stand before him to receive our crown for what we have done in his Kingdom work. With our rewards bestowed upon us, we shall enter with our Savior to share with him the marriage supper of the Lamb.

W. A. Criswell

WHAT A DIFFERENCE
But what a difference in the death of the men who believed and loved the Bible. D. L. Moody said, "This is my coronation day; don't try to call me back." Charles Spurgeon, when facing death, said, "Can this be death? Why it is better than living."

John R. Bisagno

A PETITION
Monarch of all things, fit us for thy mansions;
Banish our weakness, health and wholeness
   sending;
Bring us to heaven, where thy saints united
       Joy without ending.

Gregory

Mark Twain made a wry observation: "Now then, in the earth these people cannot stand much church—an hour and a quarter is the limit, and they draw the line at once a week. That is to say, Sunday. One day in seven; and even then they do not look forward to it with longing. And so—consider what their heaven provides for them: 'church' that lasts forever, and a Sabbath that has no end." If the worship of God is to occupy us in heaven—and some New Testament evidences points to that possibility (see Rev. 11:15-18)—then a little practice here on earth would be time and effort well spent!

Ralph L. Murray

102

HOLY SPIRIT

And it shall come to pass afterward, that I will pour out my spirit
upon all flesh . . .

Joel 2:28

But the fruit of the Spirit is love, joy, peace, longsuffering, gentleness, goodness, faith, meekness, temperance . . .

Galatians 5:22–23

PENTECOSTAL POWER

Heaven is still as full of stores of spiritual blessing as it was then. God still delights to give the Holy Spirit to them that ask Him. Our life and work are still as dependent on the direct impartation of Divine Power as they were in Pentecostal times.

Andrew Murray

COME IN

Thou hast bought me to possess me;
In Thy fullness Lord, come in!

GOD FILLED HIM

Jack R. Taylor relates how the pastor of a growing church was filled with the Holy Spirit: "After the service we went to my study and began our visit. He told of pastoring a growing church where, within the past year, the Sunday School attendance and budget offerings had doubled. He related how a great many had been baptized. But his tone changed as he confessed to an inner defeat and discouragement. He could not, would not, go on as he had before. He was sick and tired. I related how a man could be filled with the Spirit and begin the adventure of allowing God's power to be released through him. I shared with him how that a man must die to all his preconceived plans, images, and pride before God would fill him. We went to prayer. I never heard a man pray just like that! But God met him and at last report the power of God was flowing through his life."

THE COMFORTER AND CONVICTOR

He has proved that He is indeed the Comforter. If the conviction and consciousness of sin arise from any other source, then indeed it is enough to crush us with shame, and to harrow us with unimaginable fears. But when it comes from the Spirit of God, it comes with healing and comfort on its wings.

J. C. Hare

TEACHER OF THE TEACHER

One who teaches others must be in the continual process of being taught by the Holy Spirit. He receives, so he is qualified to give. John 14:6 gives the pattern: "The Holy Spirit whom the Father will send in my name, will *teach you* everything, and will call to mind all that I have told you." The coin must be seen in relation to the fountain. The divine presence of the Holy Spirit must be the teacher of the teacher!

Ralph W. Neighbour, Jr.

THE REALITY OF HIS PRESENCE

Much is being said and written about the Holy Spirit in our day. Discussion is plentiful concerning when the Holy Spirit enters the life of a Christian.

John indicated that by the power of the Holy Spirit repentant and believing souls are regenerated (John 3:5). At the moment of regeneration the Holy Spirit moves into the Christian's life.

Our recognition that we need help when life overpowers us and our plea for his help will bring out the reality of his presence.

Willard Dawson

There is constant peace, joy, and victory. The besetting sins have been conquered through His Spirit. 'Greater is he that is in you, than he that is in the world' (1 John 4:4). It is a day by day reality, moment by moment. What a thrill to begin each day with a fresh commitment to the Lord Jesus, thanking Him for *literally* living within my body and praising Him for victory over lust, pride, and the other onslaughts that will be coming my way through the day. And what a joy to come to the end of the day praising Him for His goodness, confessing every known sin, and going to sleep committing myself to Him all over again.

Cecil McGee

THE SPIRIT OPENS OUR EYES

The Holy Spirit was sent into our lives to draw us to Jesus Christ. The Spirit opens our prejudiced eyes to see that Christ's death on the cross is a very personal act. He died for each one of us. Not only was the nature of God in that body on the cross: our sin was also poured into that precious body. He died with our sin within Him! In doing so, He provided the only available connection between the Father and mankind.

Ralph W. Neighbour, Jr.

ENTHUSIASM

There is no doubt that enthusiasm is a plus factor in our lives. It often makes the difference between success and failure. But there are two kinds of enthusiasm: the kind which we work up like at a rally or pep meeting, and the kind which comes from within, the real kind.

The word "enthusiasm" comes from two Greek words, "en" and "theos," meaning God in us. Genuine enthusiasm is just that. It is God's Spirit working in and through us. The other kind is counterfeit, spurious, unreal. The world can do without a phony enthusiasm, but it desperately needs the real thing.

Carlton Myers

THE MIND OF THE SPIRIT

"And he that searcheth the heart knoweth the mind of the Spirit," because he maketh intercession for the saints according to the will of God, and he leads Christians to pray for just those things, with groanings that cannot be uttered. When neither the word nor providence enables them to decide, then let them be filled with the Spirit, as God commands them to be. He says, "Be ye filled with the Spirit." And *He* will lead their minds to such things as God is willing to grant.

Charles G. Finney

No instinct can be put in you by the Holy Spirit but one He purposes to fulfill.

HONOR THE SPIRIT

"Honor the Holy Ghost!" was the plea of an old man to Dwight L. Moody in the beginning days of his evangelistic ministry. He never forgot that admonition. That movement or person which does not honor the Spirit cannot succeed. Those who honestly, scripturally, and sanely honor the Holy Spirit as He magnifies Christ cannot fail.

Jack R. Taylor

THE FIRE OF THE SPIRIT

When Blaise Pascal died in 1662, it was found that he had stitched into his coat, between cloth and lining, so that it would lie next to his heart, a foolscap sheet of paper covered with hasty scribbles, and a good copy on parchment. Under a cross surrounded by the rays of the rising sun was the year of his conversion (1654), and the day and the hour: "From about half-past ten at night till about half-past twelve." Then, in a line by itself, and in big capital letters, the single word "FIRE." Below that, in a series of exclamations in the French language, were the words: "I know! I know! I feel! Joy! Peace!"

The summation word was "fire." Why fire? We can only guess, but we know the gifted Pascal must have had his reasons. Could they have been something like these? Fire illuminates. So does the spirit. Fire purges. So does the Spirit. Fire fuses. So does the Spirit. Fire transforms dull matter into blazing, life-giving energy. And so does the Holy Spirit of God.

Ralph L. Murray

Spirit of the living God,
    Fall fresh on me.
Break me, melt me, mould me, fill me
Spirit of the living God,
    Fall fresh on me.

Arranged by B. B. McKinney

Breathe on me, Breath of God . . .

Edwin Hatch

DEFINITION OF THE SPIRIT
The Bible teaches that the Holy Spirit is co-equal with God the Father and co-equal with God the Son. The Bible also teaches that the Holy Spirit is a Person. He is never to be referred to as "it." He's not just an agent. He's not just an influence. He is a mighty Person: the Holy Spirit of God.
Billy Graham

When the Holy Spirit is ignored in our work, the wheels may keep turning but life is gone. Things become mechanical. God's Word that comes out of a Spirit-filled heart will quicken and heal; break and restore; rend and revive. *Read John 16:7-22.*
Rosalee Mills Appleby

And so the yearning strong,
With which the soul will long,
    Shall far outpass the power of human telling;
For none can guess its grace,
Till he becomes the place
    Wherein the Holy Spirit makes his dwelling.
Bianco da Siena

GOD'S RATIFICATION
Salvation is not a human achievement. Not only was God's coming in Christ necessary to draw us to God, but his coming in the Holy Spirit is necessary to make salvation effective in our lives. The decision that we make is to ask God to take our lives. This decision is meaningful only because God ratifies it by coming to live with us.
Joseph F. Green

Holy Spirit, dwell with me:
I myself would holy be;
Separate from sin, I would
Choose and cherish all things good;
And whatever I can be,
Give to him who gave me thee.
T. T. Lynch

God gives power only to men who need it. He does not waste power. He gives it to those who have tackled something so big, so overwhelming, that their own resources are quite insufficient. Such a tackling of a task too big for human power is the opening of the door through which there comes the rushing of a mighty wind of the Spirit.
Halford E. Luccock

THE WINGED LIFE
The life of the Spirit-filled heart is the *winged life*. The unsurrendered life is the life of the cage. The best that the cage can give is a momentary thrill that soon gives place to a pitiful beating against the bars.

INWARD AND OUTWARD
It is not enough that we have the objective revelation in the written word, we must also have the inward illumination of the Holy Spirit to enable us to comprehend it. It is a great mistake to try to comprehend a spiritual revelation with the natural understanding.
R. A. Torrey

REGENERATION AND GIFTS
At the moment I am born over again – as I am placed in Jesus Christ's holy life – as the Holy Spirit occupies my life as His temple – at this moment, which we refer to as the instant of conversion, I receive all the spiritual gifts I shall ever possess. It is at the time of salvation that I am, once and forever, "brought into one body by baptism, in the one Spirit . . ." (1 Corinthians 12:13). The Spirit of God is His greatest gift to me at the time of my conversion. To understand 1 Corinthians 12, we must understand that the coming of the Holy Spirit involves Him joining me to the Body of Christ.
Ralph W. Neighbour, Jr.

FALSE "SPIRITUALITY"

Some who claim to be Spirit-filled reveal pride in their attempt to impress people with their spirituality. They try to "snow" folks with the fact that they have something special that not everyone has. No one is more repulsive than the individual trying to impress others with his spirituality.

Landrum Leavell

HOLY SPIRIT: AUTHOR

When reading the Bible in even a casual way, one will readily see that it was necessary for the Holy Spirit carefully to guard and to guide every step of the way so that a true and perfect message would be delivered. No one else other than the Holy Spirit could accomplish such a miracle. The Bible actually is that miracle. As the books of the Testaments were being written down through the centuries, different men spoke as they were moved by the Holy Spirit and, God being the author of the Word through the generations, the words all attest to one great truth, point to one great God, and offer to us one marvelous way of salvation.

W. A. Criswell

THE WITNESS OF THE SPIRIT

What is a witness? *A witness is one who can no longer be himself!* He finds himself inhabited by the Holy Spirit of God, the indwelling Spirit of Christ. All he does at work, at home, at play bears the evidence of that fact. That is "witness." Witness is more than living according to a certain pattern; it is simply the very person of God within me, revealing something of Himself in all that I am and in all that I do, in every situation.

Ralph W. Neighbour, Jr.

We remember that Peter and John were alluded to in Acts 4:13 as "ignorant and unlearned"; yet, Peter, using all of his talent and empowered of the Holy Spirit, delivered the message at Pentecost, in response to which thousands of people became Christians.

Chester Swor

REDEMPTION ROAD

Our Father,
as we travel
the long and winding road
of redemption,
some of us sit
at roadside tables of indifference
watching life go by and muttering
"let it be, let it be."
some of us broil in anger
before the swift vehicles of dehumanization
screaming "revolution, revolution."
some of us see the hurt of wrecked lives,
but do nothing except preach
"all you need is love, all you need is love."
some of us find the traffic too heavy and
too fast and, standing in dumb amazement,
mutely long for yesterday.

But then some of us just keep traveling,
making wrong turns,
getting hurt,
helping and being helped,
receiving love,
looking for you.

Grant us the presence of your Spirit
on the long and winding
road of redemption.
Amen.

Francis Martin

ACTIVE SPIRITUALITY

Some people think that spirituality comes through inactivity—meditating, thinking. They forget that the time in Christian history when spirituality was perhaps at its highest was just after Pentecost. We read in Acts that men were so filled with the Spirit of God that the most active chapter in all of Christianity was written in bold, Christlike deeds. The greatest indication of the Holy Spirit's presence in the life of an individual is the way he responds to its presence in his person.

James L. Sullivan

THE SPIRIT AND GOD'S WILL

The Holy Spirit was sent to us because we cannot do God's will with human mind and hands. Man's brain, clever and ingenious as it might be, can never devise ways and means of achieving spiritual ends by especially thought–up, man–made devices. Without this inner force we would soon falter, and even despair. Under the Spirit's leadership we do find ways of accomplishment, methods of achievement, and the high incentive which make Christian work so rewarding.

James L. Sullivan

THE SPIRIT IN CONTROL

I lay prostrate before God and waited for Him to pour into me what He wished . . . and He did! The Holy Spirit took control, immersing me in peace and joy. The room glowed with His Presence. It has not been the same since. My conversion and call have a new meaning. God worked anew in my life, my church, and my family. He was in control. Joy continues to flow as I continue to drink at that fountain, knowing always every day is really sweeter than the day before.

C. B. Hogue

SPIRIT–FILLED EVANGELISM

Spirit-filled evangelism will magnify Jesus as Lord. It will be based on the conviction that it is enough to praise Him and to raise His banner: He *will* draw all men unto Himself if He is lifted up.

Ralph W. Neighbour, Jr.

A PIERCING QUESTION

Will a Spirit-filled Christian give the impression that prayer meeting is anathema? Will a Spirit-filled Christian hold grudges, bear hatreds, animosity, or ill will toward other people?

Landrum Leavell

THE SPIRIT APPLIES THE CROSS

There is no other way to overcome the self-life than through the work of the Holy Spirit constantly applying the meaning of the cross. Without the constant work of the Holy Spirit filling our lives with Himself, we are forever "stirring in the coffin." Our constant consent to His constant application of the deeper meaning of the cross keeps us in the *position of death* that we might constantly know the *power of His Life.*

Jack R. Taylor

CLAIMING THE SPIRIT'S WORK

But all that belongs to us as our birthright in Christ becomes ours in actual and experimental possession through the Holy Spirit's work in us as individuals. To the extent that we understand and claim for ourselves the Holy Spirit's work, to that extent do we obtain for ourselves the fulness of power in Christian life and service that God has provided for us in Christ.

R. A. Torrey

THE BAPTISM OF THE SPIRIT

The baptism of the Spirit is a *once and for all* experience by which we are immersed into Christ. The fulness of the Spirit is an event which is followed by a continuing disposition of faith. Paul's injunction, in Ephesians 5:18 literally rendered, would read, "Be ye continually always being filled with the Holy Spirit."

Jack R. Taylor

But there is such a thing as being so deeply imbued with the Spirit of God, that you must and will act so as to appear strange and eccentric, to those who cannot understand the reasons of your conduct.

Charles G. Finney

We must empty by filling.
Nothing is ever displaced until it is replaced.

HOME

A Field of Diamonds

Bless the four corners of this house,
And be the doorway blest; its nooks, its sun,
Its rooms, its chambers every one.

There's a blessing on the hearth,
A special providence for fatherhood.
Robert Browning

Youth fades; love droops; the lessons of friend-
ship fall;
A mother's secret hope outlives them all.
Oliver Wendell Holmes

HOME IS . . .
Where joy is shared,
And sorrow eased.
Where fathers and mothers
Are respected and loved,
Where children are wanted.
Where the simplest food
Is good enough for kings
Because it is earned.
Where money is not so important
As loving kindness:
Where even the teakettle
Sings for happiness.

THAT IS HOME. GOD BLESS IT!

'Mid pleasures and palaces though we may roam,
Be it ever so humble, there's no place like home.
John Howard Payne

When I was a boy of 14, my father was so ignorant I could hardly stand to have the old man
around. But when I got to be 21, I was aston-
ished at how much the old man had learned in
seven years.
Mark Twain

PRAYER FOR MY CHILDREN
Their faith is strong, their hearts are sure that
    God made all things good and pure.
Oh Holy Spirit, so divine, completely fill this
    heart of mine;
Teach me the words that I should say to guide
    my children day by day.
On up the path that leads above to never doubt
    God's perfect love,
Give me that child-like faith I pray - oh, make
    me a child today.

WE KISS'D AGAIN WITH TEARS
As through the land at eve we went,
    And pluck'd the ripen'd ears,
We fell out, my wife and I,
O we fell out I know not why,
    And kiss'd again with tears.
And blessings on the falling out
    That all the more endears,
When we fall out with those we love,
    And kiss again with tears!
For when we came where lies the child
    We lost in other years,
There above the little grave,
O there above the little grave,
    We kiss'd again with tears.
Alfred Lord Tennyson

Children begin by loving their parents; as they
grow older they judge them; sometimes they
forgive them.
Oscar Wilde

Happy the man, whose wish and care
    A few paternal acres bound,
Content to breathe his native air
    In his own ground.
Alexander Pope

Thou shalt *teach thy child* to love and trust in
God, and thou shalt wisely help him to choose
Jesus Christ as his Lord and Saviour.

Following a revival meeting the minister asked a young man what it was that caused him to come forward and accept Christ. "It was not your preaching, sir, but my mother's practicing, that made me want to be a Christian." Perhaps if more parents would practice Christianity at home, the pastor's preaching would bring better results.

SWEETEST SOUNDS

The sweetest sounds to mortals given
Are heard in Mother, Home and Heaven.
W. G. Brown

TRIBUTES TO MOTHER

A kiss from my mother made me a painter.
Benjamin West

A mother is a mother still, the holiest thing alive.
Coleridge

Mother is the name for God in the lips and hearts of children.
Thackeray

All that I am or hope to be, I owe to my angel mother.

Lincoln

AN EVANGELIST'S MOTHER

"All that I have ever accomplished in life," declared Dwight L. Moody, the great evangelist, "I owe to my mother."

WHAT IS A BOY?

A boy is a bank where you may deposit your most precious treasures—the hard-won wisdom, the dreams for a better world. A boy can guard and protect these, and perhaps invest them wisely and win a profit—one larger than you ever dreamed. A boy will inherit your world. All your work will be judged by him. Tomorrow he will take your place, run your country, your company, your town, your church. He deserves more of your attention NOW.

ON DAD'S HOMEGOING

All this long day since you have slipped beyond us
And headed on to find your dreamed-of land,
One picture more than all you told of heaven
Stands in my mind and helps me understand.
I've heard you talk of God as the kind Father,
Standing with outstretched arms at heaven's door,
Waiting in love to greet his little children
When they return to him forevermore.
It comforts me to know that tonight, Daddy,
You don't have to be the strongest one of all,
Nor have so many people leaning on you,
Nor have to stand so firm, nor yet so tall.
Tonight you can be once more, just a boy, Dad,
Racing with joy up to your Father's door,
And feel his gentle loving arms about you,
His child, his son, at home with him once more.
Ida Nelle Hollaway

LULLABY FOR MY MOTHER

Where have you gone, my mother?
Blue ribbons tied in your hair,
A rag doll cuddled close in your lap
You rock so quietly there.
Where have you gone, my mother?
Your voice is low and mild;
When you speak my name uncertainly
You, not I, seem the child.
You loved me dearly, my mother;
Your counsel was gentle and wise.
You helped me to cradle my babies
And hush their new-born cries.
I bring you handfuls of hyacinths
And ribbons of yellow and blue;
Rock in your dream world, my Raggedy Anne,
I will stay here and watch over you.
Bettie M. Sellers

All happy families resemble one another; every unhappy family is unhappy in its own way.
Leo Tolstoy

There's no place like a Christian home.

Sweet is the smile of home; the mutual look,
When hearts are of each other sure.

John Keble

THAT LITTLE GIRL

She can muss up your home, your hair and your
dignity—spend your money, your time and your
temper—then just when your patience is ready to
crack, her sunshine peeks through and you've
lost again.

Yes, she is a nerve-racking nuisance, just a
noisy bundle of mischief. But when your dreams
tumble down and the world is a mess, when it
seems you are pretty much of a fool after all, she
can make you a king when she climbs on your
knee and whispers, "I love you best of all!"

Alan Beck

The love of fatherhood and motherhood is a
divine revelation and miracle. It is a creative act
of God in us.

Walter Rauschenbusch

MATERIALS FOR A HOME

Anyone can build an altar; it requires God to provide the flame. *Anybody can build a house; we
need the Lord for the creation of a home.* The
New Testament does not say very much about
homes; it says a great deal about the things that
make them. It speaks about life and love and joy
and peace and rest! If we get a house and put
these into it, we shall have secured a home.

John Henry Jowett

What is a home without a Bible?
Tis a home where day is night,
Starless night,
For o'er life's path way,
Heaven can shed no kindly light.

Home is where the heart is.

ADOPTED—IN LOVE

And when we got there you came out, and gently
took me in your arms as you called me your
"poor little boy," and you led me gently in; and
there was the blazing warm fire, the bright light,
and the table spread, and the supper all waiting
for me! And that was my home! . . . How you
soothed me, and warmed me, and put me to bed
in the strange room, and heard me say my
prayers, and stayed with me till I was fast asleep!

John Todd to his "foster" mother

HE IS NOT DEAD

When the little brown thrush that harshly chirred
Was dear to him as the mocking bird;
And he pitied as much as a man in pain
A writhing honey-bee wet with rain.—
Think of him still as the same, I say:
He is not dead—he is just away!

James Whitcomb Riley

A MOTHER WATCHING HER CHILDREN PRAY

And tho sometimes a smile may play upon my
lips when I hear them pray,
For blessings on the frog and toad, from
my heart lifts a mighty load
Of fear, that they may someday stray to
earth's own evil, wicked way . . .

THAT BOY

A boy is a magical creature—you can lock him
out of your workshop, but you can't lock him
out of your heart. You can get him out of your
study, but you can't get him out of your mind.
Might as well give up—he is your captor, your jailer,
your boss, and your master—a freckle-faced, pint-
sized, cat-chasing bundle of noise. But when you
come home at night with only the shattered
pieces of your hopes and dreams, he can mend
them like new with the two magic words—
"Hi Dad!"

Alan Beck

INFLUENCE

Those things, which ye have both learned, and received, and heard, and seen in me, do: and the God of peace shall be with you.

Philippians 4:9

And he did evil in the sight of the Lord, and walked in the way of Jeroboam, and in his sin wherewith he made Israel to sin.

1 Kings 15:34

IF

If Christ is the Way, we are the signboards.
If Christ is the Truth, we are the examples.
If Christ is the Life, we are the messengers.
If Christ is the Door, we are the doorkeepers, to
   open it to others.
If Christ is the Vine, we are the fruit bearing
   branches.

CHRIST'S INFLUENCE

Nothing could be more simple, more intelligible, more natural, more supernatural. It is an analogy from an everyday fact. Since we are what we are by the impacts of those who surround us, those who surround themselves with the highest will be those who change into the highest. If to live with men, diluted to the millionth degree with the virtue of the Highest, can exalt and purify the nature, what bounds can be set to the influence of Christ?

Henry Drummond

I BELIEVE IN YOU

I think of a missionary doctor on a lonely village station, a very able doctor, but even more effective as a Christian and a leader in evangelization. Not long ago a convert was being baptized–a rare event in that difficult area–and he was answering questions to test his very simple faith. One answer he began safely enough. "I believe in God Almighty, and in the Lord Jesus," but then his training gave way to his experience, and turning to the doctor he burst out, "and sahib, I believe in you."

Frank Lenwood

JUST SHINE

It is a great deal better to live a holy life than to talk about it. Lighthouses do not ring bells and fire cannons to call attention to their shining. They just shine!

D. L. Moody

O, that my tongue might so possess
   The accents of His tenderness
That every word I breathe should bless!

JESUS—OUR EXAMPLE

When Peter speaks of Jesus having left us an "example" he chose for "example" the Greek word signifying "the headline of a copybook." Jesus is for our imitation; he is our "copy." And a test of discipleship is the progress we make in the reproduction of the copy he has set.

DEAD TO THE DIVINE

Now, take a man that is spiritually dead. Pinch his conscience; he does not start. Bring before him the law, and let it thunder in his ears; it makes no impression upon him. Pierce him with the sword of the Spirit; he does not feel it; he is not susceptible to fear; he has no moral sensibility. And you say that that man is spiritually dead because he is not alive to Divine influences.

Henry Ward Beecher

GRANNY GRUNT

Granny Grunt on grumble street
Lived for many years.
She ever complained to all she'd meet
And filled their life with tears.

Her closest friend, Miss Discontent,
Spread grief where'er she went.
No smile worthwhile she ever gave
To those who passed her by.

But one day they both fell ill
Beyond this world's repair—
Then reminisced in deep despair
The days they griped away.

Jimmy Martin

Select your words as you would choice flowers for a friend.

Every time I receive notice from a certain insurance company that a premium is due a card is enclosed containing this inquiry: "Are you carrying all the insurance you should for the protection of your family?" It reminds me to ask Christians this question: "Are you increasing your interest in the Kingdom of Christ?"

INFLUENCE OF THE GOSPEL
Decades ago Charles Bradlaugh, an atheist, challenged Hugh Price Hughes, a godly minister, to debate with him the truth of the Christian faith. The challenge was immediately accepted in these words: "The courts as a rule, in rendering their verdicts, do not rely solely upon the arguments of the lawyers on either side. They carefully scrutinize the evidence offered by those who have firsthand knowledge of the facts. I will bring with me to the debate one hundred men and women who have been saved from lives of sin by the Gospel of Christ. They will give their evidence and you will be allowed to cross-examine them. I will ask that you bring with you one hundred men and women who have been similarly helped by the gospel of infidelity which you preach." The debate was abandoned.

NEGATIVE INFLUENCE
Stay in bed until ten; read Sunday paper until one; feed your face until three; loll around until nine; nothing doing; nothing done; good night!

A CHRISTIAN IS:

A MIND — through which Christ thinks;
A HEART — through which Christ loves
A VOICE — through which Christ speaks;
A HAND — through which Christ helps.

He preaches well who lives well.
Miguel Cervantes

FOUR "BODIES"
Fred Somebody, Thomas Everybody, Pete Anybody and Joe Nobody were neighbors.

Everybody went fishing on Sunday or stayed home to visit with friends. Anybody wanted to worship but was afraid Somebody wouldn't speak to him. Nobody did the visitation. Nobody worked on the church building.

Once they needed a Sunday School teacher. Everybody thought Anybody would do it; and Somebody thought Everybody would do it. Guess who did it finally? That's right . . . Nobody. It happened that a fifth neighbor—an unbeliever—came to live among them. Everybody thought that Somebody should try to win him; Anybody could have at least made an effort, but guess who finally won him to Christ? NOBODY!!

TRANSFIGURATION
A single ray of sunlight
  Upon a cloud-filled day,
Can flood the soul with splendor,
  And chase all care away.

A single strain of music,
  To one whose soul is night,
Can fill the heart with gladness,
  And make the day all bright.

A single word well-spoken,
  To one who's gone astray,
Can turn the footsteps forward
  To Him who is the Way!
R. Paul Caudill

A careless word may kindle strife,
A cruel word may wreck a life.
A bitter word may hate instill,
A brutal word may smite and kill.
A gracious word may smooth the way,
A joyous word may light the day.
A timely word may lessen stress,
A loving word may heal and bless.

Upon his retirement a Christian leader received this letter . . .

"Dear Bishop Burt:

Your years have passed like sunlight. They were beautiful, and filled with service in the old world and the new. God has been with you, and you have been with God.

Would you might live a hundred years to bless mankind, but wherever you are, in earth or heaven, you will like the place. You make it good to live where you are around.

You have blessed my life, and I want to live with you forever in the skies.

Your brother everywhere,

William A. Quayle."

THE REAL SAVAGES

When Indians hear the horrid filth
Of Irish, English men:
The horrid oaths and murders late,
Thus say these Indians then:
We wear no clothes, have many gods,
And yet our sins are less:
You are barbarians, pagans wild,
Your land's the Wilderness.

Roger Williams

BEAUTY OF LANGUAGE

There is a beauty of language, just as there is a beauty of face. There is a harmony of words, just as there is a harmony of sky and stars, green foliage, and crystal waters. There is a delicacy of speech, just as there is a delicacy of tints in the masterpiece on canvas, in the shimmer of light on the dewdrop, in the semi-transparent petal of the woodland flower.

INFLUENCE OF ACTIONS

The microscopic creatures, thousands of which will go into a square inch, make the great white cliffs that beetle over the wildest sea and front the storm. So, permanent and solid character is built up out of trivial actions . . .

Alexander Maclaren

WATCH YOUR WORDS

Keep a watch on your words, my darlings,
For words are wonderful things;
They are sweet, like the bees' fresh honey,
Like the bees, they have terrible stings.
They can bless like the warm, glad sunshine,
And brighten a lonely life;
They can cut, in the strife of anger,
Like an open, two-edged knife.

AN ERRANT ARROW

I shot an arrow into the air,
It fell to earth, I knew not where . . .

Henry Wadsworth Longfellow

NO ROOM TO TALK

There is so much good in the worst of us,
And so much bad in the best of us,
That it hardly becomes any of us
To talk about the rest of us.

PASS IT ON

Have you had a kindness shown?
Pass it on;
'Twas not given for thee alone,
Pass it on;
Let it travel down the years,
Let it wipe another's tears,
Till in Heaven the deed appears—
Pass it on.

Henry Burton

INFLUENCE OF CHRIST

All friendship, all love, human and Divine, is purely spiritual. It was after He was risen that He influenced even the disciples most. Hence in reflecting the character of Christ it is no real obstacle that we may never have been in visible contact with Him. Be more under His influence than under any other influence.

Henry Drummond

JESUS CHRIST

I KNOW A NAME
I know a soul that is steeped in sin,
    That no man's art can cure;
But I know a Name, a Name, a Name
    That can make the soul all pure.

I know a life that is lost to God,
    Bound down by the things of earth;
But I know a Name, a Name, a Name
    That can bring that soul new birth.

I know of lands that are sunk in shame,
    Of hearts that faint and tire;
But I know a Name, a Name, a Name
    That can set those lands on fire.

Its sound is sweet, its letters flame,
    Oh, I know of a Name, a wonderful Name,
        'TIS JESUS.

CHRIST IS PRESENTED IN
Matthew as the King.
Mark as the Servant.
Luke as the Son of Man.
John as the Son of God.
Acts as the Lord of all.
Romans as the Mercy Seat.

To the artist he is the One Altogether Lovely.
To the architect he is the Chief Cornerstone.
To the baker he is the Living Bread.
To the banker he is the Hidden Treasure.
To the builder he is the Sure Foundation.
To the doctor he is the Great Physician.
To the educator he is the Great Teacher.
To the farmer he is the Sower and the Lord of
    Harvest.

But Thee, but Thee, O sovereign Seer of Time,
But Thee, O poet's Poet, Wisdom's Tongue,
But Thee, O man's best Man, O love's best Love,
O perfect life in perfect labor writ,
O all men's Comrade, Servant, King, or Priest—
                        Sidney Lanier

About this time lived Jesus, a wise man—if indeed one may call him a man. For he, as a teacher of those men who receive the truth joyfully, did marvelous things. And he attracted many Jews and men of Hellenic birth. He was the Christ. And when Pilate had condemned him to be crucified on the evidence of our leaders, those who had loved him from the first did not desert him. For he appeared to them on the third day alive, the prophets having foretold this and ten thousand other wonders concerning him. And to this day the tribe of the Christians, who are called after him, has not failed.
                        Flavius Josephus

What the hand is to the lute,
What the breath is to the flute,
What is fragrance to the smell,
What the spring is to the well,
What the flower is to the bee,
That is Jesus Christ to me.

What's the mother to the child,
What the guide in pathless wild,
What is oil to troubled wave,
What is ransom to the slave,
What is water to the sea,
That is Jesus Christ to me.
                        Charles Haddon Spurgeon

CHRIST IS SEEN IN
1 Corinthians as the Wisdom and Power of God.
2 Corinthians as the Yea and Amen.
Galatians as the Crucified.
Ephesians as the Center of all the Father's
                        counsels.
Philippians as the Life, Example, Goal, Power.
Colossians as the Head of the body (as the risen
                        Man).

How sweet the name of Jesus sounds
In a believer's ear!
                        John Newton

To the florist he is the Lily of the Valley and the Rose of Sharon.

To the geologist he is the Rock of Ages.

To the judge he is the Righteous Judge.

To the lawyer he is the Counselor, the Lawgiver, the Advocate.

To the newspaperman he is the Good Tidings of Great Joy.

To the philanthropist he is the Unspeakable Gift.

To the philosopher he is the Wisdom of God.

THE OMNIPRESENT CHRIST

Christ be with me, Christ within me,
Christ behind me, Christ before me,
Christ beside me, Christ to win me,
Christ to comfort and restore me,
Christ beneath me, Christ above me,
Christ in quiet, Christ in danger,
Christ in hearts of all that love me,
Christ in mouth of friend and stranger.

Patrick of Ireland

CHRIST IS PORTRAYED IN

1 Thessalonians as the Deliverer from the wrath to come

2 Thessalonians as the Destroyer of Antichrist.

1 Timothy as the Mediator.

2 Timothy as the Resource in a day of ruin.

Titus as God our Saviour.

Philemon as Surety (the Spirit of Christ in Paul, "Put that on mine account").

Life or death has little meaning without Christ. Character and ideals are empty words without the supreme character. Suffering becomes sacred when Jesus is in it. Hope has no foundation and holiness ceases to exist apart from him. Read Philippians 3:7-11.

Rosalee Mills Appleby

Thou hast conquered, O Galilean!

Emperor Julian

PERFECT CURRICULUM

Dr. John R. Mott asked Professor Drummond to name three courses of study which might be recommended to Christians for spiritual profit. After a few moments of thought he replied, "I would recommend that they study first, the life of Jesus Christ; secondly, the life of Jesus Christ; and thirdly, the life of Jesus Christ!"

LOVING STEPS

Every step he made from the sands of Egypt to the carpenter shop in Nazareth, to the Jordan River, through the hills of Judea, on the Lake of Galilee, in the road to Bethlehem, to the house of trouble, to the bed of sickness, to the grave of the dead, to the temple in Jerusalem, through the shadows of Gethsemane, through the agonies of Pilate's court, along the streets of the city that "stoned the prophets and killed them that were sent unto her," up the dark slopes of Calvary, out from the grave in Joseph's garden, along the road to Emmaus, on out to Olivet where, "with the wind as his steeds and the cloud as his chariot" he went back to the Father—every step was a step of love.

R. G. Lee

To the preacher he is the Word of God.

To the lonely he is the Friend that sticketh closer than a brother.

To the servant he is the Good Master.

To the toiler he is the Giver of Rest.

To the sorrowing he is the Comforter.

To the bereaved he is the Resurrection and the Life.

To the sinner he is the Lamb of God that taketh away the sin of the world.

He is the Star of Astronomy, the Rock of Geology, the Lion and the Lamb of Zoology, the Harmonizer of all discords and the Healer of all the diseases. Great men have come and gone, yet He lives on.

ONE SOLITARY LIFE

Here is a man who was born in an obscure village, the child of a peasant woman. He grew up in another obscure village.

He worked in a carpenter shop until he was thirty, and then for three years he was an itinerate preacher.

He never owned a home. He never had a family. He never went to college. He never traveled two hundred miles from the place he was born.

He never did one of the things that usually accompany greatness. He had no credentials but himself. He had nothing to do with this world except the naked power of his divine manhood.

While still a young man, the tide of public opinion turned against him. His friends ran away. One of them denied him.

He was turned over to his enemies. He went through the mockery of a trial. He was nailed upon a cross between two thieves. His executioners gambled for the only piece of property he had on earth while he was dying, and that was his coat.

When he was dead he was taken down and laid in a borrowed grave through the pity of a friend.

Nineteen wide centuries have come and gone, and today he is the centerpiece of the human race and the leader of the column of progress.

I am far within the mark when I say that all the armies that ever marched, and all the navies that ever were built, and all the parliaments that ever sat, and all the kings that ever reigned, put together, have not affected the life of man upon this earth as powerfully as has that one solitary life.

CHRIST IS SEEN IN

Hebrews as High Priest.
James as the Lord of Glory.
1 Peter as the Living Stone.
2 Peter as the Day Star.
1 John as the True God and Eternal Life.
2 John as the Son of the Father.
3 John as the Truth.
Jude as the Coming Judge.
Revelation as the Lamb enthroned.

HIS STORY

It has been said that history is really his (God's, Christ's) story, the story of how God has revealed himself to men, of how God has provided for man's redemption from sin. Some call it "salvation history."

It would be interesting and profitable to study world history from this perspective. We wouldn't be allowed to teach it this way in the public schools; but, if we really believe that the Christ-event was the central event in history (B.C.,A.D.), this would seem to be the only proper way to teach history.

It is certain that the most important future event will be the return of Christ. All that is happening now is leading up to this event. Yes, history is truly his story.

Carlton Myers

"I am the Rose of Sharon, and the Lily of the Valleys"; words most seemly in the lips of the Lord Jesus Christ, in whom it is not robbery from others, but condescension and grace, to commend Himself to the sons of men. "I am meek and lowly," would be the utterance of pride in Gabriel, but it is humility in Jesus, Who has stooped that He might become meek and lowly. "I am the true Vine," "I am the good Shepherd," etc., are the expressions alike of truth and grace, and so here.

A. Moody Stuart

If you first let Christ work IN you, He will then be able to work THROUGH you!

Christ has no hands but our hands
  To do his work today;
He has no feet but our feet
  To lead men in his way;
He has no tongues but our tongues
  To tell men how he died;
He has no help but our help
  To bring them to his side.

Annie Johnson Flint

The central theme of the Bible is Jesus Christ. It begins with Jesus Christ as the bud in Genesis that produces the flower, the finished fruit in Revelation, the coming, ruling King of kings. The Old Testament conceals Christ, the New Testament reveals Christ. The Old Testament veils Christ, the New Testament unveils Christ. The Old Testament is Christ concealed, the New Testament is Christ revealed. The Old Testament contains Christ, the New Testament explains Christ. It is, indeed, "The Jesus Book."

John R. Bisagno

SPACE LOVE

The blue of the sky
   And the stars hanging high
Sparkle and gleam
   Like a heavenly team;
And nightingales above
   In the willows make love
To the twittering glow
   Of a moon hanging low;
While the nations vie
   For a place in the sky.
And God the maker of all
   Grieves to know man must fall;
The sands of time are running low,
   And man is not prepared to go
To heavenly realms where mansions wait
   The loyal, faithful, devoted, great,
Who have followed Christ and his commands;
   While cosmonauts search for astral lands.
The love of Christ transcends all space
   Forgives and holds man by his grace.

Leola Christie Barnes

Michelangelo carved his celebrated statue of David from a block of marble which had received so deep an indentation as to be quite unserviceable under a less daring chisel. So Christ deals with humanity. No other hand but his could shape the saint, who was once a sinner.

Great things said Jesus about himself. Thinking of this world's darkness, he said: "I am the Light of the world." Thinking of humanity's homelessness: "I am the Door." Thinking of our waywardness: "I am the Way." Thinking of our need of protection: "I am the Good Shepherd." Thinking of our fruitlessness that dishonors God and burglarizes our souls: "I am the Vine." Thinking of the world's deadness in sin: "I am the resurrection, and the life." Thinking of the greatness of Jonah, behind the curtain of whose preaching Nineveh shifted scenes of riot for penitential tears: "A greater than Jonah is here." Thinking of Solomon's wisdom, glory, greatness: "A greater than Solomon is here."

R. G. Lee

THE SUPERLATIVE CHIEF

He laid aside His purple robe for a peasant's gown. He was rich, yet for our sake He became poor. How poor? Ask Mary! Ask the wise men! He slept in another's manger. He cruised the lake in another's boat. He rode on another man's ass. He was buried in another man's tomb. All failed but He never. The ever perfect One—He is the Chief among ten thousand. He is altogether lovely.

THE DOOR

Christ is the Door. No organization can take his place. None can represent him, even. We may make use of the Church as we make use of a hotel when we are traveling home to see father and mother; but no landlord of any hotel shall tell me that he is my father, or my mother, or that his hotel is my home. Churches are God's hotels, where travelers put up for the night, as it were, and then speed on their way home. Christ is the one Door. All that pass through that Door are of the one church, and belong to him.

Henry Ward Beecher

Christ is the hope of glory—*in you.*

LIGHT IN THE DARKNESS
One early winter morning the falling of ice-laden
limbs sounded to a half-asleep preacher like
someone moving about in the house. A flip of
the light switch revealed that the power had
failed. There should have been matches in the
top drawer, but after five minutes of groping in
the dark, he decided to go back to bed and let
the prowler find him.

Trying to locate those matches in the top
drawer in darkness "like midnight shut up in a a
gopher hole," set him to thinking on the tragedy
of blindness. We can imagine blindness in games
of childhood, but it is much more realistic on a
dark night when danger threatens and no light
can be found. It is a feeling surpassing
helplessness.

Jesus saw the multitudes of his day as blind.
They too were fumbling around in top drawers
in an effort to locate God and themselves. John,
the apostle, described this condition as "darkness". A light came to this darkness, but the
darkness refused to see it and the people remained
blind and continued to grope helplessly for truth.
But, some saw.

John Jeffers

NO DISAPPOINTMENT
  And His blessed kiss of peace
Has assured my heart forever
  That His love will never cease.
He is not a disappointment!
  He is all in all to me—
Saviour, Sanctifier, Keeper,
  The unchanging Christ is He!
He has won my heart's affections,
  And He meets my every need;
He is not a disappointment,
  For He satisfies indeed.

There is no name like His for us. It is more imperial than Caesar's, more musical than Beethoven's, more conquering than Charlemagne's
more eloquent than Cicero's.

R. G. Lee

He who is the bread of life began His ministry
    hungering.
He who is the water of life ended His ministry
    thirsting.
He who was weary is our true rest.
He who paid tribute is the King of kings.
He prayed yet hears our prayers.
He wept but dries our tears.
He was sold for thirty pieces of silver, yet
    redeemed us.
He was led as a lamb to the slaughter, but is the
    Good Shepherd.
He died and gave His life, and by dying destroyed
    death for all who believe.

The world cannot bury Christ. The earth is not
deep enough for his tomb, the clouds are not
wide enough for his winding-sheet; he ascends
into the heavens, but the heavens cannot contain
him. He still lives—in the church which burns un-
consumed with his love; in the truth that reflects
his image; in the hearts which flame with his love;
in the spirit which is infused with his power.

Jesus! the very thought of Thee
With sweetness fills my breast:
But sweeter far Thy face to see.
And in thy presence rest.

Bernard of Clairvaux

The great Physician now is near,
The sympathizing Jesus;
He speaks the drooping heart to cheer,
Oh, hear the voice of Jesus.

William Hunter

Daniel Webster said: "I believe Jesus Christ to be
the Son of God. The miracles which he wrought
establish, in my mind, his personal authority, and
render it proper for me to believe whatever he
asserts. I believe, therefore, all his declarations,
as well when he declares himself to be the Son of
God, as when he declares any other proposition.

JOY

Thou wilt shew me the path of life: in thy presence is fulness of joy; at thy right hand there are pleasures for evermore.

Psalm 16:11

Whom having not seen, ye love; in whom, though now ye see him not, yet believing, ye rejoice with joy unspeakable and full of glory.

1 Peter 1:8

Of all the lights you carry in your face,
Joy will reach the farthest out to sea.

Henry Ward Beecher

CHRISTIAN JOY
There is a joy which is not given to the ungodly,
but to those who love Thee for Thine own sake,
whose joy Thou Thyself art. And this is the
happy life, to rejoice to Thee, of Thee, for Thee,
this it is, and there is no other.

Augustine

. . . Spiritual joy comes of cleanness of heart
and the purity of continual prayer.

Francis of Assisi

JOY OF CHRISTIANITY
It has been thought by many that to be religious
is to be serious and even gloomy. Jesus did not
teach it this way. He said: "Peace I leave with
you, My peace I give unto you." The Psalmist
said: "In Thy presence is fullness of joy," and
Paul said: "Rejoice in the Lord and again I say
Rejoice." These are not the sayings of advocates
of a gloomy and desolate religion. Christianity
gives men and women a song and a smile, no
matter what the circumstances are.

Billy Graham

But we are pressed by heavy laws;
And often, glad no more,
We wear a face of joy, because
We have been glad of yore.

William Wordsworth

Nothing else is to be desired except the joy that
comes from truth; nothing is to be shunned
except its absence.

John Scotus

HAPINESS VS. JOY
Happiness and joy are not the same. Happiness is
determined by the happenings, events, and circumstances of life. Joy is determined by the fulness of the Holy Spirit in our lives. So it is
possible to be joyful even though you are
unhappy.
The fulness of the Holy Spirit in us is determined
by how much we have surrendered our wills to
God. It is also determined by how much of God's
word is in us.
Happiness is not something you find by searching
for it. It is a by-product of losing yourself in
serving God and others. The same is true of joy.
You cannot work it up. It is a supernatural result
of God's spirit.

Carlton Myers

Someday people will learn that material things do
not bring happiness, and are of little use in making men and women creative and powerful. Then
the scientists will turn their laboratories over to
the study of God and prayer and to the spiritual
forces. When this day comes the world will see
more advancement in one generation than it has
seen in the past four.

Charles P. Steinmetz

Smile, brother, smile,
When you smile another smiles,
And soon there's miles and miles
Of smiles, and life's worth while
Because you smile,
So smile, brother, smile.

A smile on your lips:
  Cheers your heart,
  Preserves peace in your soul,
  Promotes your health,
  Beautifies your face,
  Induces kindly thoughts,
  Inspires kindly deeds.

A SMILE

A SMILE costs nothing but gives much—it takes but a moment, but the memory of it usually lasts forever. None are so rich that can get along without it—and none are so poor but that can be made rich by it. It enriches those who receive without making poor those who give—it creates sunshine in the home, fosters good will in business and is the best antidote for trouble—and yet it cannot be begged, borrowed or stolen, for it is of no value unless it is freely given away. Some people are too busy to give you a smile—give them one of yours—for the good Lord knows that no one needs a smile so badly as he or she who has no more smiles left to give.

Phillips Brooks was once crossing the Atlantic and a young man, a fellow-passenger, having an intense desire for an interview with him, went to his cabin door and knocked gently. As no answer was received he quietly opened the door, to find the great saint of God prostrate upon the floor, his hands raised to heaven and his lips moving in prayer. These were the words which he heard: "O Lord Jesus, Thou hast filled my life with peace and gladness. To look into Thy face is earth's most exquisite joy."

Mrs. Charles E. Cowman

Your neighbor, sir, whose roses you admire,
Is glad indeed to know that they inspire
Within your breast a feeling quite as fine
As felt by him who owns and tends that vine.
Friend, from my neighbors and this vine I've
   learned
That sharing pleasure means a profit turned;
And he who shares the joy in what he's grown
Spreads joy abroad and doubles all his own.

I believe if I furnish the smile on the face, God will provide the mood in the heart.

Mary Bacheler

THE FULNESS OF JOY

God—
I want to walk with you in joy,
Laughing, singing, clasping hands,
Sharing together the worlds you've made,
The singing hills, the quiet lands;
To know the faith of buried bulb
Waiting in darkness its burst of bloom,
To know the patience of nesting bird
Sending its lilting song through the gloom;
To feel the beauty of each new day—
Washed clean, refreshing, warm with light,
To feel the wonderful, joyous calm
Of each returning, restful night.
What joy to breathe, to see, to feel,
To walk with you in sun or shade!
The fulness of joy: to walk with you
In earth or heaven you have made.

Ida Nelle Hollaway

THEY HAVE FOUND A JOY

This is a cheerful world as I see it from my garden, under the shadow of my vines. But if I could ascend some high mountain and look out over the wide lands, you know very well what I would see—brigands on the highways; pirates on the seas; armies fighting, cities burning; in the amphi-theatres men murdered to please applauding crowds; selfishness and cruelty, misery and despair under all roofs. It is a bad world.

But I have discovered in the midst of it a quiet and holy people who have learned a great secret. They have found a joy which is a thousand times better than any of the pleasures of our sinful life. They are despised and persecuted, but they care not. They are masters of their own souls. They have overcome the world. These people, Donatus, are the Christians—and I am one of them.

Cyprian

Frowning is hard work. It takes sixty-four muscles of the face to make a frown and only thirteen to make a smile.

A Field of Diamonds

THE KEY TO JOY
This is so with Christ in the heart. From attic to basement in the whole house of life there must be no room that is closed to Him. There may be rooms of the soul we would not throw open to the world, but if the Lord is to abide with us, the key even to these must be placed in His hands. Only so can we know the joy and peace and strength of His abiding presence in the heart.

Christian Observer

ONLY MAN CAN SMILE
Gems may flash reflected light, but what is a diamond-flash compared to an eye-flash and a mirth-flash? Flowers cannot smile; this is a charm that even they cannot claim. It is the prerogative of man; it is the color which love wears, and cheerfulness, and joy—these three. It is a light in the windows of the face by which the heart signifies it is at home and waiting. A face that cannot smile is like a bud that cannot blossom, and dries up on the stalk. Laughter is day, and sobriety is night, and a smile is the twilight that hovers gently between both—more bewitching than either.

Henry Ward Beecher

JOY OF SURRENDER
There is but one way to find that fulness of joy, a surrendered life. A will and life completely surrendered to the God of love will bring joy under all circumstances. In the olden days one who was thus surrendered to God was led out to be burned at the stake, and he threw his arms around the stake and cried out: "Welcome, cross of Christ! Welcome eternal life!"

R. A. Torrey

Joys are our wings; sorrows our spurs.

J. P. F. Richter

Joy is not in things; it is in us.

Wagner

THE ARITHMETIC OF HAPPINESS
When you rise in the morning, say that you will make the day blessed to a fellow creature. It is easily done: a left-off garment to the man who needs it: a kind word to the sorrowful; an encouraging expression to the struggling—trifles in themselves as light as air—will do at least for the twenty-four hours. If you send one person away happy through the day, there are 365 in the course of a year. And suppose you live forty years only. After you commence that course of medicine, you have made 14,600 persons happy, at all events for a time.

The happiest heart that ever beat
  Was in some humble breast
That found the common daylight sweet,
  And left to Heaven the rest.

John Vance Cheney

PROMISE YOURSELF . . .
To talk health, happiness, and prosperity to every person you meet.
To wear a cheerful countenance at all times and give every living creature you meet a smile.
To look at the sunny side of everything and make your optimism come true.

LET THE JOY BELLS RING
The Macedonian Christians were happy givers. A good steward, one who has given himself to the Lord, will not constantly sound the crucifical note, but will rather ring the joy bells. The annunciation angel sang, "Behold, I bring you good tidings of great joy" (Luke 2:10). Jesus said, "These things have I spoken unto you, that my joy might remain in you, and that your joy might be full" (John 15:11). In Hebrews 12:2 we read of Jesus as follows: "For the joy that was set before him [he] endured the cross, despising the shame."

J. E. Dillard

126

LOVE

For God so loved the world, that he gave his only begotten Son, that whosoever believeth in him should not perish, but have everlasting life.

John 3:16

Herein is love, not that we loved God, but that he loved us, and sent his Son to be the propitiation for our sins.

1 John 4:10

A GLORY OF CHRISTIANITY

One of the glories of Christianity is the place it gives to love. It sums up all religious duty in love to God, and all ethical duty in love to man. It has set before humanity as the fullest revelation of God and the highest expression of manhood the life of Jesus Christ, whose name is a synonym of love. It has made love the dominant characteristic in the nature of God himself, and therewith has written love across the whole universe.

Walter Rauschenbusch

LOVE OF THE CHRISTIANS

But it is the exercise of this sort of love which doth, with some, chiefly brand us with a mark of evil. "See," say they, "how they love each other"; for they themselves hate each other: and "see how ready they are to die for each other"; for they themselves are more ready to slay each other.

Tertullian

WHAT IS LOVE?

It is silence when your words would hurt,
It is patience when your neighbor is curt;
It is defense when a scandal flows,
It is thoughtfulness for another's woes;
It is promptness when a stern duty calls,
It is courage when misfortune falls.

Love is love only when it is the sacrifice of one's self. Only when a man gives to another, not merely his time and his strength, but when he spends his body for the beloved object, gives up his life for him,—only this do we all acknowledge as love; and only in such love do we all find happiness, the reward of love. And only in virtue of the fact that there is such love toward man, only in this, does the world stand.

Leo Tolstoy

Love can be measured by the sacrifice it makes.

SAY IT, BACK IT!

The cry for love is universal. The need for someone to care and to care for someone is constant. A place to belong—where roots may deepen and secured against the changing winds of time, forever makes the difference between a reason for life's being and drifting aimlessly.

For the sake of love, love "suffereth long, and is kind."
For the sake of love, love turns from self to love expressed in selflessness.
Love expressed by word alone is but a passing breath and emptiness remains.
Love expressed in active deed secures the way to harmony and peace and life's fulfillments come.

The cry for love is as close as the nearest breath of life. Dare one turn a deaf ear to need as it grieves upon the wind?

"Say it with your mouth, then back it up with your heart." Can love ever do less than this?

Louise Barker Barnhill

LOVE OF ENEMY

. . . He truly loveth his enemy, who murmurs not for the injury done to himself, but, for the love of God, is consumed with grief for the sin in his enemy's soul, and who manifests his love for him in deeds.

Francis of Assisi

LOVE IS NOT A CRITIC

Love makes him hold others innocent in his heart; even when he sees infirmity or fault in his neighbor, he reflects that very likely all is not as it seems on the outside, but the act may have been done with a good intention.

John Tauler

'Tis better to have loved and lost
Than never to have loved at all.

Alfred Lord Tennyson

. . . that the neighbour may be loved with perfect righteousness it is necessary that God should be in our thoughts. How otherwise is it possible for one to love his neighbour rightly who doth not love him in God? Moreover he cannot love aught in God, who loveth not God Himself. God therefore must first be loved, that the neighbour may be loved in God.

Bernard of Clairvaux

I LOVE YOU!

On deeper musing, the wonder of the eternal Father's love for his children was more clearly revealed. Of a truth there are no wire-spanned miles to separate Spirit from Spirit–only the measure of error that stands as a partition between. However, when error is forgiven and the weight of guilt removed, then all distance is spanned and Spirit dwells with Spirit.
I love you! In the mystery of these words is found the link of heart to heart, and of immortal soul to the heart of the everlasting Father, God.

Louise Barker Barnhill

The Spectrum of Love has nine ingredients:
Patience . . . . . "Love suffereth long."
Kindness . . . . . "And is kind."
Generosity . . . . "Love envieth not."
Humility . . . . . "Love vaunteth not itself, is not puffed up."
Courtesy . . . . . "Doth not behave itself unseemly."
Unselfishness . . . "Seeketh not her own."
Good Temper . . . "Is not easily provoked."
Guilelessness . . . "Thinketh no evil."
Sincerity . . . . . "Rejoiceth not in iniquity, rejoiceth in the truth."

Henry Drummond

Love is the force that draws man and man together, the great social instinct of the race.

Walter Rauschenbusch

If we give love and sympathy
  Even to those who hate us
We fill them so with mystery
  They know not how to rate us.

Helen King

EARTHLY LOVES

We know of earthly loves which cannot die. They have entered so deeply into the very fabric of the soul, that, like some cloth dyed ingrain, as long as two threads hold together they will retain the tint.

Alexander Maclaren

MY GIFTS

No offering of my own I have,
  Nor works my faith to prove;
I can but give the gifts he gave,
  And plead his love for love.

A RED, RED ROSE

O, my luve is like a red, red rose,
  That's newly sprung in June.
O, my luve is like the melodie,
  That's sweetly played in tune.

Robert Burns

ALL BESIDES LOVE IS BUT WORDS

Words do not come
with facility . . .
nor does love.
Words can bring the
beauty of
communal fellowship
or
threat of war.
Somehow,
words that do not come
easily
are less important
than love.
Love only brings love.

Harvey L. Nowland

It's love, it's love that makes the world go round.
W. S. Gilbert

With all thy faults, I love thee still.
William Cowper

NEVER DOUBT I LOVE

Doubt thou the stars are fire;
  Doubt that the sun doth move;
Doubt truth to be a liar;
  But never doubt I love.
William Shakespeare

LOVE IS . . .

Love is swift, sincere, pious, pleasant, gentle, strong, patient, faithful, prudent, long-suffering, manly, and never seeking her own; for wheresoever a man seeketh his own, there he falleth from love. Love is circumspect, humble, and upright; not weak, not fickle, nor intent or vain things; sober, chaste, steadfast, quiet, and guarded in all the senses. Love is subject and obedient to all that are in authority, vile and lowly in its own sight, devout and grateful towards God, faithful and always trusting in Him even when God hideth His face, for without sorrow we cannot live in love.
Thomas a Kempis

Give me a man who before all things loves God with his whole soul; who loves himself and his neighbor in so far as they love God, his enemy also as one who may sometime love him; who loves his relatives according to the flesh in a brotherly fashion by reason of nature, his spiritual instructors more abundantly by reason of grace, his love for other things being thus regulated by his love for God . . .
Bernard of Clairvaux

Christian love means "having to say you're sorry."

A FULLER LOVE

Many of the current Gospels are addressed only to a part of man's nature. They offer peace, not life; faith, not Love; justification, not regeneration. And men slip back again from such religion because it has never really held them. Their nature was not all in it. It offered no deeper and gladder life-current than the life that was lived before. Surely it stands to reason that only a fuller love can compete with the love of the world.
Henry Drummond

LOVE — MERCY — HUMILITY

Love to the Saviour rises in the heart of a saved man in proportion to the sense which he entertains of his own sinfulness on the one hand, and of the mercy of God on the other. Thus the height of a saint's love to the Lord is as the depths of his own humility: as this root strikes down unseen into the ground, the blossoming branch rises higher in the sky.
William Arnot

LOVE

I love you
Because you have done
More than any creed
Could have done
To make me good,
And more than any fate
Could have done
To make me happy.
  . . . .
You have done it
Without a touch,
Without a word,
Without a sign.
You have done it
By being yourself,
Perhaps that is what
Being a friend means,
After all.
Roy Croft

MEDITATION

But his delight is in the law of the Lord; and in his law doth he meditate day and night.

Psalm 1:2

Meditate upon these things; give thyself wholly to them; that thy profiting may appear to all.

1 Timothy 4:15

If you sit down at set of sun
And count the acts that you have done,
  And counting find
One self-denying deed, one word
That eased the heart of him who heard;
  One glance most kind,
That fell like sunshine where it went—
Then you may count that day well spent.

George Eliot

STUDY

Study to know the grace our Lord bestowed on
    thee;
Study to know the love He had for you and me.
Study to lift thy soul above the din of things;
Study to hear His voice which through the ages
    rings.
Study about the price He paid upon the tree;
Study to know His plans that span eternity.
Study that thou a workman unashamed may be,
Study to share the Word of truth entrusted unto
    thee.

J. E. Lambdin

If we would really welcome the Lord Jesus, we
must make a road for Him by abasing our pride,
elevating our thoughts, removing our evil habits,
and preparing our hearts. Never did a soul cast
up a highway for the Lord, and then fail to enjoy
His company.

Charles Haddon Spurgeon

I have seen Jesus, and my heart is dead to all be-
side;
I have seen Jesus, and my wants are all supplied;
I have seen Jesus, and my heart is satisfied,
        Satisfied with Jesus.

A. B. Simpson

God makes no duplicates. Each life is purpose-
ful, original, precious.

GOD'S NEARNESS

Speak to Him thou for He hears, and
  Spirit with Spirit can meet—
Closer is He than breathing, and nearer
  than hands and feet.

Alfred Lord Tennyson

WHEN I MET THE MASTER

I had walked life's way with an easy tread,
  Had followed where comforts and pleasure led,
Until one day, in a quiet place,
  I met the Master, face to face.

With station and rank and wealth for my goal,
  Much thought for my body, but none for my
    soul,
I had entered to win in life's big race,
  When I met the Master, face to face.

I had built my castles and reared them high,
  With their towers had pierced the blue of the
    sky,
I had sworn to rule with an iron mace,
  When I met the Master, face to face.

I met Him and knew Him, and blushed to see
  That His eyes full of sorrow were fixed on me,
And I faltered and fell at His feet that day
  While my castles melted and vanished away.

Melted and vanished, and in their place
  Naught else did I see but the Master's face,
And I cried aloud, "Oh, make me meet
  To follow the steps of Thy wounded feet!"

My thought is now for the souls of men,
  I have lost my life to find it again,
E'er since that day in a quiet place,
  When I met the Master, face to face.

And, oh, how sweet it is to know
  Thy loving, mighty, tender clasp
Will never let me go.

Make Christ your most constant companion.

Turn your eyes upon Jesus,
Look full in His wonderful Face,
And the things of earth will grow strangely dim,
In the light of His glory and grace.
Helen Howarth Lemmel

NOT I, BUT CHRIST

Not I, but Christ, be honored, loved, exalted;
Not I, but Christ, be seen, be known, be heard;
Not I, but Christ, in every look and action;
Not I, but Christ, in every thought and word.

Not I, but Christ, in lowly, silent labor;
Not I, but Christ, in humble, earnest toil;
Christ, only Christ—no show, no ostentation;
Christ, none but Christ, the Gatherer of the spoil.

Redeem the time! God only knows
How soon our little life may close,
With all its pleasures and its woes.
Redeem the time!

"He who wastes time insults Providence!"

I NEED THEE

"I need Thee, loving Shepherd,
I need Thy constant care,
To guide me on life's journey,
And all the way prepare.
I need Thine arms around me,
To hold me lest I fall:
O more and more I need Thee—
My only Hope, my All."

Lord, I have shut my door!
Come Thou and visit me. I am alone!
Come as when doors were shut Thou cam'st of
yore
And visited Thine own!
My Lord, I kneel with reverent love and fear
For Thou art here!

HIS WILL

Tho' the pathway be drear, and sacrifice dear,
In the way of His will there is peace.
In the place of His will there is joy,
There praises our hearts will employ,
Amid sorrow and pain, when tears flow like rain,
In the place of His will there is joy.
In the place of His will there is power,
His Spirit flows in every hour,
Tho' our strength may be small, tho' we have
none at all,
In the place of His will there is power.

RECOMPENSE

Today the skies are clear and blue,
The rains have passed away;
And stormy clouds of angry mien
No longer hold their sway.

Like temperamental, cloud–swept skies
Are days all filled with strife;
And sorrow's tears soon lose their sway,
Sweet recompense of life.
R. Paul Caudill

A CALL

Among the things that this day brings
Will come to you a call,
The which, unless you're listening,
You may not hear at all;
Lest it be very soft and low,
Whate'er you do, where'er you go,
Be listening.

When God shall come and say to you,
'Here is the thing that you must do,'
Be listening.

THE MORNING WATCH

Some minutes in the morning,
Ere the cares of life begin,
Ere the heart's wide door is open
For the world to enter in.

O Saviour, bid me "go and sin no more,"
   And keep me always 'neath the mighty flow
Of Thy perpetual fountain; I implore
   That Thy perpetual cleansing I may fully
     know.
            Frances Ridley Havergal

MEETING WITH GOD
O let us keep that meeting place—
The secret tryst with God.
At such a time He shows His face,
O holy tryst with God.
Never mind though friends and others call,
His love impels our best, our all;
Let us come alone, before Him fall
And keep our tryst with God.

SERENITY IN GOD
My path may lead through wood at night,
   Where neither moon nor any light
Of guiding star or beacon shines;
   He will not let me miss my signs.
Lord, grant to me a quiet mind,
   That, trusting Thee—for Thou art kind—
I may go on without a fear,
   For Thou, my Lord, art always near.

The Master always kept a space of silence around
His soul; that inner serenity which is, perhaps,
one of the most important things a busy life can
possess.
            Mrs. Charles E. Cowman

MEDITATION FOR TODAY
Lord, for all who are taxed physically, undertake
with Thy sweet strength and sustaining. Prevent
the exacting of Satan, and may the joy and
strength of God be marvelous today. Cleanse
me from flurry, and keep me purely and calmly
Thine. Gather me into concentrated peace on
Thee. Come in Thy great and quiet almightiness.
            Oswald Chambers

Oh, let me live as if He died
   But yestertide;
And I myself had seen and touched
   His pierced side.

A QUIET PLACE
I want to make a quiet place
Where those I love can see God's face,
Can stretch their hearts across the earth,
Can understand what spring is worth,
Can count the stars,
Watch violets grow,
And learn what birds and children know.

He said not,
   "Thou shalt not be
     Tempested;
Thou shalt not be
     Travailed;
Thou shalt not be
     Afflicted:"
But He said,
   "Thou shalt not be
     Overcome!"
            Julian of Norwick

ANOTHER WORLD IS MINE
Another world is mine tonight,
   As on the shimmering beams of light,
I glide along through star-lit skies
   On silvery wings of restful flight.
Above me lies the broad expanse
   Of heaven's endless, bright domain,
All filled with music of the stars
   That blend their songs in sweet refrain.
Below me lies the troubled world,
   Where man contends for selfish gain,
Oblivious to the law of life,
   That gain ill got is wreathed with pain.
How strange it seems to mind and heart,
   So far removed from things of earth;
Methinks I see the face of God,
   And feel my soul reclaim new birth.
            R. Paul Caudill

NATION

That land is great which knows the Lord,
Where freedom's guided by His word.

AMERICA, BEWARE!
The average age of the world's great civilizations
has been 200 years. These nations progressed
through this sequence:
From BONDAGE to Spiritual Faith
From SPIRITUAL FAITH to Courage
From COURAGE to Liberty
From LIBERTY to Abundance
From ABUNDANCE to Selfishness
From SELFISHNESS to Complacency
From COMPLACENCY to Apathy
From APATHY to Dependency
From DEPENDENCY, back again into
   BONDAGE

AMERICA
America! America!
  God shed His grace on thee.
                    Katharine L. Bates

My country, 'tis of thee,
Sweet land of liberty,
Of thee I sing;
                    Samuel Francis Smith

America is great because she is good, and if
America ever ceases to be good, America will
cease to be great.
                    Alexis De Tocqueville

Religious liberty is the mother of all true liberty.
It is based upon the dignity of each individual
made in the "image of God" (Gen. 1:27) and his
competency to stand before God without the
mediation of earthly priest or king (1 Tim.
2:1-6). It is not a privilege granted by man, but
a right given of God.
                    Herschel H. Hobbs

Once to every man and nation comes the moment
  to decide
In the strife of Truth and Falsehood, for the good
  or evil side . . .
                    James Russell Lowell

God of our fathers, known of old,
  Lord of our far-flung battle-line,
Beneath whose awful Hand we hold
  Dominion over palm and pine—
Lord God of Hosts, be with us yet,
Lest we forget—lest we forget!
                    Rudyard Kipling

And the star-spangled banner in triumph shall
  wave
O'er the land of the free and the home of the
  brave.
                    Francis Scott Key

FREEDOM OF WORSHIP
Aye, call it holy ground,
  The soil where first they trod!
They left unstained what there they found—
  Freedom to worship God.
                    Felicia D. Hemans

The administration of justice is the firmest pillar
of government.
                    George Washington

Observe good faith and justice toward all nations;
cultivate peace and harmony with all. Religion
and morality enjoin this conduct; and can it be
that good policy does not equally enjoin it?
                    George Washington

Government of the people, by the people, and
for the people.
                    Abraham Lincoln

"Posterity! You will never know how much it cost the present generation to preserve your freedom! I hope you will make a good use of it. If you do not, I shall repent it in heaven that I ever took half the pains to preserve it."

John Adams

THE CURE
There is nothing wrong with America that the faith, love of freedom, intelligence and energy of her citizens cannot cure.

Dwight D. Eisenhower

LIBERTY OR DEATH
Why stand we here idle? What is it that gentlemen wish? What would they have? Is life so dear, or peace so sweet, as to be purchased at the price of chains and alavery? Forbid it, Almighty God! I know not what course others may take, but as for me, give me liberty, or give me death!

Patrick Henry

ALL TOGETHER
As long as we can *all* stand up *together,* God will bless America.
For whether God blesses America or not does not depend so much upon God as it does upon us Americans.

Carl Heath Kopf

Let us have faith that Right makes Might, and in that faith let us to the end dare to do our duty as we understand it.

Abraham Lincoln

LIBERTY OF CONSCIENCE
I desire not that liberty for myself which I would not freely and impartially weigh out to all the consciences of the world besides; therefore, I humbly conceive that it is the express and absolute duty of the civil powers to proclaim an absolute freedom of conscience in all the world.

Roger Williams

GOD AND LIBERTY
"Cradle of American Liberty!" it is a great name; but there is something in it which saddens my heart. You should not say "American liberty." You should say "liberty in America." Liberty should not be either American or European,— it should be just "liberty." God is God. He is neither America's God nor Europe's God. He is God. So shall liberty be.

Louis Kossuth

TO NEW CITIZENS
You have just taken an oath of allegiance to the United States. Of allegiance to whom? Of allegiance to no one, unless it be God—certainly not of allegiance to those who temporarily represent this great Government. You have taken an oath of allegiance to a great ideal, to a great body of principles, to a great hope of the human race.

Woodrow Wilson

Its soul, its climate, its equality, liberty, laws, people, and manners. How little do my countrymen know what precious blessings they are in possession of, and which no other people on earth enjoy.

Thomas Jefferson

THE AMERICAN CREED
"I believe in the United States of America as a government of the people, by the people, for the people; whose just powers are derived from the consent of the governed; a democracy in a republic; a sovereign nation of many sovereign states; a perfect union, one and inseparable; established upon those principles of freedom, equality, justice, and humanity for which American patriots sacrificed their lives and fortunes. I therefore believe it is my duty to my country to love it, to support its constitution, to obey its laws, to respect its flag, and to defend it against all enemies."

William Tyler Page

A Field of Diamonds

Our country is the world–our countrymen are all mankind.

William Lloyd Garrison

THE MELTING POT
America is God's Crucible, the great Melting–Pot where all the races of Europe are melting and reforming . . .

Israel Zangwill

MY NATIVE LAND
Breathes there a man with soul so dead,
Who never to himself hath said,
    This is my own, my native land?
Whose heart hath ne'er within him burn'd
As home his footsteps he hath turn'd
    From wandering on a foreign strand?

Sir Walter Scott

RECOGNITION OF NEED
One of the healthiest and most promising signs on the national horizon is the realization of spiritual and moral need that is sweeping this nation. Many of our most cynical leaders are now admitting that America needs a religious and moral bath that will cleanse it from deception, immorality and lethargy.

Billy Graham

AN AMERICAN
I was born an American; I will live an American; I shall die an American; and I intend to perform the duties incumbent upon me.
For this we muster the spirit of America and the faith of America.
We do not retreat. We are not content to stand still. As Americans, we go forward, in the service of our country, by the will of God.

Daniel Webster

God bless America so she may be a blessing.

PROGRESS AND REGRESS
On Friday morning, November 22, 1963, in Dallas, a young President was jovial and exuberant. His straw–like hair was blowing in the breeze, and his wide smile turned to strangers. Then in five seconds of time, the damage was done. Two terrible bullets from a sniper's $12.00 gun hit his head and neck. Lyndon B. Johnson called it the "foulest deed of our time." What progress science and technology had made--an accurate gun! What regress in morals and religion--a wild hatred! A crackpot had listened to the apostles of bitterness and bigotry. (The clock had been turned back 100 years when another President had been assassinated.) This was one in a series of assassinations that took America from the space age to the stone age. True progress will come when people will acknowledge Christ as the Leader of their thoughts and lives. Pray that the future will bring some great progress of the soul to keep up with the discoveries of science.

John Warren Steen

The same sense of a great change comes over any one who watches the life of this nation with an eye for the stirring of God in the souls of men. There is a new shame and anger for oppression and meanness; a new love and pity for the young and frail whose slender shoulders bear our common weight; a new faith in human brotherhood; a new hope of a better day that is even now in sight.

Walter Rauschenbusch

INSCRIBED ON THE STATUE OF LIBERTY
"Give me your tired,
    your poor,
Your huddled masses yearning to
    breathe free,
The wretched refuse of your teeming shore.
Send these, the homeless, tempest-tost to me,
I lift my lamp beside the golden door."

Emma Lazarus

PEACE

And he shall judge among many people, and rebuke strong nations afar off; and they shall beat their swords into plowshares, and their spears into pruninghooks: nation shall not lift up a sword against nation, neither shall they learn war anymore.

Micah 4:3

Peace I leave with you, my peace I give unto you: not as the world giveth, give I unto you. Let not your heart be troubled, neither let it be afraid.

John 14:27

Oh, precious peace within my heart;
    Oh, blessed rest to know
A Father's love keeps constant watch,
    Amid life's ebb and flow;
I ask no more than this; I rest
    Content, and know His way is best.

True peace is found by man in the depths of his own heart, which is the true Dwelling-place of God.

John Tauler

THE CHRISTIAN'S PEACE
The Christian has a deep, silent, hidden peace, which the world sees not—like some well in a retired and shady place, difficult of access. He is the greater part of his time by himself, and when he is in solitude, that is his real state. What he is when left to himself and to his God, that is his true life.

John Henry Newman

Thou awakest us to delight in Thy praise; for Thou madest us for Thyself, and our heart is restless, until it repose in Thee.

Augustine

PEACE AND HIS WILL
God for His service needeth not proud work of
    human skill;
They please Him best who labour most in peace
    to do His will.

William Wordsworth

PEACE OF SOUL
Peace and tranquillity of the soul is above all glory of any house; for *peace passeth all understanding*. This is that peace above all peace which shall be granted . . . when He shall destroy all Principalities and Powers . . . And thus there will be peace over all . . .

Ambrose

Lord, make me an instrument of your
    peace!
Where there is hatred, let me sow love;
Where there is injury, pardon;
Where there is doubt, faith;
Where there is despair, hope;
Where there is darkness, light;
Where there is sadness, joy.
O Divine Master, grant that I may not
    so much seek
To be consoled, as to console;
To be understood, as to understand;
To be loved, as to love.
For it is in giving that we receive;
It is in pardoning that we are pardoned;
It is in dying that we are born to eternal life.

Francis of Assisi

LIFE AND PEACE
A man has found himself when he has found his relation to the rest of the universe, and here is the book [the Bible] in which those relations are set forth. And so when you see a man going along the highways of life with his gaze lifted above the road, lifted to the sloping ways in front of him, then be careful of that man and get out of his way. He knows the kingdom for which he is bound. He has seen the revelation of himself and of relations to mankind. He has seen the revelations of his relation to God and his Maker, and therefore he has seen his responsibility to the world. This is the revelation of life and of peace.

Woodrow Wilson

PATHS OF PEACEFULNESS
Lead me, dear Lord, in paths of peacefulness.
    But if, perchance, Thy paths should ever lie
O'er mountain trails, though they be rough and
    bleak,
    Then may I answer, "Master, here am I."

I. S. Ellis

First keep thyself in peace, and then shalt thou be able to be a peacemaker towards others.

HYMN OF PEACE

When winds are raging o'er the upper ocean,
  And billows wild contend with angry roar,
'Tis said, far down beneath the wild commotion,
  That peaceful stillness reigneth, evermore.

Far, far beneath, the noise of tempests dieth,
  And silver waves chime ever peacefully,
And no rude storm, how fierce soe'er it flieth,
  Disturbs the Sabbath of that deeper sea.

Harriet Beecher Stowe

FDR'S DYING WISH

"We seek peace—enduring peace. More than an end to war, we want an end to the beginnings of all wars—yes, an end to this brutal, inhuman, and thoroughly impractical method of settling differences between governments. The mere conquest of our enemies is not enough. We must go on to do all in our power to conquer the doubts and the fears, the ignorance and the greed which made this horror possible. Today we are faced with the pre-eminent fact that, if civilization is to survive, we must cultivate the science of human relationships—the ability of all peoples, of all kinds, to live together and work together, in the same world, at peace."

Franklin Delano Roosevelt

With peace in his soul a man can face the most terrifying experiences. But without peace in his soul he cannot manage even as simple a task as writing a letter.

"Blessed are the peacemakers."—So said Jesus, but a visit to our nation's capital would seem to indicate that it was, "Blessed are the warmakers." In the parks, the public buildings, and the National Cemetery are countless great monuments and statues erected in memory of the gallant heroes of war. But one has to keep his eyes opened to discover honors accorded heroes of peace. Some day we will agree with Milton: "Peace hath her victories no less renown'd than war."

PRAYER LEADING TO PEACE

A prayer wells up, "Make thyself real to me now. Speak to my heart. Put me in contact with thee. Help me to worship thee in spirit and in truth. Give me a heart that is alert and receptive and a will that is submissive. Unveil the face of Jesus. I need thy balm for the wounds of yesterday; thy strength for the burdens of this day; and thy vision for the years ahead."
In our innermost being there is a meaningful silence. Peace and consciousness of his presence invade the soul.

Rosalee Mills Appleby

PEACE BEYOND UNDERSTANDING

The peace which goes beyond the understanding says: "I have done all this as well as I know how, but there are regions of danger which I cannot explore, there are perilous forces which I cannot measure. The universe is large, and out of any distant corner of it there may come a sudden blow striking right at my life. Beyond what I can provide for, then, I find out Him who is in all the universe, and, loving Him, I trust myself upon His love. It is not knowledge, now, of what will come or how it can be met; it is only the sympathetic apprehension of His love and care who is all-strong, all-wise. This is what I rest upon. This is the confidence in which I sleep by night and work by day." It is a peace which passeth understanding and fulfils itself in love.

Phillips Brooks

During World War II a European Christian said: "On the surface there is storm, but twenty fathoms down it is quite calm."

PEACE AND WAR

Peace hath her victories
  No less renown'd than war.

John Milton

PEACE AND JOY

"These things write we unto you, that your joy may be full." What is fulness of joy but *peace?* Joy is tumultuous only when it is not full; but peace is the privilege of those who are "filled with the knowledge of the glory of the Lord, as the waters cover the sea." "Thou wilt keep him in perfect peace, whose mind is stayed on Thee, because he trusteth in Thee."

John Henry Newman

OUR LAST CHANCE

At the close of World War II General MacArthur said: "We have had our last chance. If we do not now devise some greater and more equitable system, Armageddon will be at our door. The problem basically is theological and involves a spiritual recrudescence and improvement of human character. . . . It must be of the spirit if we are to save the flesh."

In His will is our peace.
(*In la sua voluntade e nostra pace.*)

Alighieri Dante

Why do they prate of the blessings of peace? we
    have made them a curse, . . .
And lust of gain, in the spirit of Cain, is it better
    or worse
Than the heart of the citizen hissing in war. . . .

Alfred Lord Tennyson

AT PEACE

Grant me Thy grace, most merciful Jesus, that it may be with me, and work in me, and persevere with me, even unto the end. Grant that I may ever desire and wish whatsoever is most pleasing and dear unto Thee. Let Thy will be mine, and let my will alway follow Thine, and entirely accord with it. May I choose and reject whatsoever Thou dost; yea, let it be impossible for me to choose or reject according to Thy will.

Thomas a Kempis

SWEET PEACE, THE GIFT OF GOD'S LOVE

There comes to my heart one sweet strain,
A glad and a joyous refrain;
I sing it again and again,
Sweet peace, the gift of God's love.

Peter P. Bilhorn

THE HEIRS OF HEAVEN

Set thyself in peace and then shalt thou be able to set others at peace. A peaceable man availeth more than a great learned man.

It is not a great thing for a man to be conversant with good men and mild men: for that pleaseth all men naturally and every man gladly hath peace with them that feel as he doth; and such he loveth. But for a man to live peaceably with hard and overthwart men indisciplined and contrarious is a great grace and a commendable and a manly deed.

There are some that keep themselves at peace and have peace with others also; and there be some also that neither have peace themselves nor suffer others to have peace; to others they be grievous but most grievous to themselves. And there be some that keep their peace in themselves and study to reduce other men to peace. He that can well suffer shall find most peace; he is an overcomer of himself, lord of the world, the friend of Christ and the heir of heaven.

Thomas a Kempis

LOVE OF PEACE

A Christian, according to the teaching of the Lord, should be guided in his relations toward men only by the love of peace, and therefore there should be no authority having power to compel a Christian to act in a manner contrary to God's law, and contrary to his chief duty toward his fellow-men.

Leo Tolstoy

In a world of strife the attainment of peace is never easy. Our personal peace cost the Lord Jesus Christ his life.

POTPOURRI

And there are also many other things which Jesus did, the which, if they should be written every one, I suppose that even the world itself could not contain the books that should be written.

John 21:25

And ye shall know the truth, and the truth shall make you free.

John 8:32

WHAT A RELIGION!

If you could get religion like a Methodist, experience it like a Baptist, be positive of it like a Disciple, be proud of it like an Episcopalian, pay for it like a Presbyterian, propagate it like an Adventist, and enjoy it like a black man—that would be some religion!

The glory is not in never failing, but in rising every time you fall.

SUCCESS?

At the peak of his glory,
He stood alone.
His was the age old story:
His friends were stepping stones.

Jimmy Martin

RESOLVED—

I will make it a year of faith and prayer,
    A year of high endeavor;
I will crowd it with deeds both brave
    and fair,
I will act the hero ever.
I will travel God's path at God's own rate;
I will welcome both gain and loss;
Nor will I rebel when heaven's gate
    Looks tragically like a cross.

Life owes me nothing. One clear morn
Is boon enough for being born;
    And be it ninety years or ten,
    No need for me to question when.
While Life is mine, I'll find it good,
And greet each hour with gratitude.

An artist who was asked, "What is your best picture?" answered, "My next." Make tomorrow your best day!

THERE IS A MYSTERY IN HUMAN HEARTS

There is a mystery in human hearts,
And though we be encircled by a host
Of those who love us well and are beloved,
To every one of us, from time to time,
There comes a sense of utter loneliness.

THANK GOD FOR FOOLS!

Thank God for fools!—abused, of low estate.
    We rear our temples on the stones they laid;
Theirs is the prize our timid souls might not wait;
    Theirs—the triumph of the unafraid.

When duty calls me, Lord, let pleasure wait.
    Let me fulfill my calling. Let Thy will,
Not mine, be done. Oh, let me ever hear
    Thy calm, approving voice, Thy guidance still.

IMAGE BEARERS

Standing between two eternities, the eternal purpose in which we were predestinated to be conformed to the image of the first-born Son, and the eternal realization of that purpose, when we shall be like Him in His glory. We hear the voice from every side: O ye image-bearers of God! on the way to share the glory of God and of Christ, live a God-like, live a Christlike life!

Andrew Murray

We must be emptied of self before we can be filled with grace; we must be stripped of our rags before we can be clothed with righteousness; we must be unclothed that we may be clothed; wounded, that we may be healed; killed, that we may be made alive; buried in disgrace, that we may rise in holy glory. These words, "Sown in corruption, that we may be raised in incorruption."

Charles H. Spurgeon

REST

Are you very weary? Rest a little bit.
In some quiet corner, fold your hands and sit.
Do not let the trials that have grieved you all the day
Haunt this quiet corner; drive them all away!
Let your heart grow empty of every thought
    unkind
That peace may hover round you, and joy may
    fill your mind.
Count up all your blessings, I'm sure they are
    not few,
That the dear Lord daily just bestows on you.
Soon you'll feel so rested, glad you stopped a bit,
In this quiet corner, to fold your hands and sit.

THE TONGUE

The philosopher being asked which was the best
member of the body answered, "The tongue,"
and being asked again which was the worst, answered, "The tongue"—if good, the only trumpet
of God's glory; if bad, a very firebrand of hell.

FOR THOSE WHO FAIL

"All honor to him, who shall win the fight,"
The world has cried for a thousand years,
But to him who tries and who fails and dies,
I give great honor and glory and tears;
Give glory and honor and pitiful tears
To all who fail in their deeds sublime;
Their ghosts are many in the van of years,
They were born with time in advance of time.

HOLINESS IN CHRIST

I then saw that there was a holiness to be found
in the gospel, in which the inner conflict ceased,
and it was for me to find the key. The Lord led
me by many paths, but He never allowed me to
lose sight of this goal—this holiness that is possible in Christ. When we turn our eyes away from
ourselves and fix them in faith on Him—then He
gives us His righteousness, not only imputed
righteousness, but also the power to live righteous lives in Him.

Sister Eva of Friedenshort

HIS BIDDING

There is only joy as we seek His pleasure;
    There is only a rest as we seek His will—
And some day after life's fitful fever,
    I think we shall say in the home on high:
"If the hands that He touched but did His
    bidding
    How little it matters what else went by!"

NEW YEAR ASSURANCE

I said to the man who stood
    at the gate of the year,
"Give me a light that I may
    tread safely into the unknown."
And he replied,
"Go out into the darkness and put
    your hand
Into the hand of God;
That shall be to you better than light
    and safer than a known way."

M. Louise Haskins

Even the woodpecker owes his success to the fact
that he uses his head and keeps pecking away
until he finishes the job he starts.

CHRISTIAN APPAREL

They that put on the Lord Jesus are clothed with
a fourfold garment:
  1. With a garment of Christ's imputed
     righteousness.
  2. With a garment of sanctification.
  3. With a garment of protection.
  4. With a garment of glory.

YOU WILL NEVER BE SORRY

For telling the truth.
For living a pure life.
For your faith in Christ.
For confessing your sins.
For doing your best.
For thinking before acting.
For hearing before judging.

LEARN FROM THE CAMEL

The camel, at the close of day,
Kneels down upon the sandy plain
To have his burden lifted off
   And rest again.
My soul, thou too shouldst fall to thy knees
When daylight draweth to a close,
And let thy Master lift the load
   And give repose.
The camel kneels at morning's dawn
To have the guide replace his load—
Then rises up anew, to take
   The desert road . . .

Wheaton Anthology

GRAMMAR FOR LIVING

Live in the Active voice, not the Passive.
   Think more of what you make happen
   than about what happens to you.
Live in the Indicative Mood, rather than the Sub-
   junctive. Be concerned with things as they
   are, rather than as they might be.
Live in the Present Tense, facing the duty at
   hand without regret for the past or worry
   over the future.
Live in the First Person, criticizing yourself
   rather than finding fault with others.
Live in the Singular Number, caring more for the
   approval of your own conscience than for
   the applause of the crowd.

William Dewitt Hyde

THAT IS SUCCESS

Before God's footstool to confess
A poor soul knelt, and bowed his head;
"I failed," he cried. The Master said,
"Thou didst thy best—that is success!"

PROVE MY SOUL

   I go to prove my soul!
I see my way as birds their trackless way.
I shall arrive! what time, what circuit first,
I ask not . . .

Robert Browning

PLEA FOR A NEW YEAR

Just one thing, O Master, I ask today,
Now that the old year has passed away,
And a promising new year, through grace
   of Thine,
With all the dreams of youth is mine—
Just one thing I ask, and nothing more,
Not to linger behind, nor run before,
O Master! This is my only plea—
Take hold of my life and pilot me.

NOT A DISAPPOINTMENT

He is not a disappointment!
   Jesus is far more to me
Than in all my glowing daydreams
   I had fancied He could be;
And the more I get to know Him,
   So the more I find Him true,
And the more I long that others
   Should be led to know Him too.

Build thee more stately mansions, O my soul,
   As the swift seasons roll!
   Leave thy low-vaulted past!

Oliver Wendell Holmes

No truer word, save God's, was ever spoken,
Than that the largest heart is soonest broken.

Walter Savage Landor

CHRISTIANITY is a battle, not a dream.

Wendell Phillips

PATIENCE

Let us, then, be up and doing,
   With a heart for any fate;
Still achieving, still pursuing,
   Learn to labor and to wait.

Henry Wadsworth Longfellow

"The *Heavenly Father* knows best."

PRAISE

Praise ye the Lord. I will praise the Lord with my whole heart, in the assembly of the upright, and in the congregation.

Psalm 111:1

. . . the garment of praise for the spirit of heaviness; that they might be called trees of righteousness, the planting of the Lord, that he might be glorified.

Isaiah 61:3

Use yourself then by degrees thus to worship
Him, to beg His grace, to offer Him your heart
from time to time, in the midst of your business,
even every moment if you can. Do not always
scrupulously confine yourself to certain rules, or
particular forms of devotion; but act with a general confidence in God, with love and humility.

William Law

PRAISE FOR ANSWERED PRAYER

I asked for power
That I might have the praise of men
I asked for all things
That I might enjoy life
    I was given life
        That I might enjoy all things
I have nothing that I asked for
But everything that I hoped for
        My prayer is answered
        I am most blessed.

PRAISE FOR CREATION

God has joy in his creation. The abundance is
evidence of his overflowing joy. He looks on
everything that he has made and sees that it is
good. So should we. Creation calls us to join in
his praise.

Creation calls us to awe, reverence, wonder,
and worship. Everywhere we turn, we discover
some new evidence of God's power and wisdom.
We are called to gratitude that he has chosen to
make us, to give us life, to give us a chance to
share in the wonder of his world.

Joseph F. Green

GOD IS GLORIOUS

Praise the Lord, for he is glorious!
    Never shall his promise fail;
God hath made his saints victorious;
    Sin and death shall not prevail.
Praise the God of our salvation;
    Hosts on high, his power proclaim;
Heaven and earth, and all creation,
    Laud and magnify his name!

WE PRAISE THEE THIS DAY

We praise Thee this day,
O Lover Divine,
For the music and laughter and joy
Which are not of this world,
Which are surer and deeper, beyond all telling,
Than aught that this world can give.

We praise Thee this day
For the music and laughter and joy
Of Thine own eternal life;
For the heart overflowing with gladness
Because it has Thee;
For the zest and delight of the humblest life
        lived on earth
That is kindled aflame with the friendship of
        God.

F. S. Hoyland

PRAISE, THE HIGHEST FUNCTION

Praise is the highest function that any creature
can discharge. The rabbis have a beautiful bit of
teaching buried among their rubbish about
angels. They say that there are two kinds of
angels, the angels of service and the angels of
praise, of which two orders the latter is the
higher, and that no angel in it praises God twice;
but having lifted up his voice in the psalm of
heaven, then ceases to be. He has perfected his
being, he has reached the height of his greatness,
he has done what he was made for; let him fade
away. The garb of legend is mean enough, but
the thought it embodies is that ever true and
solemn one, without which life is naught:
"Man's chief end is to glorify God."

Alexander Maclaren

Come, my soul, thou must be waking;
    Now is breaking
    O'er the earth another day:
Come to him who made this splendour;
    See thou render
    All thy feeble strength can pay.

Friedrich von Camitz

PRAISE FOR THE MORNING
Morning has broken
  Like the first morning,
Blackbird has spoken
  Like the first bird.
    Praise for the singing!
    Praise for the morning!
    Praise for them, springing
      Fresh from the Word!

Mine is the sunlight!
Mine is the morning
Born of the one light
  Eden saw play!
    Praise with elation,
    Praise every morning,
    God's re-creation
      Of the new day!

Eleanor Farjeon

Stand up, and bless the Lord,
  Ye people of his choice:
Stand up, and bless the Lord your God
  With heart and soul and voice.

Though high above all praise,
  Above all blessing high,
Who would not fear his holy name,
  And praise and magnify?

James Montgomery

CROWN HIM!
Hark, those bursts of acclamation!
Hark, those loud triumphant chords;
Jesus takes the highest station:
O what joy the sight affords!
Crown Him, crown Him, crown Him, crown Him!
King of Kings, and Lord of lords.

Thomas Kelly

To God be the glory, great things He hath done;
So loved He the world that He gave us His Son.

Fanny J. Crosby

God is love: let heaven adore him;
  God is love: let earth rejoice;
Let creation sing before him,
  And exalt him with one voice.
He who laid the earth's foundation,
  He who spread the heavens above,
He who breathes through all creation,
  He is love, eternal love.

Timothy Rees

God has certainly not been selfish to any man, sinner or Christian, and to deny him a single moment of time is dangerously selfish. To deny him heart and soul is eternally punishable. And yet we cannot give any of these without the other.

How long does it take to praise God? A minute-- two minutes? To ask God for forgiveness of our wrongdoings? Or, to thank him for all He has given you?

So why deny God his time? Think of him at lunch, while you work, at home--anywhere and everywhere you go. You do not have to be at a place of regular worship to praise God and meditate upon him. Any place becomes a chapel when God is truly there and this includes your heart and soul.

Hubert Shipman

PRAISE
Praise him for his grace and favour
To our fathers in distress;
Praise him still the same for ever,
Slow to chide and swift to bless.
Praise him! Praise him! Praise him! Praise him!
Glorious in his faithfulness.

Fatherlike, he tends and spares us;
Well our feeble frame he knows;
In his hands he gently bears us,
Rescues us from all our foes.
Praise him! Praise him! Praise him! Praise him!
Widely as his mercy flows.

H. F. Lyte

THE COURT OF PRAYER

PRAISE has to do with adulations directed to God for who He is rather than what He has done. This is the court of prayer. I am convinced that this is how we get into praying in the Spirit. Praise is a facet of prayer about which the average Christian knows so very little. Yet it is vital that we learn to praise, for the vitality of every kind of prayer rests on praise. The Psalmist has given me inestimable help in learning to praise. There are dozens of songs in our hymn books which are made to be sung as praise to Jesus, the Father, and the Holy Spirit.

Jack R. Taylor

O Lord Jesus, I ask no other reward, no other happiness, except that of Thy pure words, which are inspired by the Holy Spirit, without any erroneous or fallacious theories, so that I may perceive where Thou dwellest, and by earnest searching and diligence be introduced to that abode.

John Scotus

THE SHRINE

I stumbled on it, in a quiet wood,
A simple rugged boulder, sculptured by
Rough winds and beating rain; in strength it
    stood
Beneath the arched blue dome of autumn sky.
Its altar cloth was just a drift of leaves,
Dry, yet ablaze with red, with burning gold,
The kind a brooding, aging season weaves,
The pattern ripped and blown apart and old.
The air was filled with throbbing, soundless
    hymns,
With psalms unchanted, with the voice of God
In answer. Light thinned as a candle dims
At evening when a small head starts to nod.
Love hovered, shining, there; what could I say?
What could I do but bow my head and pray?

Geraldine Ross

LOUD PRAISES

Eternal Father, who didst all create,
    In whom we live, and to whose bosom move,
    To all men be thy name known, which is Love,
Till its loud praises sound at heaven's high gate.

R. Bridges

HOW RICH THY GRACE!

Jesus, my Lord, how rich thy grace,
    How fair thy bounties shine!
What can my poverty bestow,
    When all the worlds are thine?

Philip Doddridge

PRAISE OF JESUS

There was One who loved all mankind, and who loved them more than Himself, and who gave Himself to die that they might live; there was One who went into the gates of death, that the gates of death might never hold us in; there was One who lay in the grave, with its dampness, its coldness, its chill, and its horror, and taught humanity how it might ascend above the grave; there was One who, though He walked on earth, had His conversation in heaven, who took away the curtain that hid immortality from view, and presented to us the Father God in all His glory and in all His love.

Matthew Simpson

LONGING FOR GOD

As pants the hart for cooling streams
    When heated in the chase,
So longs my soul, O God, for thee,
    And thy refreshing grace.

N. Tate and N. Brady

Praise to God, immortal praise,
For the love that crowns our days;
Bounteous source of ev'ry joy,
Let thy praise our tongues employ. . .

Anna L. Barbauld

PRAYER

If thou shouldst never see my face again,
Pray for my soul. More things are wrought by
  prayer
Than this world dreams of. Wherefore, let thy
  voice
Rise like a fountain for me night and day.
For what are men better than sheep or goats
That nourish a blind life within the brain,
If, knowing God, they lift not hands of prayer
Both for themselves and those who call them
  friend?

Alfred Lord Tennyson

Pray and stay are two blessed monosyllables.

John Donne

If you are too busy to pray, you are TOO BUSY
(see Luke 18:1)!

"Prayer changes things." What does it change?
God? Man? God does not change. Prayer may
so markedly change a man and his life-style that
those around him feel God may have changed.

"BEGGING"

Sir Walter Raleigh one day asking a favor from
Queen Elizabeth, the latter said to him, "Raleigh,
when will you leave off begging!" To which he
answered, "When your Majesty leaves off giving."
Ask great things of God. Expect great things
from God. Let His past goodness make us
"instant in prayer."

The *Christian Endeavor World* tells of a little girl
who came to her mother in tears, asking,
"Mamma, how can I untrouble trouble?" Jesus
gives the answer to this question. He denatures
trouble, enables his followers to find pleasure in
being persecuted, and even takes away the sting
of death. "Trouble may drive you to prayer, but
prayer will drive away trouble."

LINCOLN'S PRAYER TESTIMONY

Abraham Lincoln, during the Civil War, said: "I
have been driven many times to my knees by the
overwhelming conviction that I had nowhere else
to go. My own wisdom and that of all about me
seemed insufficient for the day."

POWER TO PRAY

Grant me comfort, or deny;
    Visit, or from me depart;
Only let Thy Spirit cry,
    "Abba, Father," in my heart!
"Abba, Father," would I say,
    Only give me power to pray.

HE HEARS

I may not always understand
    Just why he sends to me
Some bitter grief, some heavy loss,
    But, though I cannot see,
I kneel, and whisper through my tears
    A prayer for help, and know He hears.

A GOOD QUESTION

One day a little girl, about five years old, heard a
preacher praying most lustily, till the roof rang
with the strength of his supplication. Turning to
her mother, and beckoning the maternal ear
down to a speaking-place, she whispered:
"Mother, don't you think that if he lived nearer
to God he wouldn't have to talk so loud?"

PREJUDICED PRAYER

Some go to prayer, not to quietly ascertain the
will of God, but to ask Him to do that to which
they have already fully set their minds.

We can read, or speak; we can sow, or sing,
    And serve in the busiest way;
But it seems so often the hardest thing
    Is to find a fit time to pray.

PRESENCE OF GOD
Begin all prayer, whether mental or vocal, by an act of the Presence of God. If you observe this rule strictly, you will soon see how useful it is.
Francis de Sales

No man has backslid from the life and power of Christianity who continues instant and fervent . . . in private prayer.
Adam Clark

Never think that God's delays are God's denials; hold on, hold fast, hold out; patience is genius.
Buffon

A LIVING ANSWER
You can be—yes—you—
An answer to prayer.
There is work to be done;
A field is to be won;
And millions are praying—
Hands lifted, hearts saying:
O Lord, yet how long
Until right conquer wrong?
You can answer that prayer—
You—answer that prayer.

Our truest prayers are but the echo of God's promises. God's best answers are the echo of our prayers. As in two mirrors set opposite to each other, the same image is repeated over and over again, the reflection of a reflection, so here, within the prayer, gleams an earlier promise, within the answer is mirrored the prayer.
Alexander Maclaren

If man is man and God is God, to live without prayer is not merely an awful thing: it is an infinitely foolish thing.
Phillips Brooks

Prayer is the nearest approach to God, and the highest enjoyment of Him, that we are capable of in this life.

It is the noblest exercise of the soul, the most exalted use of our best faculties, and the highest imitation of the blessed inhabitants of Heaven.
William Law

THE NEED OF PRAYER
I believe it is impossible to live well without prayer, and that prayer is the necessary condition of a good, peaceful, and happy life. The Gospels indicate how one should pray, and what prayer should consist of.
Leo Tolstoy

DON'T "SAY" PRAYERS
To *say* my prayers is not to pray
Unless I *mean* the words I say;
Unless I *think* to *whom* I speak,
And with my heart His blessing seek.
Then let me, when I come to pray,
Not only heed the words I say,
But let me seek with earnest care
To have my thoughts go with my prayer.

CONVERSATION WITH GOD
There is not in the world a kind of life more sweet and delightful, than that of a continual conversation with God: those only can comprehend it who practice and experience it: yet I do not advise you to do it from that motive; it is not pleasure which we ought to seek in this exercise; but let us do it from a principle of love, and because God would have us.
Brother Lawrence

In prayer the lips ne'er act the winning part
Without the sweet concurrence of the heart.
Robert Herrick

Do not pray for easy lives; pray to be strong men.
Do not pray for tasks equal to your powers; pray
for power equal to your tasks.
Phillips Brooks

Do not travel on in darkness,
    When you may walk in sunshine fair,
You can find the light, and the pathway bright,
    By the aid of a whispered prayer.

NEW YEAR'S PRAYER
At the gateway of the year now let us kneel to
pray—asking God to bless us ere we go upon our
way. . . . We dare not take one step along the
road that lies ahead—without a prayer for guidance on the path that we must tread.

Let us pray for strength, endurance, courage,
fortitude—so that we may venture out with hope
and faith renewed . . . mighty weapons, final
victory.

Patience Strong

SIX TIMES
Jesus repeated to his disciples before leaving
them this possibility of their coming to him in
prayer. "Whatsoever ye ask in my name, that
will I do." Recently a great Christian wrote
back from the Orient, "I am thousands of miles
removed from you in physical distance, but only
a second away in prayer." At times we feel that
heaven is far from us, but in the inner closet, we
have immediate contact with heaven. *Read
Nehemiah 1:3-11.*

Rosalee Mills Appleby

Prayer is the soul's sincere desire,
    Uttered or unexpressed;
The motion of a hidden fire,
    That trembles in the breast.
James Montgomery

And fools who came to scoff, remained to pray.
Oliver Goldsmith

Today
Lord, give me strength, I pray,
To live my life this day!
    To live it right,
    With all my might,
    Without mistake,
    And for Thy sake.
When fear besets my way,
Let me the question lay
    Before Thy throne,
    Where all is known,
    Where what is best
    Will meet Thy test.
Should my day be drear,
Keep Thou me near
    To hear Thy voice,
    And thus rejoice
    That Thou art mine,
    And I am Thine.

DEVOTIONAL LIFE
Select a topic for a year's Bible study, as
"Prayer." Any Christian who wishes to deepen
his devotional life may do so if he will pay the
price in time, in willingness and in earnestness.
We have his promise. If we would know God,
we must be still, even amid life's rush and noise.
R. A. Torrey

PLACE OF PRAYER
I journeyed north, south, east, and west,
An endless trail, a hopeless quest;
At last, at last, I came to where
Was a little, walled-in place of prayer.

Jacob, though a man, a single man, a travelling
man, a tired man, yea, though a worm, that is
easily crushed and trodden under foot, and no
man (Is. 41:14), yet in private prayer he is so
potent, that he overcomes the Omnipotent God.
Thomas Brooks

Prayer strums the heartstrings of God.

HE PRAYETH BEST

He prayeth well who loveth well
Both man and bird and beast.
He prayeth best who loveth best
All things both great and small;
For the dear God who loveth us,
He made and loveth all.

S. T. Coleridge

HYPOCRITICAL PRAYER

. . . unless the common course of our lives be according to the common spirit of our prayers, our prayers are so far from being a real or sufficient degree of devotion, that they become an empty lip-labour, or, what is worse, a notorious hypocrisy.

William Law

A CHILD'S PLEA

Now I lay me down to sleep
I pray the Lord my soul to keep;
If I should die before I wake,
I pray the Lord my soul to take.

New England Primer

They never sought in vain that sought the Lord aright!

Robert Burns

Prayer is so simple;
It is like quietly opening a door
And slipping into the very presence of God,
There in the stillness
To listen to His voice;
Perhaps to petition,
Or only to listen;
It matters not.
Just to be there
In his presence
Is prayer.

The man who bows the lowest in the presence of God stands the straightest in the presence of sin.

ELIZABETHAN PRAYER FOR ENEMIES

Most merciful and loving Father, we beseech Thee most humbly, even with all our hearts, to pour out upon our enemies with bountiful hands whatsoever things Thou knowest may do them good.

BOLDLY PRAY

This word *boldly* signifies liberty without restraint. You may be free, for you are welcome. You may use freedom of speech. The word is so used in Acts 2:29 and 4:13. You have liberty to speak your minds freely, to speak all your heart, your ails, and wants, and fears, and grievances. As others may not fetter you in speaking to God by prescribing what words you should use; so you need not restrain yourselves, but freely speak all that your condition requires.

David Clarkson

PRAYER FOR ADVERSARIES

Almighty God, have mercy on N and N and on all that bear me evil will, and would me harm, and their faults and mine together, by such easy, tender, merciful means as Thine infinite wisdom best can divine, vouchsafe to amend and redress, and make us saved souls in heaven together where we may ever live and love together with thee and thy blessed saints, O glorious Trinity, for the bitter passion of our sweet Saviour Christ, Amen.

Sir Thomas More

Praise His blessed Name forever!
    There is nought that can compare
To the glories of a contact
    With the Prince of Peace—through prayer!

THE LAST PRAYER

When the last fire is out and the last guest departed,
    Grant the last prayer that I shall pray, Be good
    to me, O Lord!

John Masefield

Who rises from Prayer a better man, his prayer is answered.

George Meredith

"THE CHURCH FURNACE"

Charles Haddon Spurgeon was one day showing some visitors through the Tabernacle. After taking them to the main part of the building he said, "Come and I'll show you the heating apparatus." Not caring to see the apparatus they would have declined, but out of courtesy they consented. Imagine their surprise when he took them to a room where four hundred were gathered in a prayer meeting. His figure of speech was well chosen. The church with warmth of spirit must have the warmth-producing prayer meeting.

LOVING–PRAYING

There is nothing that makes us love a man so much as praying for him; and when you can once do this sincerely for any man, you have fitted your soul for the performance of everything that is kind and civil towards him.

William Law

THAT DEFINITE OBJECT

A man must have some definite object before his mind. He cannot pray effectually for a variety of objects at once. The mind of man is so constituted that it cannot fasten its desires intensely upon many things at the same time. All the instances of effectual prayer recorded in the Bible were of this kind. Wherever you see that the blessing sought for in prayer was attained, you will find that the prayer which was offered was prayer for that definite object.

Charles G. Finney

If you do take time for prayer you will have a real, living God, and if you have a living God you will have a radiant life.

R. A. Torrey

We are never so high as when we are on our knees!

WANT TO BE RADIANT?

Would you like to be a radiant Christian? You may be! Spend time in prayer. You cannot be a radiant Christian in any other way. Why is it that prayer in the name of Christ makes one radiantly happy? It is because prayer makes God real. *The gladdest thing upon earth is to have a real God!* You cannot have vital faith in God if you give all your time to the world and to secular affairs, to reading the newspapers and to reading literature, no matter how good it is.

Mrs. Charles E. Cowman

AN EFFECTIVE PRAYER

O Saviour, pour upon me thy Spirit of meekness
    and love,
Annihilate the Selfhood in me, be thou all my
    life,
Guide thou my hand which trembles exceedingly
    upon the rock of ages.

William Blake

GATES OF HEAVEN

The Persian kings took state upon them, and enacted that none should come near to them uncalled, on pain of death. But oh! sirs, the gates of heaven are always open; you have liberty night and day of presenting your petition, in the name of Christ, to the King of the whole earth.

Ralph Erskine

Our prayers are our bills of exchange, and they are allowed in heaven when they come from pious and humble hearts; but if we be broken in our religion, and bankrupt of grace, God will protest our bills; He will not be won with our prayers.

Thomas Adams

PROVIDENCE

The eternal God is thy refuge, and underneath are the everlasting
arms . . .

Deuteronomy 33:27

He shall cover thee with his feathers, and under his wings shalt thou
trust: his truth shall be thy shield and buckler.

Psalm 91:4

A Field of Diamonds

HE KEEPS HIS PROMISE
"When once His word is past,
  When He hath said, 'I will,'
The thing shall come at last;
  God keeps His promise still."

ALL EVERGREENS
The Lord's trees are all evergreens. No winter's cold can destroy their verdure; and yet, unlike evergreens in our country, they are all fruit-bearers.

Charles Haddon Spurgeon

HE GUIDES MY FEET
I may not always know the way
  Wherein God leads my feet;
But This I know, that 'round my path
  His love and wisdom meet,
And so I rest content to know
  He guides my feet where'er I go.

The eternal God, who hath, in and by his eternal powerful arm, preserved me through all my troubles, trials, temptations, and afflictions, persecutions, reproaches, and imprisonments, and carried me over them all, hath sanctified all these things to me, so that I can say, all things work together for good to them that love God, and are beloved of him.

George Fox

WAY OF HIS WILL
In the way of His will there is peace,
There doubtings and restlessness cease.

Storm and tempest all the way,
Dark the night, and stern the day,
Wild the winds, and broken sail,
Still my Pilot must prevail.
Through the roaring of the swell
I can hear the harbor bell.

THE ALMIGHTY WILL
The child, the seed, the grain of corn,
  The acorn on the hill,
Each for some separate end is born
  In season fit, and still
Each must in strength arise to work the Almighty Will.

Robert Louis Stevenson

GOD CARES
Give free and bold play to those instincts of the heart which believe that the Creator must care for the creatures He has made, and that the only real effective care for them must be that which takes each of them into His love, and knowing it separately surrounds it with His separate sympathy. There is not one life which the Life-giver ever loses out of His sight; not one which sins so that He casts it away; not one which is not so near to Him that whatever touches it touches Him with sorrow or with joy.

Phillips Brooks

PROVIDENCE
My belief in a special Providence grows yearly stronger, unsubduable, impregnable.

Thomas Carlyle

HE KEEPS THE CITY
  And when the hours of rest
Come, like a clam upon the mid-sea brine,
  Hushing its billowy breast—
The quiet of that moment, too, is thine;
  It breathes of Him who keeps
The vast and helpless city while it sleeps.

William Cullen Bryant

GOD SENDS THE WEATHER
It hain't no use to grumble and complane;
  It's jest as cheap and easy to rejoice.
When God sorts out the weather and sends rain,
  W'y, rain's my choice.

James Whitcomb Riley

But in the day of conflict, fear, and grief,
   When the strong hand of God, put forth in
      might,
Plows up the subsoil of the stagnant heart,
   And brings the imprisoned truth-seed to the
      light.
                  . . .
Wrung from the troubled spirit in hard hours
   Of weakness, solitude, perchance of pain,
Truth springs, like harvest, from the well-plowed
      field,
   And the soul feels it has not wept in vain.
                              Horatius Bonar

All mankind is of one Author, and is one volume;
when one Man dies, one chapter is not torn out
of the book, but translated into a better language; and every Chapter must be so translated;
God employs several translators; some pieces are
translated by age, some by sickness, some by
war, some by justice; but God's hand is in every
translation; and His hand shall bind up all our
scattered leaves again, for that Library where
every book shall lie open to one another.
                              John Donne

UNSEEN GROUND
Pile your riches fathoms deep;
   Rob the mountains of their gold.
All earthly riches are too cheap
   To buy the kingdom of the soul.
Build your stately mansions 'round
   Upon the flimsy crumbling sod . . .
I'll build my home on unseen ground,
   Where dwells my King, almighty God.
                              M. F. Graham

He that doth the ravens feed
Yea, providentially caters for the sparrow,
Be comfort to my age!
                     William Shakespeare

He's got the whole world in His hands.

HAVE BEEN WITH JESUS
Oh, may it be
That some who scorn, today
Are speaking thus of you—and me:
Some wonder has been wrought—
Where once she was so cold,
She now is kind!
            . . .
And thankfully we say—
Though none but God may hear:
"Rejoice! Rejoice!
For He is guiding me—
I, too,
Have been with Jesus."

A MYSTERIOUS WAY
God moves in a mysterious way
   His wonders to perform;
He plants his footsteps in the sea
   And rides upon the storm.
                        William Cowper

Yet, in the maddening maze of things,
   And tossed by storm and flood,
To one fixed trust my spirit clings;
   I know that God is good.
                     John Greenleaf Whittier

There's a divinity that shapes our ends,
Rough-hew them how we will.
                           Shakespeare

In the simple astronomy of early times, there
was no failure, nor decay, nor change, in the
calm heavens. The planets, year by year, returned punctually to their places; and, unhasting
and unresting, rolled upon their way. Weakness
and weariness had no place there; and the power
by which the most ancient heavens were upheld
and maintained was God's unwearied might.
                           Alexander Maclaren

PILOT ME
Jesus, Saviour, pilot me,
   Over life's tempestuous sea;
Unknown waves before me roll,
   Hiding rocks and treach'rous shoal;
Chart and compass came from Thee;
   Jesus, Saviour, pilot me.

Edward Hopper

Years ago Bishop Bashford, in one of his tours in China, was one night compelled to sleep out-doors, under the trees, the hotel keeper warning him about marauders. Being watchful and wake-ful awhile, he thought of these words of the Psalmist, and then said to the Lord, "There is no use both of us being awake," so he slept the sleep of the just. In the morning he saw a watcher standing guard under a tree; the unsaved man was helping God guard his own.

OUR SHELTER
O God, our help in ages past,
   Our hope for years to come,
Our shelter from the stormy blast,
   And our eternal home.

Isaac Watts

IN HIS HAND
Our times are in his hand
Who saith, "A whole I planned."

Robert Browning

THE MASTER MUSICIAN
So I think, perchance, the Master
   At the close of life's weary day,
Will take from our trembling fingers
   The tune we cannot play.
He will hear through the jarring discord
   The strain, although half expressed,
He will blend it in perfect music
   And add it to all the rest.

TAUGHT BY THE LEAVES
Did the leaves say nothing to you as they mur-mured when you came hither today? They were not created this spring, but months ago, and the summer just begun will fashion others for another year. At the bottom of every leaf-stem is a cradle, and in it is an infant germ; and the winds will rock it, and the birds will sing to it all summer long; and the next season it will unfold. So God is working for you, and carrying forward to the perfect development all the processes of your lives.

Henry Ward Beecher

HIS LOVE AND CARE
And so beside the Silent Sea
   I wait the muffled oar;
   On ocean or on shore.
No harm from him can come to me

      . . .

I know not where his islands lift
   Their fronded palms in air;
I only know I cannot drift
   Beyond his love and care.

LEAVING GOD TO THINK FOR HIM
That little bird has chosen his shelter; above it are the stars and the deep heaven of worlds; yet he is rocking himself to sleep without caring for to-morrow's lodging, calming clinging to his little twig, and leaving God to think for him.

Martin Luther

Not only around our infancy
Doth heaven with all its splendors lie;
Daily, with souls that cringe and plot,
We Sinais climb and know it not.

James Russell Lowell

The best that man can invent or discover is only a pale reminder of what God has done through the ages.

Alexander Maclaren

SALVATION

Neither is there salvation in any other: for there is none other name under heaven given among men, whereby we must be saved.

Acts 4:12

For the Son of man is come to seek and to save that which was lost.

Luke 19:10

STRANGELY WARMED

"In the evening I went very unwillingly to a society in Aldersgate Street, where one was reading Luther's preface to the Epistle to the Romans. About a quarter before nine, while he was describing the change which God works in the heart through faith in Christ, I felt my heart strangely warmed. I felt I did trust in Christ, Christ alone, for salvation; and an assurance was given me, that He had taken away *my* sins, *even mine,* and saved *me* from the law of sin and death."

John Wesley

Man cannot be saved by perfect obedience, for he cannot render it; he cannot be saved by imperfect obedience, for God will not accept it.

In creation God shows us His hand, but in redemption God gives us His heart.

Adolphe Monod

CONVERSION

Conversion is a work of *argument,* for the judgment is gained by the truth. It is a work of *conviction,* for the awakened are pricked in their hearts. It is a work of *enquiry,* for they ask, "What must we do to be saved?" And, lastly, it is a work of *comfort,* for its subjects have received remission of sins, and the gift of the Holy Ghost.

Joseph Sutcliffe

What is a little sparkle of fire, if it fall into the main sea? The same are the sins of a penitent person when dealt with by the mercy of God.

Thomas Horton

And I believe that there is no other way of salvation than through the merits of his atonement.

Daniel Webster

A SOLDIER'S CONVERSION

Moody told of having asked a soldier for the process of his conversion. The soldier's graphic answer was: "Halt!" "Attention!" "Right-about face!" "March!"

"HE JUST GIVE HIMSELF"

The story is told of an Indian chief who sought the peace and joy of salvation. He had heard the missionary tell about Jesus. So he prayed, confessed his sins, and made sacrifices, but no peace came. Then he cried: "Poor old Indian chief done give his bows and arrows to King Jesus; done give his blanket and tomahawk to King Jesus; done give his horse and gun to King Jesus; poor old Indian got nothing more to give—he just give himself to King Jesus." It was then that he found pardon and the peace that passeth understanding.

There is not a single half-promise, not a single promise of partial deliverance from sin in the Bible. "The blood of Jesus Christ his Son cleanseth us from *all* sin." (1 John 1:7.)

Mrs. Charles E. Cowman

RED ON RED TURNS WHITE

Two men were watching a troop of British soldiers in red uniforms. "Look at those coats through this glass," one said to his companion. "What do you see?" The other answered, "White." White those coats seemed indeed, for red seen through red turns white.

Our sins are scarlet in the sight of God. The fact grieves us, for it can neither be denied nor altered. But God looks at the sins of the believer through a color as red as themselves—the blood of Christ. Scarlet sin becomes white as wool, white as snow. "There is therefore now no condemnation to them which are in Christ Jesus."

Jesus is a specialist in salvation.

Salvation is a sudden experience. Negatively the Bible calls it repentance; positively, faith. But there is no genuine repentance without saving faith; and there is no saving faith without genuine repentance.

A. C. Dixon

Into my heart. Into my heart.
Come into my heart, Lord Jesus;
Come in today, come in to stay;
Come into my heart, Lord Jesus.

Harry D. Clarke

Amazing grace! how sweet the sound,
    That saved a wretch like me!
I once was lost, but now am found,
    Was blind, but now I see.

John Newton

UNITED IN LOVE
The Spirit came—by faith I see the mystic union—
The soul of man united to his God in love!
Redeemed, he stands before the Throne in holy
    adoration,
Redeemed on earth, but home at last in heaven
    above.

ATONING LOVE
What is the atonement? That Christ gave God the right to be compassionate? That he came down to this world, and made a bargain, and agreed that he would suffer so much if God afterwards would exercise compassion and leniency towards men? Away with your shop logic! Away with your commerical theories! Go down among the moles and bats, and grope with such detestable notions of truth as that by agreement Christ came among men to suffer and give God a chance to be gracious! Over all these heresies of hell I lift up the glorious words, "God so loved the world that he gave his Son." Love before Christ came was the bow which sent that silver arrow into the world.

Henry Ward Beecher

We all need not only to recognize the utter insufficiency and worthlessness of our own righteousness, which is the lesson of the opening chapters of the epistle to the Romans, but also the utter insufficiency and worthlessness in the things of God, of our own wisdom, which is the lesson of the first epistle to the Corinthians, especially the first to the third chapters. (see *e.g.* 1 Cor. 1:19-21,26,27.)

R. A. Torrey

Salvation is a GIFT to be RECEIVED: not a GOAL to be ACHIEVED!

SAVED BY GRACE
Naught have I gotten but what I received;
Grace hath bestowed it since I have believed;
Boasting excluded, pride I abase;
I'm only a sinner saved by grace!

J. M. Gray

A NEW creature! The *new* birth! 'Except a man be born again'—what does it mean? I cannot explain the mystery of birth, but what does it matter? Here is *the child*. I cannot explain the truth that something darting like a flash of lightning into the soul of that Oxford student transformed his whole life, but, explained or unexplained, here is *George Whitefield!*

Dr. Boreham

Salvation is a spiritual life insurance policy:—
Jesus has paid all the "premiums"—you receive all the "benefits."

EARTHQUAKE OR QUIET
It matters not whether you are trembling in an earthquake of excitement, or in the quiet of a chariot ride; but what does matter is that you turn from sin to Jesus Christ as your Saviour.

A. C. Dixon

. . . how shall we obtain salvation, but from Thy hand, remaking what is made?

Augustine

No debt need be carried forward to another page of the book of our lives, for Christ has given Himself for us, and He speaks to us all—"Thy sins be forgiven thee."

Alexander Maclaren

COME!
When Christ calls He also draws. 'Come!' says the sea to the river. 'Come!' says the magnet to the steel. 'Come!' says the spring to the sleeping life of the field and forest.

C. Stanford

ONLY ONE REMEDY
Man calls sin a weakness: God calls it willfulness. There is only one remedy for sin—the precious blood of Christ, which was shed for the remission of sins on Calvary's Cross.

WAY OF SALVATION
I urge thee to be saved. This is the wish of Christ; in one word, He freely grants thee life. And who is He? Understand briefly: the Word of truth; the Word of incorruption; He who regenerates man by bringing him back to the truth; the goal of salvation; He who banishes corruption and expels death; He who has built His temple in men, that in men He may set up the shrine of God.

Clement of Alexandria

Freedom from sin is the greatest of all liberties.

Life with Christ is an ENDLESS HOPE; without Him it is a HOPELESS END!

From the cross the Lord Jesus calls on you to return. Hasten home!

The door of heaven shuts from below, not from above. "Your iniquities have separated," saith the Lord.

Williams of Wern

SAVED BY GRACE
From this hell upon earth there is no escape, save through the grace of the Saviour Christ, our God and Lord. The very name Jesus shows this, for it means Saviour; and He saves us especially from passing out of this life into a more wretched and eternal state which is rather a death than a life.

Augustine

HOPE THROUGH THE BLOOD
What hope then is there for any of us; for we have "all sinned and come short of the glory of God?" There is hope for us because God himself has provided a propitiation, through faith, by his blood." The wrath of God at sin strikes on Him instead of striking on us.

R. A. Torrey

Whenever we are hearing a new teacher and a new message, let us look for the sign of blood. Jesus says of Himself that He had come "to give his life a ransom for many." Beware of any prophet who does not say as much for Christ!

WHAT JESUS DOES
He cures the mind of its blindness, the heart of its hardness, the nature of its perseverance, the will of its backwardness, the memory of its slipperiness, the conscience of its benumbness, and the affections of their disorder, all according to His gracious promises (Ezek. 36:26-27).

John Willison

SERVICE

Knowing that of the Lord ye shall receive the reward of the inheritance; for ye serve the Lord Christ.

Colossians 3:24

For they themselves shew of us what manner of entering in we had unto you, and how ye turned to God from idols to serve the living and true God.

1 Thessalonians 1:9

A Field of Diamonds

The greatest hour in any person's life is when he comes face to face with Jesus Christ and hears the Master's call to the fellowship and service of His Kingdom.

"YE DO IT UNTO ME"

And may we not forget as we go forth again upon the highways of life, where many are left destitute and robbed and bruised and broken, where we see ten thousand tragedies of sin, that the least expensive side is the costliest often, and that we represent him poorest who gave himself for men when we pass by on the other side, keeping our "wine and oil and money" for ourselves, riding our "lone saddle alone." May we hear Jesus saying to us across the centuries, "Inasmuch as ye do it unto one of the least of these my brethren, ye do it unto me."

R. G. Lee

RISE UP AND FOLLOW THEE

In simple trust like theirs who heard
   Beside the Syrian sea
The gracious calling of the Lord,
Let us, like them, without a word
   Rise up and follow Thee.

John Greenleaf Whittier

TEACH ME . . .

Teach me to do Thy will, Thy pattern show me;
   Reveal Thy purpose for my life each day.
Then for Thy service with fresh oil anoint me,
   And with Thy presence hallow all my way.

Freda Hanbury Allen

NO WOUND? NO SCAR?

   No wound? No scar?
Yet, as the Master shall the servant be,
And pierced are the feet that follow Me;
   But thine are whole; can he have followed far
   Who hath no wound nor scar?

NOT STOREHOUSES

We are not storehouses, but channels
   We are not cisterns, but springs,
Passing our benefits onward,
   Fitting our blessings with wings;
Letting the water flow onward
   To spread o'er the desert forlorn;
Sharing our bread with our brothers,
   Our comfort with those who mourn.

This verse is on an old slab in the cathedral of Lubec, Germany:
Thus speaketh Christ our Lord to us:
"Ye call me Master, and obey me not;
Ye call me Light, and see me not;
Ye call me Way, and walk me not;
Ye call me Life, and desire me not;
Ye call me Wise, and follow me not;
Ye call me Fair, and love me not;
Ye call me Rich, and ask me not;
Ye call me Eternal, and seek me not;
Ye call me Gracious, and trust me not;
Ye call me Noble, and serve me not;
Ye call me Mighty, and honor me not;
Ye call me Just, and fear me not;
If I condemn you, blame me not."

May I not covet the world's greatness if it cost me the crown of life!

John Henry Jowett

GIVING—NOT GETTING

It is in loving, not in being loved
   The heart finds its quest;
It is in giving, not in getting
   Our lives are blest.

GO, LABOR ON

Go, labor on; spend and be spent
   Thy joy to do the Father's will;
It is the way the Master went;
   Shall not the servant tread it still?

Horatius Bonar

GOD'S COUNTING ON YOU
No matter what others are doing, my friend,
Or what they are leaving undone,
God's counting on you to keep on with the job
'Til the very last battle is won.
He's counting on you to be faithful;
He's counting on you to be true.
Yes, others may work, or others may shirk,
But, remember—God's counting on You!

UP AND BE DOING!
Up and be doing! The time is brief,
And life is frail as the autumn leaf.
The day is bright and the sun is high;
Erelong it will fade from the glowing sky;
And the harvest is ripe and the fields are wide;
And thou, at thine ease, mayest not abide.
The reapers are few and far between,
And death is abroad with his sickle keen.
Go forth and labor! A crown awaits.

WHY ME?
Why am I put here?
    What reason untold?
Some kind of meaning
    My being must hold.
God holds the answer
    Under His lock and key.
If He's choosing His kingdom
    Why did He choose me?
When He calls me, I shun Him,
    Ignore Him, and then
The next time He wants me
    He calls me again.
I don't say, "I know Him"
    Each chance that I get.
Then He gently reminds me of
    The first time we met.
Oh, Lord, now forgive me,
    Take first place in my heart.
Give me strength to witness
    and know that "Thou art."

                    Linda Wingfield

"INASMUCH"
With trembling hand the lonely beggar knocks. Cautiously the door cracks narrowly ajar and fear peers out on ragged want. At once the door slams shut, and as the beggar turns to go, the winds of cold indifference buffet him anew. For one brief pause he looks upon the passing throng, then quietly he moves to lose himself therein. Where does he go? Beggars? The world is filled with those who starve-hungering, ever hungering for love. Hear them as they cry:
    "Love me with your heart, not with your
    shallow self alone."
    "Love me for what I am-my frailties-my
    differences-not by the measure of society."
    "Love me for the sake of love-enough to help
    me feel a little more secure in my world of
    fear-filled adversity."
Time is autumn-old, and ere its chill becomes the frost and snow of winter's dress, compassion fires must burn with brighter glow. Jesus said: "Inasmuch as ye did it unto the least of these, my brethren, ye have done it unto me."
(Matthew 25:40)
Even now a beggar knocks.

                    Louise Barker Barnhill

HUMAN SERVICE
I settled with myself that I would consider myself justified in living till I was thirty for science and art, in order to devote myself from that time forward to the direct service of humanity . . . What would be the character of the activities thus planned for the future was not yet clear to me. I left it to circumstances to guide me. One thing only was certain, that it must be directly human service, however inconspicuous the sphere of it.

                    Albert Schweitzer

Service is the rent we pay for the space we occupy.

Christ sends none away empty but those who are full of themselves.

Charles Haddon Spurgeon

FREEDOM IN SERVICE

The Apostle (Paul) has taught me something even beyond freedom itself, namely that to serve is real freedom. Though I be free from all, he says, yet have I made myself servant unto all, that I might gain the more. What is that which surpasses liberty but to have the Spirit of grace, to have charity? Liberty renders us free to men, but charity renders us beloved by God.

Ambrose

It is better to bring a cheap bouquet
To a living friend this very day,
Than a bushel of roses, white and red
To lay on his casket when he's dead

Since from His bounty I receive
  Such proofs of love divine,
Had I a thousand hearts to give,
  Lord, they should all be Thine.

Thomas Hastings

I GO

Is it enough?
I go!
His hand points to the farthest shore
Where human hands outstretched are begging for
The Christ who conquered—lo,
It is enough,
I go!

Bring to God your gift, my brother,
He'll not need to call another,
  You will do;
He will add His blessing to it,
And the two of you will do it,
  God and you.

R. E. Neighbour

NO ENGROSSING TASK?

I thought because I could not teach or preach
  That God had no engrossing task for me;
But now I know life cannot reach
  Beyond His love and man's necessity.
And so I yield in service all he lends
  Of time and strength, of money and of skill,
As one who for a gracious Master spends
  His bounty in accordance with his will.

Thy love shall chant its own beatitudes
After its own life workings;
A child's kiss set on thy sighing lips shall make
    thee glad;
A poor man helped by thee shall make thee rich;
A sick man nursed by thee shall give thee health;
A weak one helped by thee shall give thee
    strength;
An ignorant one taught by thee shall make thee
    wise;
Thou shalt be served thyself
By every sense of service which thou renderest!

Elizabeth Barrett Browning

The Lord had a job for me, but I had so much to
    do,
I said, "You get somebody else, or wait till I get
    through."
I don't know how the Lord came out, but He
    seemed to get along,
But I felt kind o' sneakin' like—knowed I'd done
    God wrong.
One day I needed the Lord—needed him right
    away;
And He never answered me at all, and I could
    hear Him say,
Down in my accusin' heart: "Not now, I'se got
    too much to do;
You get somebody else, or wait till I get
    through."

Paul Laurence Dunbar

An old song goes:
"Give to the world the best you have and the best will come back to you."

SIN

For all have sinned, and come short of the glory of God.

Romans 3:23

Of sin, because they believe not on me.

John 16:9

A Field of Diamonds

PAYDAY SOMEDAY
And when I see Ahab fall in his chariot and when I see the dogs eating Jezebel by the walls of Jezreel, I say, as the Scripture saith: "O, that thou hadst hearkened to my commandments; then had thy peace been like a river, and thy righteousness as the waves of the sea!" And as I remember that the gains of ungodliness are weighted with the curse of God, I ask you, "Wherefore do ye spend money for that which is not bread? and your labor for that which satisfieth not?"

R. G. Lee

In Adam's fall
We sinned all.

New England Primer

CLIMBING TO HELL
I had Ambition, by which sin
  The angels fell;
I climbed and, step by step, O Lord,
  Ascended into Hell.

W. H. Davies

Wherever God erects a house of prayer,
The Devil always builds a chapel there;
And 'twill be found upon examination,
The latter has the largest congregation.

Daniel Defoe

THE DEVIL
Forthwith the Devil did appear,
For name him, and he's always near.

Matthew Prior

The devil can cite Scripture for his purpose.

Shakespeare

The Christian's sins pierce Christ's heart.

The end of all Christian preaching is to cast the sinner trembling at the feet of mercy.

Vinet

A SINNER'S CONFESSION
I lived for myself, I thought for myself,
  For myself, and none beside—
Just as if Jesus had never lived,
  As if He had never died.

A STEP HELLWARD
As the first step heavenward is humility, so the first step hellward is pride. Pride counts the gospel foolishness, but the gospel always shows pride to be so. Shall the sinner be proud who is going to hell? Shall the saint be proud who is newly saved from it? God had rather His people fared poorly than lived proudly.

Mason

Man-like is it to fall in sin,
Fiend-like is it to dwell therein,
Christ-like is it for sin to grieve,
God-like is it all sin to leave.

Henry Wadsworth Longfellow

THE ANONYMOUS SINNER
We should have read his there—the rich young
    ruler—
  If he had stayed that day;
Nameless—though Jesus loved him—ever name-
    less
  Because—he went away.

SINS—BIG AND LITTLE
You and I are apt to talk about "big" and "little" sins. There is an Indian proverb which says, "There is no distinction between big and little when talking about snakes." They are all alike—snakes.

A. E. Richardson

170

TWO VIEWS OF SIN

Man calls sin an accident: God calls it an abomination.
Man calls sin a blunder: God calls it blindness.
Man calls sin a chance: God calls it a choice.
Man calls sin a defect: God calls it a disease.
Man calls sin an error: God calls it enmity.
Man calls sin fascination: God calls it fatality.
Man calls sin infirmity: God calls it iniquity.
Man calls sin a luxury: God calls it lawlessness.
Man calls sin a trifle: God calls it tragedy.
Man calls sin a mistake: God calls it madness.

GREAT SINNER

The great Scotch surgeon, Sir James Simpson, was once approached by a young man who wished to compliment him by asking what he regarded as his greatest discovery, and the simple reply of this eminent scientist was, "My greatest discovery is that I am a great sinner and that Jesus is a great Saviour."

If a man is a perfectionist, and thinks he is sinless, it is proof not that he is better, but only that he is blinder, than his neighbors.

Richard Glover

ALL GUILTY

"All men have sinned." That statement declares that men, *all* men everywhere, are guilty—consciously guilty, evilly guilty, terribly guilty, guilty with aggravations, guilty without excuse.

R. G. Lee

That's the greatest torture souls feel in hell:
In hell, that they must live and cannot die.

John Webster

The descent to hell is easy.

FUTILITY

We toil for fame,
We live on crusts,
We make a name,
   Then we are busts.

L. H. Robbins

HORRID REUNION

The deeds we do, the words we say,
   Into still air they seem to fleet,
     We count them ever past;
     But they shall last,—
In the dread judgment they
   And we shall meet.

John Keble

And the Devil did grin, for his darling sin
   Is pride that apes humility.

Samuel Taylor Coleridge

CONFESSION

Owning her weakness,
Her evil behaviour,
And leaving with meekness,
Her sins to her Saviour!

Thomas Hood

SPIRITUAL PRIDE

Spiritual pride. By how many artifices does it contrive to show itself! If at any time I am favored with clearer discoveries of my natural and acquired depravity and hatefulness in the sight of God, and am enabled to mourn over it, in comes spiritual pride with, Aye, this is something like. This is holy mourning for sin; this is true humility. . . . What a proof that the heart is the natural soil of pride, when it thus contrives to gather strength from the very exercises which one would think must destroy it utterly.

A. J. Gordon

MY SINS
The sins that tarnish whore and thief
  Beset me every day.
My most ethereal belief
  Inhabits common clay.

Gamaliel Bradford

I can resist everything except temptation.

Oscar Wilde

THE SINNER'S EXISTENCE
To-morrow, and to-morrow, and to-morrow,
Creeps in this petty pace from day to day
To the last syllable of recorded time.

Shakespeare

The sins ye do by two and two ye must pay for
one by one.

Rudyard Kipling

WHAT THEN?
"When the choir has sung its last anthem,
And the preacher has made his last prayer;
When the people have heard their last sermon
And the sound has died out on the air;
When the Bible lies closed on the altar
And the pews are all empty of men
And each one stands facing his record—
And the great Book is opened—WHAT THEN?"

THE SCARS OF SIN
Wounds of the soul, though healed, will ache;
The reddening scars remain
  And make confession.
Lost innocence returns no more,
We are not what we were
  Before transgression!

"Trifles unnoticed by us may be links in the
chain of sin."

"A *bad habit* is first a *caller*, then a *guest*, and at
last a *master*."

Talmud

I have lived long enough; my way of life
Is fall'n into the sear, the yellow leaf:

Shakespeare

LAST DITCH PRIDE
Lord Byron, a short time before death, was heard
to say, "Shall I sue for mercy?" After a long
pause, he added, "Come, come, no weakness;
let's be a man to the last!"

COBWEBS TO CHAINS
"Sir," said Samuel Johnson, "the chains of habit
are generally too small to be felt until they are
too strong to be broken. Habits are at first cob-
webs—at last cables."

DEATH OF A SCOFFER
The French nurse who was present at the death-
bed of Voltaire, being urged to attend an English-
man whose case was critical, said: "Is he a
Christian?" "Yes," was the reply, "he is, a
Christian in the highest and best sense of the
term—a man who lives in the fear of God: but
why do you ask?" "Sir," she answered, "I was
the nurse who attended Voltaire in his last illness, and for all the wealth of Europe I would
never see another infidel die."

Unbelief is not humility, but thorough pride. It
refuses to believe God because it does not find
in self a reason for believing. This is the very
height of presumption.

Ignorance is not innocence, it is often a sin; and
one sin is no salvation from another.

THANKSGIVING

HUMBLE THANKSGIVING

Now know, that of ourselves, we have nothing; for this and all other gifts are from above. Therefore he who would receive from above, must of necessity place himself beneath, in true humility.

John Tauler

A THANKFUL HEART

Lord, Thou hast given me a cell
   Wherein to dwell,
A little house whose humble roof
   Is weatherproof . . .
Low is my porch as is my fate,
   Both void of state,
And yet the threshold of my door
   Is worn by the poor
Who hither come and freely get
   Good words or meat.
'Tis Thou that crown'st my glittering hearth
   With guileless mirth.
All these and better Thou dost send
   Me to this end,
That I should render for my part
   A thankful heart.

Robert Herrick

THANKSGIVING THOUGHT

"O give thanks to the Lord," said the Psalmist. Jesus frequently was an example as He said, "I thank Thee, O Father." Ten lepers were healed. Only one "turned back" to glorify God, "giving thanks." We scold nine but fail to pause and ask if we would have raised the ratio.

J. Ray Grissett

I say to myself, why shouldst thou not be thankful? God is good, all this life is a heavenly miracle, great, though stern and sad . . . The universe is full of love . . . and it remains for ever true that God reigns.

Thomas Carlyle

HIGH FORM OF THANKSGIVING

Thus, if God is to be worshipped with forms of thanksgiving, he that makes it a rule to be content and thankful in every part and accident of his life, because it comes from God, praises God in a much higher manner than he that has some set time for singing of psalms. He that dares not say an ill-natured word, or do an unreasonable thing, because he considers God as everywhere present, performs a better devotion than he that dares not miss the church.

William Law

THANKFUL FOR CRUSTS

A group of prisoners of war wrote a book on their experiences behind barbed wire. One man wrote, "A crust of dry bread has a flavor unbelievable to the well-nourished." To us a crust of dry bread is hardly a blessing. That harsh experience in a prison camp made this man appreciate what he had never appreciated at home.

There was a man in Boston who, though not rich, was accustomed to go into the courts of justice every morning to give bail for culprits that had no friends; and it was his testimony that of all those for whom he gave bail, not one betrayed him,—not one left him in the lurch. And do you suppose that those creatures whom Christ has helped, and whom he has given a hope of eternal salvation, would turn against him, their best friend, and the one to whom they are indebted for their choicest blessings? Would that be human nature? Is there anything on God's earth like gratitude to inspire a soul to act in the right direction?

Henry Ward Beecher

As Christians, then, let us thank God for his creation. We could not have existed without him, and we should see that our existence is good. He did good in making us.

Joseph F. Green

OUR THANKSGIVING ACCEPT
Lord, for the erring thought
Not into evil wrought;
Lord, for the wicked will,
Betrayed and baffled still;
For the heart from itself kept,
Our thanksgiving accept!
William Dean Howells

THANK GOD FOR . . .
We should thank God for his creation. We should
thank him for the actual world he has made—the
world of human life, where such things as money,
sex, and politics are necessary.
Joseph F. Green

THANK GOD FOR TROUBLE?
In everything give thanks! In Christian circles it
is common to hear expressions of thanks and
praise to God for His abundant blessings—and
this is right! But did you ever thank God for
trouble? Have you ever thanked God for allowing problems and heartaches and difficulties to
come your way? In trouble—more than in blessing—I believe we come to know God better and
appreciate Him more deeply, for:
"Out of the presses of pain,
Cometh the soul's best wine;
And the eyes that have shed no rain,
Can shed but little shine."
M. R. DeHaan

A BLANKET OF THANKFULNESS
Lights are out. The day puts itself to bed.
Again the house is quiet. I, alone, am awake.
Fatigue pulls at my eyelids, as my thoughts
And memories weave a blanket of thankfulness
For God's nearness and His goodness.
Now is the time for prayer. . . .
Iris O'Neal Bowen

An unthankful man is like a hog eating acorns
under an oak tree, and never so much as looking
up to see where they came from.

GOD, JESUS, AND BEING HUMAN
Our Father,
You know how human we are.
You know how sometimes we feel
so estranged from you, as though
we were motherless children.
But you know too how sometimes we feel
so close to you, as though we were
nestled in the bosom of motherly love.
Thank you for our humanness.

You know, too, how human Jesus is.
We remember how Jesus cried,
"My God, my God, why have
you abandoned me?"
But we remember also how
Jesus said,
"My Father and I are one."
Thank you for Jesus' humanness.

You know what it is to be human.
Thank you for our humanness.
Thank you for Jesus' humanness.
In the name of Jesus, the optimal
human being, we pray.
Amen.
Francis Martin

THANK YOU
To say "thank you" is to acknowledge that the
one to whom you are directing this expression of
gratitude has fulfilled a need in your life.
When the psalmist said, "O give thanks to the
Lord" (Psalms 107:1, RSV), he was saying that
the Christian should acknowledge that God is
the fulfiller of needs in his life.
It is a great moment for man when he says,
"Thank you, God." Self has been cast aside and
the channel is open for God's power and love to
flow in and radiate out of his life.
Willard Dawson

Remember: ingratitude is one of man's most-
despised sins.

A Field of Diamonds

THE TRAVELER
I used to kneel in simple prayer
And dare implore, "Lord, take me there.
Allow me to abide with you,
Walk in your garden, touch heaven's fresh dew."

Of course, he heard my childish pleas.
Grant, he heeded not, demands such as these.
Instead, softly he whispered into my ear
"The world needs your faith to cast away fear!"

"But Lord," I beseeched, lamenting my woes,
Claiming my faults, subjecting my no's.
Tarried he not, as he brushed doubt aside,
"Child, I made you from 'love', not from the
    world to hide."

"In boldness, in splendor, reach out for the
    dawn,
Claim earth's tomorrows like a flute-noted song.
Gather the rain drops, make friends with each
    cloud,
Do so with wonderment, and in you, I'll be
    proud!"

Now when I kneel, my prayer is thus,
"Thank you God, for staying with us." Amen.
                    Ruth McPherson Kilby

GRATITUDE
Thanksgiving seems to have to do with gratitude
for what God has done. It is the enumeration of
all that the Lord has wrought. As there is thanksgiving, the mood of the heart will turn to one of
thanksgiving. There often must be thanksgiving
before there will come a thankful spirit. We are
ordered by the will to be thankful for everything.
"In every thing give thanks: for this is the will
of Christ Jesus concerning you" (1 Thess. 5:18).
                    Jack R. Taylor

I had most need of blessing, and "Amen"
Stuck in my throat.
                    William Shakespeare

COME, YE THANKFUL PEOPLE, COME
Come, ye thankful people, come.
Praise the song of harvest home!
All is safely gathered in,
Ere the winter storms begin;
God, our Maker doth provide
For our wants to be supplied:
Come to God's own temple, come,
Praise the song of harvest home.
                    Henry Alford

MEMORIES: PAST, PRESENT, AND FUTURE
Our Father,
We thank you
for the past made present
through our memories.
    We thank you
    for the memories
    of wedding days and
    of birthdays.
    We thank you
    for the memories
    of big and little decisions
    that were right and
    for the memories
    of every day made holy
    by acts of love.
We thank you
for the past made present
through our memories.
    We pray that
    the roots of the past
    may take hold in the soil
    of the present and
    grow into a meaningful future.
    We pray that we may live
    in the Spirit of Jesus
    whose present grew
    out of his past and
    whose present made a future
    for himself and
    for all of us. Amen.
                    Francis Martin

Lord, thank you even for our unknown blessings.

176

WISDOM

Then I saw that wisdom excelleth folly, as far as light excelleth darkness.

Ecclesiastes 2:13

But the wisdom that is from above is first pure, then peaceable, gentle, and easy to be intreated, full of mercy and good fruits, without partiality, and without hypocrisy.

James 3:17

A Field of Diamonds

FOUR CLASSES OF MEN
Men are four:
He who knows not, and knows not he knows
    not,
  He is a fool; shun him.
He who knows not, and knows he knows not,
  He is simple; teach him.
He who knows, and knows not he knows,
  He is asleep; waken him.
He who knows, and knows he knows,
  He is wise; follow him.
Lady Burton

If you can talk with crowds and keep your vir-
    tue,
Or walk with kings—nor lose the common touch;
If neither foes nor loving friends can hurt you;
If all men count with you, but none too much;
If you can fill the unforgiving minute
With sixty-seconds' worth of distance run—
Yours is the Earth and everything that's in it,
And—which is more—you'll be a Man, my son!
Rudyard Kipling

KNOWLEDGE OF GOD
Not to the contemplation of things without will
I devote myself, but I will meditate upon what I
find within me, and from things of lowly import
within me I will ascend to those above me; so
that I may be able to know whence I came, and
whither I go; what I am, and from whom I am,
and thus from knowledge of myself may be able
to come to the knowledge of God. For the more
I advance in knowledge of myself, the more do I
progress towards a knowledge of God.
Bernard of Clairvaux

Wisdom alone is free, she sets the poor over the
rich, and makes the servants lend at usury to their
own masters; lend, that is, not money but understanding, lend the talent of that Divine and eternal Treasure which is never wasted, the mere loan
of which is precious.
Ambrose

Give me the patience to accept those things
which cannot be changed, the courage to change
those things which can be changed, and the wisdom to know the difference.

GIVE AND TAKE
In worldy town on worldy street
Where worldly people live,
A feud arose on part of those
Who wished their way imposed.
Some said give;
Some said take.
But what Give would give
Take just would not take.
And what Take would take,
Give just would not give.
Then one day a stranger came—
Wisdom was his name.
With no renown, he settled down
In the midst of Worldly town.
Soon a line of truce was drawn
In the midst of Worldy Street,
And all agreed, who disagreed
Here, their foe to meet.
Then Wisdom spoke of Love and peace
For all the hearts of men,
If only they would give and take
With foe as well as friend.
A stake of gold with "TRUTH" inscribed
Was placed in Wisdom's hand
To mark the place where love and grace
Had spread from man to man.
Then Wisdom chose a sacred place,
Now hailed by ev'ry race,
For Wisdom drove the golden stake
HALFWAY BETWEEN GIVE AND TAKE.
Jimmy Martin

The wisest man in the world readily acknowl-
edges his lack of wisdom. The man who boasts
of his wisdom has already shown that he is
unwise. Wisdom begets humility.

Wisdom lies in being able to apply knowledge.

No one in this world is so perfect that if he were to examine his own heart, he would not find sin enough of which to rid himself, so that he would not be able justly to reprove others.

John Tauler

To those who would give advice, the best advice that I know is: If you can't be kind, be quiet.

M. D'Alroy

Read and think. Study now, and now garden. Go alone, then go abroad. Speculate awhile, then then work in the world.

Ralph Waldo Emerson

HEIGHTS
The heights by great men reached and kept
Were not attained by sudden flight,
But they, while their companions slept
Were toiling upward in the night.

Henry Wadsworth Longfellow

ENLARGE THY SOUL
Narrow is the mansion of my soul; enlarge Thou it, that Thou mayest enter in.

Augustine

Trust thou more in promises carved in melting ice
   Than in vain delusions that crumble into dust.
Misleading in rewards, its virtue only hidden vice,
   This world never hath welcomed days of loving trust.

Bernard of Clairvaux

A sadder and a wiser man,
He rose the morrow morn.

Samuel Taylor Coleridge

To know what to do is wisdom.
To know how to do it is skill.

Knowledge comes, but wisdom lingers.

Alfred Lord Tennyson

WISDOM'S TEST
Wisdom is not finally tested by the schools,
Wisdom cannot be pass'd from one having it to another not having it,
Wisdom is of the soul, is not susceptible of proof, is its own proof.

Walt Whitman

We look backward too much and we look forward too much. Thus we miss the passing moment.

William Lyon Phelps

A RULE OF THREE
Three things to govern—temper, tongue and conduct.
Three things to cultivate—courage, affection and gentleness.
Three things to commend—thrift, industry and promptness.
Three things to despise—cruelty, arrogance and ingratitude.
Three things to wish for—health, friends and contentment.
Three things to admire—dignity, gracefulness and intellectual power.
Three things to give—alms to the needy, comfort to the sad and appreciation to the worthy.

I have studied now Philosophy
And Jurisprudence, Medicine
And even, alas, Theology
From end to end with labor keen;
And here, poor fool, with all my lore
I stand no wiser than before.

Johann Wolfgang von Goethe

A little learning is a dangerous thing.

Alexander Pope

HOW WE LEARN

Great truths are greatly won. Not found by
  chance,
Nor wafted on the breath of summer dream,
But grasped in the great struggle of the soul,
Hard buffeting with adverse wind and stream.

. . .

Not in the general mart, 'mid corn and wine,
Not in the merchandise of gold and gems,
Not in the world's gay halls of midnight mirth,
Not 'mid the blaze of regal diadems. . .

Horatius Bonar

REFLECTED GLORY

I'm not much within myself,
  And probably never will be.
But I like being near those who are
  And pretending that I could be.
I like standing near the guy
  Whose life reads like a story.
Like I said,—"I'm not too much"—
  But I love that reflected glory.
I must be content with who I am
  And know I'm not "he who hath"
So I'll wave the banner for the other fella
  And be proud of who I'm with.

Linda Wingfield

You cannot prevent the birds of sorrow from flying over your head, but you can prevent them
from building nests in your hair.

THE BOOK

I entered the world's great library doors,
I crossed their acres of polished floors;
I searched and searched their stacks and nooks,
But I settled at last on the Book of books.

I've shut the door on yesterday
  And thrown the key away—
To-morrow holds no fears for me,
  Since I have found to-day.

Vivian Y. Laramore

REST

What secret trouble stirs thy heart?
  Why all this fret and flurry?
Dost thou not know that what is best
In this too restless world is rest
  From overwork and hurry?

Henry Wadsworth Longfellow

PRAYER FOR TRUTH

Grant us Thy truth to make us free,
And kindling hearts that burn for Thee,
Till all Thy living altars claim
One holy light, one heavenly flame.

Oliver Wendell Holmes

A SPIRIT OF PATIENCE

What I have suffered in my estate, body, name,
spirit, I hope through the help from Christ and
for his sake I have desired to bear with a spirit of
patience and respect and love, even to my perse-
cutors.

Roger Williams

Nothing useless is, or low;
  Each thing in its place is best;
And what seems but idle show
  Strengthens and supports the rest.

Henry Wadsworth Longfellow

Great is the conduct of a man who lets rewards
take care of themselves—come if they will or fail
to come—but goes on his way, true to the truth
simply because it is true, strongly loyal to the
right for its pure righteousness.

Phillips Brooks

SPEAK THE TRUTH

Speak the truth, and the very roots of the grass
underground there, move and stir to bear you
witness. Speak the truth, and the innocent day
loves you and serves you.

Ralph Waldo Emerson

YOUTH

Remember now thy Creator in the days of thy youth, while the evil days come not, nor the years draw nigh, when thou shalt say, I have no pleasure in them.

Ecclesiastes 12:1

Let no man despise thy youth; but be thou an example of the believers, in word, in conversation, in charity, in spirit, in faith, in purity.

1 Timothy 4:12

DUTY

So nigh is grandeur to our dust,
So near is God to man,
When Duty whispers low, "Thou must,"
The youth replies, "I can."

Ralph Waldo Emerson

FREEDOM

The sand flea is an interesting little creature. He cannot live in the open air or in the sea. In order to survive, he must abide in the confining area of wet sand that borders the pounding surf.

When compared to other creatures, man's freedom of movement is amazing indeed. He can live for months under the sea, or above earth's atmosphere. And yet even man's freedom has its limits. He must adapt himself to his surroundings in a proper kind of vehicle. Should he violate his known limitations, he---like the same flea---invites sudden death.

Wise is the youth who recognizes that his purpose in going to school is to bury himself in his curriculum. Unless he does, he misses the point and presently may find himself academically dead; but wise also is the youth who recognizes that he is not constantly confined to this major purpose. He does have more freedom than the sand flea. He can get out and go places. Wise is the youth who also recognizes that his freedom to do other things is not unlimited. To break over the traces, completely disregarding God's limits to his freedom, is to invite certain calamity.

John Jeffers

PRESS ON

Press on, O Youth, press on!
Join hands with those who dare ascend,
With courage strong, surmount the crest;
And when the battle's strife shall end
Attain with joy the victor's rest.
Press on, O Youth, press on!

This cloudy day is our day of opportunity . . .

G. Kearnie Keegan

THEY STARTED YOUNG

Benjamin Franklin was writing for publication at sixteen. At twenty-two George Whitefield was one of the world's greatest preachers. Dwight L. Moody was preaching at eighteen, and Charles Spurgeon at sixteen. William Cullen Bryant wrote "Thanatopsis" at eighteen. Robert Southey was famous at the same age. John Milton wrote one of his best poems at the age of twenty-two. Henry Wadsworth Longfellow was professor of modern languages at nineteen, a much-loved poet at twenty-six. Robert Burns was a gifted writer at sixteen. William Gladstone belonged to the House of Lords at twenty-three. Demosthenes was the greatest orator of old Greece at twenty-five. Solomon at eighteen began a reign which was marked by wealth and wisdom.

THE LORD IS MY MAJOR PROFESSOR
(Paraphrase Psalm 23)

The Lord is my major professor:
I will not fail.

He causes me to walk the campus with serenity: he guides me to the waters of wisdom

He refreshes my mind; he helps me to find eternal truth for he is truth.

Even though I walk through the difficult days of semester examinations, I will not be afraid; for he has taught me well. His encouragement and tutoring have prepared me.

Ed Seabough

In the lexicon of youth, which fate reserves for a bright manhood, there is no such word as "fail."
Owen Meredith

God, make me big—bigger of mind and soul than I was yesterday, bigger in attitude toward all men, bigger in Christlike love for all men.
G. Kearnie Keegan

HOW?
(Paraphrase Romans 10:14)

For how will students at the
university call on Christ if they
do not believe?

And how can they believe if they
have not heard of him?

And how can they hear if a student
does not tell them?

And what student will tell them of
Christ if you do not?

Ed Seabough

COMMENCEMENT
Proud parents, grandparents, friends and sweet-
hearts waited for the impressive ceremonies to
begin. Rows of meticulously clad young men,
four years of ROTC behind them, listened for
their cue to walk to the platform, salute, shake
hands, and receive their coveted commissions.
These commissions are a recognition of achievement, but more, they are a charge to serve.

The crowning moment of graduation comes
when the senior reaches forth to receive his di-
ploma. This is a commission, too. It declares
that knowledge has been gained which fits the
recipient to perform adequately in a given field.
In short, it says, "go to work."

Jesus commissioned his followers. He commissions those who choose to follow Him today.
Our credentials—a personal faith in Him which
transforms our lives. Our task—to tell others of
His transforming love and power. Our field—the
world. "Go Ye."

John Jeffers

Young people, your parents want desperately to
be understood, just as you do. I sense their
frustration as they talk to me. They feel that you
really do not understand them. Now that's a
switch.

William L. Self

CONTRASTS FOR GRADUATES
All around me, 250 of my friends sat. Some were
holding back tears. Others were folding up their
programs. Maybe others were anticipating a cele-
bration party. We all had one thing in common—
in a few moments we, as a group, would quickly
move 250 tassels, and our high school careers
would be complete.

It was hard to concentrate during the commencement exercise. Speeding trucks made it
difficult to think at the out-of-doors ceremony.
And even when a thought pattern traveled to the
brain, it collided with another thought bearing the
exact opposite meaning.

For this graduation was a study in contrasts:
. . . it marked the end of 12 years, but it
signified the beginning of a lifetime; . . . it
brought sad thoughts about the friends and
teachers we were leaving behind but furnished
happy thoughts and dreams of what the future
would bring; . . . it served as a climactic pinnacle for some, while only a stepping stone to
higher education for others; . . . it took
everyone off high school's one-way street and
gave us all the chance to pick out our own calm
avenue, bustling expressway, dangerous foot
trail, or fatal dead-end road.

Warren Steen, III

WHO AM I?
That really hits me where it helps! It means
basically:
know yourself well
question yourself consistently
aim for the highest that you can be
struggle, but with hope.
You will very likely find the answer to the
question "Who am I?" to be very exciting:
something like,
"A great human being—
worth knowing
worth being
worth loving."
That kind of answer makes a question worthwhile!

Grady Nutt

"YOUNG OLD" PEOPLE
By contrast, aged people need youth. Visit any college campus and nearby you will find some of the youngest old people on earth. These professors and staff members and other workers have been around youth so long and in such numbers that they think young, act young, and dream like young people.

James L. Sullivan

THE CHALLENGE
I have found in our Crusades throughout the world, that young people will respond if the challenge is tough enough and hard enough.

Billy Graham

YOUTH
Today is yours, and yours the confidence
  Of garnered knowledge and our past mistakes:
Subdue the hosts of ignorance and pretense:
  Bring back the only cup our thirsting slakes.

YOUTH WITH HIS DREAM
Youth with his dream went forth,
"Christ must rule o'er the world," he said;
Held in his hand a Cross,
And followed where'er the dream led.

YOUTH'S OPPORTUNITY
The time has come to make it a reality. The opportunity for the adult generation is rapidly passing away with every clock-tick of Father Time. Youth's opportunity has come! Let us share together the happy and adventurous path!

A short life which fulfills its mission is a success. "That life is long which answers life's great end."

Young

"Died of old age at 21," read the note of a young man who committed suicide.

BECOMING
(Paraphrase Romans 12:1-2)

Christian collegian, because God loves us, I urge you: Give your life back to God; commit yourself to him; let him work through you. This is the true worship of God.

Do not let the ideologies of the campus mold you, but let God transform your mind and your whole being. Then you will begin to understand God's working in your life; and then you will begin to be the person you are capable of becoming.

Ed Seabough

A FLAMING QUESTION
Flaming youth has become a flaming question. And youth comes to us wanting to know what we may propose to do about a society that hurts so many of them.

Franklin Delano Roosevelt

A BENEDICTION
May peace guard your lives, and ever
  From the time of your early youth,
May the words that you daily utter
  Be the words of beautiful truth.

And youth must strike for goals afar which old men dare not try.

It is better to *live* thirty years, than *exist* seventy!

A short life in the saddle, Lord,
Not long life by the fire.

Louise Imogene Guiney

Arise, O youth of God!

William P. Merrill

INDEX

A

Abelard, Peter 68
Abraham 82
Ackland, Donald 33
Adam 170
Adams, Eva 75, 91
Adams, John 137
Adams, John Quincy 18
Adams, Thomas 89
ADORATION 9-14, 64, 89, 147, 148, 149, 150
Advancement 124
Adulthood 16
AGE 15-18
Aldersgate Street 162
Allen, Freda Hanbury 166
Allen, Hervey 16
Alexander the Great 66, 76
Alexander, Cecil F. 62, 64
Alexander, James W. 22
Alford, Henry 176
Ambrose 48, 79, 80, 140, 168, 178
America 136, 137, 138
Amiel, Henri Frederic 62
Ancestors 32
Anderson, John 16
Angel(s) 41, 42, 126
Apollos 96
Appleby, Rosalee Mills 10, 70, 97, 106, 119, 141
Aquinas, Thomas 89
Armageddon 142
Aspiration 54, 55, 56, 72, 152, 167, 179, 180, 184
Assisi, Francis of 10, 24, 32, 124, 128, 140
ASSURANCE 19-22
Atonement 22, 65, 67, 68, 162, 163, 164
Augustine 11, 20, 52, 88, 124, 140, 164, 179
Awe 62

B

Babcock, Maltbie D. 56
Bacheler, Mary 125
Bacon, Francis 62
Baird, E. C. 42
Barbauld, Anna L. 150
Barnhill, Louise Barker 58, 59, 75, 128, 129, 167
Barnes, Leola Christie 120
Barrie, J. M. 79
Bashford (Bishop) 160
Bates, Katharine L. 136
Beaumont, Joseph 100

Beatitudes 38
Beck, Alan 112
Beecher, Henry Ward 26, 34, 55, 114, 121, 124, 126, 160, 163, 174
Beethoven, Ludwig von 122
Believe 79, 80
Benson, Arthur Christopher 56
Bernard of Clairvaux 59, 88, 91, 122, 129, 130, 178, 179
Bernard, George 64
Best 70, 71
Bethlehem 40, 75, 119
BIBLE 23-28, 106, 180, 102, 112, 121, 170
Effect of 23, 24, 25, 26, 27, 50, 79
Genius of 28
Guidance from 23, 27, 28
Study of 23, 24, 26, 27
Bilhorn, Peter P. 142
Bisagno, John R. 14, 24, 102, 121
Blake, William 58, 86, 156
Blessed 11, 141
Blessing(s) 50, 85, 110, 137, 142, 145, 166, 175, 176
Bliss, P. P. 96
Blood 22, 65, 67, 68, 162, 164
Boaz 40
Bok, Edward W. 18, 37, 56
Bonaparte, Napoleon 21, 68
Bonar, Horatius 159, 166, 180
Book of Common Prayer 17, 76
Booth, General William 45
Boreham, Frank W. 94, 163
Bowen, Iris O'Neal 18, 60, 74, 101, 175
Bowring, John 64
Bradford, Gamaliel 172
Bradlaugh, Charles 115
Brady, N. 150
Bravery 53, 54, 55, 56
Bridges, R. 150
Bronte, Emily 52, 54
Brooks, Phillips 24, 40, 42, 55, 72, 84, 125, 141, 152, 153, 158, 180
Brooks, Thomas 52
Broughton, Len G. 45
Brown, A. D. 30
Brown, Helen Felts 42, 91
Brown, W. G. 111
Browning, Elizabeth Barrett 168
Browning, Robert 16, 32, 61, 62, 110, 146, 160
Brugman, Sophie 95
Bryant, William Cullen 84, 156, 158, 182
Buffon, Georges Louis Leclerc de 153
Burket, Gail Brook 55
Burns, Islay 46

Burns, Robert 16, 30, 71, 129, 155, 182
Bunyan, John 25, 84
Burroughs, P. E. 98
Burt (Bishop) 116
Burton, Henry 116
Burton (Lady) 178
Byron (Lord) 61, 172

C

Caesar, Julius 66, 76, 122
Cain 32, 142
Calvary 64, 65, 67, 68, 75, 119, 164
Calvin, John 65
Campus life 182, 183, 184
Carlyle, Thomas 56, 78, 89, 158, 174
Caudill, R. Paul 66, 80, 100, 115, 133, 134
Cervantes, Miguel 115
Challenge 44, 54, 56, 125, 184
Chalmers, James 95
Chambers, Oswald 71, 134
Chapman, J. Wilbur 36, 71, 86
CHARACTER 29-34, 100, 114, 115, 145
Charlemagne 122
Cheney, John Vance 126
Chesterton, G. K. 54
CHILDHOOD 35-38, 110, 155
CHRIST, JESUS 117-122, 13, 30, 31, 101, 133
Birth of 38-42
Death of 22, 63, 64, 65, 66, 67, 68, 98, 114, 162, 163, 164
Resurrection of 67, 73, 74, 75, 76
Christian(s) 85, 95, 98, 125
Christian Endeavor World 152
Christianity, effects of 54, 98, 114, 115, 124, 140, 146
CHRISTMAS 38-42
Chrysostom, John 88
CHURCH 43-48, 85, 102
City 158
Clark, Adam 153
Clarke, Harry D. 163
Clarkson, David 155
Clement of Alexandria 72, 164
Coffin, Henry Sloane 48, 65, 67, 90
Coleridge, Samuel Taylor 25, 27, 111, 155, 171, 179
College 182, 183, 184
COMFORT 49-52, 21, 152
Comforter 104
Commencement 183

190

Worship   10, 13, 14, 62, 102, 174
    Wright, Maie Everett   102

Y

Year   144, 145, 146
    Yeats, William Butler   17
    Young   184
    Young, Egerton   98
    Young, John   62
YOUTH   181–184, 98, 110

Z

    Zangwill, Israel   138
Zion   94